MANNERHEIM: MARSHAL OF FINLAND

STIG JÄGERSKIÖLD

MANNERHEIM
MARSHAL OF FINLAND

University of Minnesota Press, Minneapolis

The publication of this book was assisted by a bequest from Josiah H. Chase to honor his parents, Ellen Rankin Chase and Josiah Hook Chase, Minnesota territorial pioneers.

92
M282 j

Copyright © 1986 C. Hurst & Co. (Publishers) Ltd.

Published by the University of Minnesota Press
2037 University Avenue Southeast, Minneapolis MN 55414
Published simultaneously in Canada
by Fitzhenry & Whiteside Limited, Markham.
Printed in the United States of America

Published in Swedish as *Gustaf Mannerheim 1867–1951*
by Holger Schildts Förlag, Helsingfors, 1983,
and in Finnish as *Mannerheim 1867–1951*
by Kustannusosakeyhtiö Otava, Helsinki, 1983
© Stig Jägerskiöld, 1983
Photographs reproduced courtesy of Otava Picture Archives

Library of Congress Cataloging-in-Publication Data

Jägerskiöld, Stig Axel Fridolf, 1911–
    Mannerheim, Marshal of Finland.

    Translation of Gustaf Mannerheim, 1867–1951.
    Bibliography: p.
    Includes index.
    1. Mannerheim, Carl Gustaf Emil, friherre, 1867–1951. 2. Marshals—
Finland—Biography. 3. Finland—Presidents—Biography. I. Title.
DL1067.5.M36J34 1986   .948.97'03'0924 [B]   86-16011
ISBN 0-8166-1527-6

Gustaf Mannerheim's military and political achievements, played out within the context of Finnish history and the history of the Nordic countries as a whole, were of such great importance that the need for a full biographical record is unquestionable.

The first part of Mannerheim's military career took place in the imperial Russian army, and ended in September 1917 in the midst of the Russian Revolution. His Russian career, which in those days was a natural consequence of the place Finland had occupied within the empire since 1809, gave him a first-class military education. He acquired experience of modern warfare in the Russo-Japanese war of 1904–5 and the First World War, and of the international rules of warfare. His political perspective was enlarged: he was able to see political problems, as they arose, from the point of view of a great power. This explains his activities before and after the conflicts with the Soviet Union from 1939 till 1944, and his views on Finland's relations with Germany in 1918 and later.

On the other hand, Mannerheim's long career in Russia caused him great problems when he returned home to Finland in 1917. Many have been puzzled by the role he was able to play in the subsequent years: how could a Russian general, who at the same time was a Swedish-speaking nobleman, gain the confidence of anti-Russian Ostrobothnian peasants, most of whom were Finns? How was he able, with their help, to create the new Finnish army – the object of so many secret hopes for so long – capable of defending the newly-proclaimed Finnish independence and legal order? It was, most of all, remarkable that the 'White General' could, with the passing of the years, make the Finnish people forget the outrages committed on both sides in the fight of 1918, and unify the various classes of the country in time before the great catastrophe of the Second World War, which he had seen coming since the beginning of the 1930s. By that time, the old Marshal's authority was so firmly established that he could lead his forces through the two wars of 1939–45, notwithstanding the drastic changes in direction which changes in the international situation demanded, without any opposition or criticism. In 1944 J.K. Paasikivi, who was to succeed him as President of Finland two years later, said: 'You, and you alone, have the full confidence of the Finnish people.' How is this to be explained?

What gave Mannerheim the strength of character that in 1918 enabled

v

him to stand out firmly against the prevailing pro-German policy of his Government, and to prefer resignation at the moment of his personal triumph in order to maintain relations with the Western powers? What philosophy inspired him in 1919 and later always to refuse offers to establish a dictatorship in order to realise plans which he favoured but could not carry out within the constraints of the Constitution (which he himself had signed)? The question of intervention in the Russian civil war of 1919 was perhaps the most critical of these instances, but the temptation returned in the 1930s.

An important factor was certainly the influence of liberal thinking during his youth in his family and more generally in Finnish society, and even in many circles of St Petersburg society. He sometimes referred to this in later life, as when he wrote to the Swedish publisher K.O. Bonnier: 'I was born in a period when the liberal political ideas spread their enlightenment on mankind.' Even if the experience of revolutions and wars forced him to compromise, he still kept to ideas of freedom and legality. For example, he refused to accept Nazi demands concerning the Jews in Finland, which he considered unworthy. A state could be obliged to make concessions under protest, but there were certain limits which could never be transgressed. All these problems in Finnish history and in Mannerheim's life were often discussed among people interested in Scandinavian policy.

Thus, I had compelling reasons to accept an offer made by some members of Mannerheim's family to allow me to study those of his papers that remained. They turned to me mainly as an academic historian, but also because I had had personal contacts with the Marshal while serving in the Swedish diplomatic service, and was related to him by blood – his grandmother had been my grandfather's older sister. Having examined these sources, I decided to write a book based on this entirely new material, dealing with his youth and his first years in Russia. I could not then desist from continuing my biography to the end of his life.

*   *   *

My primary sources for this biography have been what was left of Mannerheim's private archives and, especially, his outgoing correspondence – letters he wrote to his relatives and friends. However, he destroyed much material during major political crises; he did this, for example, in 1948 when the Communist regime was established in Prague and many expected the same thing to happen in Finland. The letters he had written to his sisters, brothers, uncles and cousins were out of his reach, and were generally carefully preserved by the recipients. The Marshal enjoyed, and excelled at the art of writing. To my great satisfaction I was able to bring together and edit a collection of letters written by him from his early childhood to the last days of his life. For some short periods of his career his diaries have been preserved; I found and edited his interesting journal from the Russo-Japanese war of 1904–5, with his criticism of the Russian military system, and comments on his experiences and the political situation before and during the first, abortive Russian revolution. The notes he made during his journey across Asia in 1906–8 were already published in 1940.

For Mannerheim's military and political activities, the archives of the Finnish state contributed much important material for the periods when Mannerheim was acting in official capacities; I have had free access to all this material. The same applies to the many official archives I have consulted in the Scandinavian countries, in Germany, Great Britain, Italy, the Netherlands and to a certain extent in France. The diplomatic correspondence has sometimes been important for my researches.

A valuable source has been the reliable diaries of Mannerheim's younger friend and collaborator, Ambassador Georg Achates Gripenberg, and the diaries of the German representative at the Finnish headquarters in 1941–4, General Waldemar Erfurt. All of my books on Mannerheim had appeared when the problematical 'diaries' of his successor as President of the Republic, J.K. Paasikivi, were published; they had not previously been available to historians. The judgment of the writer of these diaries is certainly biased by his varying ambitions, and has to be treated with caution. We do not know where the entries were in fact written, or whether they have been altered at any time subsequently.

As to Mannerheim's own *Memoirs*, these were the result of collaboration among a select group of military men and civil servants. The aim was not to describe or analyse his life, but to give a description of the Finnish political and military history during his lifetime. They do not convey his personal, very impressive and brilliant style. However, Mannerheim had gone through, corrected and approved the final text before his death.

Stockholm
June 1986

STIG JÄGERSKIÖLD

CONTENTS

PLATES

between pp. 22 and 23

Carl Robert Mannerheim
Helène Mannerheim, née von Julin
Gustaf Mannerheim as a cadet
Fencing practice at the Nikolaevskoe Cavalry School
Coronation of Nicholas II, 26 May 1896
Mannerheim as commander of the 13th Vladimir Lancer Regiment, 1909
Mannerheim in the uniform of the Chevalier Guards
Anastasia Mannerheim, née Arapov, in 1898
Anastasia and Sophy Mannerheim
The fair at Uzgenn
Mannerheim in the Chapchal Pass
The mandarin general of Aksu
Mannerheim's caravan in the Muzart Pass
Mannerheim with officers of H.M. the Emperor's Guard Lancer Regiment
Mannerheim at an outdoor lunch party
Mannerheim and Georg Scalon, the Governor-General of Poland
Mannerheim with a hunting party, 1913
Mannerheim in Odessa, 1915
Mannerheim in a village in the Carpathians
Mannerheim as a divisional commander

between pp. 54 and 55

The Commander-in-Chief in 1918
Mannerheim and Svinhufvud, 16 May 1918

I
FORMATIVE YEARS
1867–1886

Carl Gustaf Emil Mannerheim, known as Gustaf, was born on 4 June 1867 on his parents' estate of Louhisaari (Villnäs),* in a picturesque district bordering the archipelago north of Turku. The main house had been built by members of the Fleming af Liebelitz family, earlier owners of the estate. Gustaf's great-grandfather Carl-Erik Mannerheim had bought Louhisaari in 1793 with the help of his wife's fortune.

Gustaf was the third child and second son of the marriage of Count Carl Robert Mannerheim and Helene von Julin. The eldest was Sophie, who was followed by Carl. After Gustaf came two sons, Johan and August, and two daughters, Anna and Eva. Both parents were of Finland-Swedish families. The Mannerheims were originally Dutch, but in the mid-seventeenth century they became merchants and industrialists in Sweden. Several later served in the army and the civil service. Gustaf's grandfather, Carl-Erik Mannerheim, was the first to settle in Finland, then part of the kingdom of Sweden. The Julins were from a different background, Gustaf's maternal grandfather Johan Jakob Julin being a pharmacist who became an energetic and enterprising foundry-master, owner of the old ironworks at Fiskars in south-west Finland. He was eventually ennobled for his services to industry. Gustaf's maternal grandmother, Charlotte Jägerskiöld, died young, and subsequently his grandfather married Charlotte's sister Louise as his second wife.

At Louhisaari, where the Mannerheim children were first brought up, an eighteenth-century tradition still survived despite a changed political atmosphere; the furniture, works of art and books bore witness to the refined culture of that time. More important, however, was the fact that Gustaf's parents shared the liberal opinions that were dominant in Europe during the revolutionary year of 1848; this was the legacy bequeathed to the Mannerheim children, and they received no other. Gustaf Mannerheim often pointed this out. Thus Carl Robert Mannerheim belonged to the 'men of 1848', espousing the ideals of freedom and equality. Helène von

---

*Finland is a country with two official languages, Finnish and Swedish, and many place names thus have two forms. Louhisaari in Finnish is Villnäs in Swedish. In general, Finnish forms are used for place-names, and a glossary on p. 199 gives Swedish equivalents.

Julin was as typically 'English' as her husband was 'French'. Contacts with England were particularly lively in her family, whose predominant way of thinking was the liberalism of the 'Manchester School'. The moral homilies which formed part of Gustaf's upbringing were often of English origin.

Gustaf Mannerheim's early childhood years at Louhisaari were happy, and later he recollected them with pleasure. There were 'good sledging, sparkling fires and tinkling sleigh-bells', and pleasant sailing trips and swimming. However, his father's financial position became increasingly embarrassed during the 1870s, and in 1880 he was compelled to leave Finland, break up his home and assign Louhisaari to his unmarried sister, Mimmi. Leaving his wife with their seven children in Finland, he went to Paris to seek a livelihood and better fortune. Helène found a refuge with her step-mother and aunt Louise von Julin on the estate of Sällvik in south-west Finland, and died there the following year, 1881.

The seven Mannerheim children were now orphans without an income. Later Gustaf Mannerheim was to write: 'Our childhood was hard.' The children also spoke of 'the time of the grey woollen mittens'. However, they were able to count on the support and help of relative and friends, who were determined to keep the family afloat. But it became generally a time of anxiety and scarcity, and the assistance they received smacked of dependence if not of actual humiliation. The children nevertheless measured up to their difficulties, becoming hard-working and capable. A strength for all of them was their determination to stick together and support each other; this family loyalty even included their father after he returned to Finland with his second wife and a little daughter, Marguerite. The children were also fortunate in enjoying the support of other relatives, notably 'Grandmother Louise', J.J. von Julin's widow and their mother's aunt. Charlotte, their true grandmother, had another daughter besides Helène: Hanna, who later married Professor Christian Lovén in Stockholm. Louise was the mother of Albert and of Sigrid, who subsequently married Axel Björkenheim. After Helène's death Hanna took charge of August and Eva Mannerheim, but her energy and interest were sufficient also to follow Gustaf's activities; she was to survive till after the Winter War. Grandmother Louise looked after Johan, while Uncle Albert assumed responsibility for Gustaf. Annika was sent to the Smolny Institute in St Petersburg, a boarding school for daughters of the nobility, but she died there in 1886.

In the autumn of 1874 the seven-year-old Gustaf was sent to school in Helsinki. He proudly informed Sophie, his elder sister by four years, 'I have gone to school. The boys call me the wild goat and the girls Squire Semolina.' School was difficult from the start; his worried mother tried to persuade him to control his temperament and behave more sedately, advice that was lost on her scamp of a son. He found it difficult to adjust, and the result was many changes of school. At last, when he was thirteen, it was decided to send him to Hamina, to try as soon as possible to enter the Cadet Corps there. This was was a foundation of the time of Alexander I with traditions going back to the period of Swedish rule. It was known to provide a good education. Many Finnish boys had passed through it during the nineteenth century and gained a livelihood at home or in the Russian empire to which Finland was joined. Here if anywhere an unruly boy should be made to conform to the demands of society. Above all, Gustaf would be able to obtain a free place, so the financial demands would be small.

It was thus principally the family's depleted fortunes that led to this choice of school. Gustaf had not chosen a military career for himself, and the decision did not correspond to the ideals of the older members of the family, who held rather critical views of the army and of things Russian. Even Gustaf could remark on his position as an alien and say ironically that he had now become 'a Russian'. Admission to the Cadet Corps itself required success in the entrance examination, and the first two years at Hamina had to be devoted to school work. On 19 June 1882 Gustaf achieved this initial aim. However, it is not surprising that life at the Cadet Corps, with its petty discipline and lack of freedom, was in many ways unpalatable to a high-spirited and clever youth; the teenage years are always a sensitive time, and perhaps they were especially difficult for Gustaf who had just lost not only his childhood home but above all his mother, and for a considerable time his father as well. However, his studies went well, and he was able to inform his relatives that he had received marks that were good and constantly improving. But where would his education lead?

Gustaf shared with several of his fellow-cadets an anxiety about the future, as recounted to his brother Carl. If after leaving the Cadet Corps you chose to enter a Finnish unit, it might be in a small place like Kuopio or Kajaani, after which you would probably try to obtain a post as manager of a more or less hopeless estate in Finland. If on the other hand you chose to enter a Russian unit, you would also have to be content with a regiment stationed in the provinces; you would 'turn sour there, eating sauerkraut'. 'I have every prospect of becoming a stranger to our own conditions if I bury myself in some squalid battalion in the interior of Russia.' However, Gustaf thought there were other ways to go; if you wanted to serve in

Russia it was best to try to transfer to schools offering more advanced training, and if you wanted to remain in Finland, a civilian career might be more attractive than a military one. These problems were to occupy him for several years to come.

Among other educational establishments the Page Corps in St Petersburg was the most attractive. He hoped for a more varied education in this famous Russian institution, if he were not to go into the navy. It was where many Finns had begun a career in the empire in all the years since 1809, when Finland was wrested from Sweden and came under Russian rule. But it appeared that Gustaf's attempts to enter the Page Corps were being thwarted by the staff of the Cadet Corps, and in addition the plan was disapproved of by the realistic Uncle Albert. Gustaf therefore became increasingly depressed. In the spring of 1886 the matter was still undecided, and clearly the outlook was not bright. Gustaf's unhappiness deepened, and his impression that the staff of the Corps, especially its new director General Enckell, were against him aroused a recalcitrant attitude in him which made matters worse.

With only a relatively short part of his time at the Cadet Corps still to go, vexation over the allowance of leave and free time made Gustaf decide in a not unusual way to visit an older friend in town outside the permitted hours, leaving a dummy in his bed. The misdemeanour was discovered by the orderly officer, and he was put on a charge. The exceptionally severe punishment was expulsion from the Corps. This might have been a catastrophe for Gustaf, who had not so far passed any examination and was both jobless and penniless. His brothers and sisters and other relatives waited tensely to see what the problem boy would do now. Then Gustaf Mannerheim showed for the first time what he was made of. He turned the self-inflicted disaster to advantage: he would take the matriculation examination at a grammar school in Helsinki, after which he would have the right to apply for admission to a military college in Russia; then his expulsion from Hamina would no longer be a fatal obstacle. It was the Nikolaevskoe Cavalry School in St Petersburg that he had in view; with his interest in horses and sport, the career of a cavalryman attracted him. But for this a better knowledge of Russian was needed that he had acquired at Hamina.

II
IN RUSSIA
1886–1904

As early as the summer of 1886 Uncle Albert helped to arrange a stay in southern Russia for his nephew. Albert's brother-in-law, Edvard Bergenheim, was in charge of the construction of a railway in the Ukraine and had his own workshops in Kharkov. There Gustaf would be able to live and learn Russian properly. Bergenheim's impression of him was thoroughly favourable: 'He is a capital young man, well behaved, attentive, well brought up, quick-witted and lively.' His reputation as a dreadful madcap was, according to Bergenheim, due only to 'a particular bit of bad luck'.

Gustaf now gained his first experience of a Russian military atmosphere – through association with an officer who gave him Russian lessons. He did not find it entirely to his liking, and would have been glad to give up his plans for a career in the empire – much to Uncle Albert's satisfaction. In any case he returned home to prepare for his matriculation examination ('I must work particularly hard at Finnish,' he wrote) in the spring of 1887, which he passed with a high mark. In the summer he again travelled to southern Russia, first to Lukianovka, the property of Mikael Scalon, whose wife Alfhild Cedercreutz was from Finland and Gustaf's godmother. She was sister-in-law to Lieutenant-General Gösta Aminoff, and in addition the family had good connections with Russian circles in St Petersburg. Here the young Mannerheim could improve his Russian in the company of carefree young people. There followed a further visit to Bergenheim and a stay in a military camp at Chuguev – the result of which was that he decided on a military career in the empire, preferably in the cavalry. 'I am better suited to fight with sabre and rifle mounted on a horse than to sit at a desk,' he wrote to his brother Carl. Among the acquaintances of General Aminoff in the imperial capital was General Alexander von Bilderling, from Courland, who also had family connections with Finland and who was commandant of the Nikolaevskoe Cavalry School. General von Bilderling willingly accepted the young Finnish baron at the School in the summer of 1887, the pre-condition being that he should pass the entrance examination, in which the Russian language usually represented the greatest difficulties. The standards were high but

5

Gustaf Mannerheim passed with flying colours.

He had now attained a goal for which he had striven. On the other hand he may have been a little apprehensive of the strange Russian environment. Much later many people have found surprising his entry into Russian military service, but in doing so they have overlooked the fact that a great number of young Finns had followed the same path since 1809 when the Swedish armed forces became almost completely closed to those who lived in the severed eastern part of the Swedish realm. Between 1809 and 1917, when Finland was joined to the Russian empire as a grand duchy, thousands of Finns made their careers in the Russian army or navy, and many reached high rank. Even in 1917 there were several Finns besides Mannerheim among Russian generals. Nevertheless Mannerheim felt a sense of strangeness – of being an alien, perhaps – in the Russian world. Many examples of this can be found as far back as his early time with the Cadet Corps. 'My dear, the way of the world is truly strange,' he wrote to Sophie. 'Seven years ago I should never have believed that I would become a Finnish cadet and, with luck, a Russian page so that I can later go away and bury myself somewhere in Russia.' Even at the Cavalry School he could emphasise to Sophie that her work as a governess in Sweden was very much to be preferred to what he was doing. It was something 'entirely different to be surrounded by Swedes, with whom one can sympathise in many respects, than to have to fight for one's bread here in Russia with a bunch of coarse Russian cavalrymen' (1.11.87).

However, Gustaf Mannerheim was soon able to adapt himself to his surroundings in St Petersburg and in the Cavalry School. Since the time of Peter the Great it had been the desire of the Russian armed forces to enlist good material from other peoples besides the Great Russians, not least from the increasing number of those who, over the course of time, had become incorporated into the empire. Until a harsh nationalism developed at the beginning of the twentieth century, the Russians displayed a judicious tolerance over this, and there was perhaps a special appreciation of Finns. Mannerheim felt sympathy towards many of his non-Russian comrades and above all found friends an all sides with comparatively liberal views – 'modern opinions', as he often put it. There were several salons where he was made to feel at home, and where he saw a connection between the surroundings he had known in Finland and those in Russia. He developed in many ways a positive attitude towards the Russians, and his warning to a German military observer during the Russo-Japanese War not to underestimate them was typical; he thought this was a mistake often made by the Baltic Germans. However, it is clear that Mannerheim preserved his own individuality and did not allow himself to be assimilated. It was characteristic of him to observe at a critical period – 1903–4 – that he had then lived for seventeen years in a strange environment, where people did not understand him or he them.

The officer cadets in the Cavalry School received a good education not merely in military subjects. They studied many academic subjects as well: Russian literature, history, languages and natural sciences. The young Mannerheim was an interested and industrious student, and he produced excellent results. He had the misfortune to suffer a bad attack of typhus in 1887, which made him fall behind somewhat, but by the end of the course after two years he had made good what he had lost. He himself thought that he should have passed out in top place in his group and thus had his name inscribed on a commemorative plaque in the hall. However, extraneous considerations worked to the advantage of a well-born Russian; nothing could be done about it, and Mannerheim thus passed out second.

An officer cadet passing out from the School could apply to continue his career in various ways. He could aim high – at a Guards regiment – or content himself with a less dazzling career in one of the numerous regiments of the line stationed in the provinces. Of course these questions of future employment filled the thoughts of the cornets at the School and were eagerly discussed. Gustaf Mannerheim had to discuss them first with Uncle Albert. 'It seems to me', observed his uncle, 'that you ought to choose a cheap regiment and make your way up by hard work and diligent studies. By this road you may not perhaps establish yourself so quickly or attain to such a high position in life. But your career will make progress and you will become a capable man, working as well as you can for the good of mankind.'

But the young Mannerheim did not want to take this advice; he was aiming higher. It was not only life in St Petersburg and splendid uniforms that attracted him; he also thought of the work involved, and wanted an appointment which offered interest and stimulating surroundings. For financial reasons he had to make a successful military career, and the guards and the General Staff Academy offered the safest routes to that end. 'I have neither influence nor means. A Guards uniform is therefore especially important. The majority of Finns who have attained success began in the Guards.' Of those regiments he preferred the Chevalier Guards, which had the Empress Dagmar* as its colonel-in-chief and which had entrée to the

*The Empress Maria Fedorovna, the consort of Alexander III,. was born Princess Dagmar, daughter of Christian IX of Denmark.

court. The regiment, founded by the Emperor Paul in 1798, had the best spirit and comradeship in the entire army. Merely to belong to it was a good recommendation. 'The officers are well educated and live simply.' The problem was that the pay was far too low, yet it was all but impossible for him to carve out a career in Russia through his own exertions and capability. With an ordinary line regiment in the country one would be lulled into indifference and apathy. Thus Gustaf Mannerheim needed a loan in order to be able to make his way forward in the Guards. Uncle Albert gradually yielded, and as for the financial side of the matter, that was eventually arranged: 'Grandmother Louise' was willing to assist with a loan so that the deficit of the early years could be covered. But in spite of all this, the Chevalier Guards proved for the moment to be only a dream; there was no vacancy there, and Gustaf was forced to apply to a regiment in the provinces in the hope that his luck would improve later. This was the 'Black Dragoons' in Kalisz, so called because of the colour of their uniforms. They were stationed in the far west of Poland, on the German frontier.

After two years the possibility arose for Gustaf Mannerheim to transfer to the Chevalier Guards. He mobilised all his connections with the authorities who had the decision in their hands. At last, in 1891, he was successful and for the next thirteen years he remained in the regiment. Service there was no disappointment. He had the advantages of able and considerate commanders and good comradeship; several of his contemporaries became lifelong friends. He now had to carry out the duties of a junior officer, mainly the training of recruits, and guard duty, including periodical attendance on the Emperor. Mannerheim soon gained the confidence of his brother-officers; he was a trustworthy friend, and not given to intrigue. According to his contemporaries in the regiment (Vladimir Murav'ev and Konstantin von der Pahlen), he was energetic, correct over money matters, a good sportsman and an excellent rider, and lived soberly. The young Finn also won the esteem of his superiors. Early in his service, the demanding Grand Duke Nicholas Nikolaevich the elder* took notice of him and his knowledge of horses.

The officers of the Chevalier Guards were popular in the social life of St Petersburg, and Mannerheim was soon received at court and in aristocratic salons. He had ample opportunities to go to the theatre and ballet, hear classical and modern music, and see good art. It was natural for him to accept the customs and values, usually international ones, of these circles around

*The third son of Nicholas I; Inspector-General of the Cavalry.

the imperial court, and all through his life he made a point of observing the standards of courtesy and solicitude for others which he learned then. In this respect he was a model, and in old age he had increasing cause to deplore the fact that 'coarse modern times have condemned many warm and pleasant traditions to disappear'.

Studies at the General Staff Academy were now forgotten; in the Russian army, service in the Guards was thought to afford adequate training even for the highest appointments. Moreover, St Petersburg was a centre of politics where anyone interested could follow developments in foreign policy and become oriented towards the view of Russia as a great power. The decade of the 1890s was an important one, and Gustaf Mannerheim often passed on his observations to his family, who had a keen interest in politics. The Franco-Russian alliance came into being at this time, and was severely criticised by Mannerheim's father, who regarded it as a betrayal of the true interests of France.

The officers of the Chevalier Guards were frequently called on to perform duties connected with the imperial court. The Guards were responsible for guard duty within the palaces, particularly the Winter Palace. On such occasions as imperial weddings and funerals and visits by foreign royalty, they had to take part in special guard duty and court functions. For these functions tall men were sought after, and Mannerheim met that requirement. When Alexander III died in 1894, he had to be on duty at the funeral ceremony, which was a magnificent but protracted affair, the procession being led by a squadron of the Chevalier Guards, in their parade uniforms with the famous silver eagle on their helmets. As the regiment always had big horses, they were clearly visible above the crowds. Two years later, on 26 May 1896, the coronation in Moscow of Nicholas II and Alexandra bore witness to the size and strength of the empire in a unique spectacle. The Chevalier Guards were sent to the ceremony, and Mannerheim was a focus of attention when, with a comrade from the regiment, he walked ahead of the young Emperor in the magnificent procession. The Finnish painter Albert Edelfelt described this historic occasion to his mother: 'Gustaf Mannerheim walked before the Emperor's baldaquin with drawn sabre and looked very handsome – truly imposing.' The tragic accident which occurred later in the day, causing hundreds of deaths, made an indelible impression on Mannerheim.

Four years previously, in 1892, Gustaf Mannerheim had married the charming and good-hearted Anastasia Arapova, the daughter of a Russian general and former Chevalier Guards officer who had died some years before. Anastasia had inherited a considerable fortune, which gave the young couple a sound financial position. Mannerheim considered her interest in music a great asset, 'and she was not at all so Russian' as he had expected. The couple had two daughters, Anastasia (born 1893) and Sofia (1895), and undoubtedly this marriage, which at first was happy, helped to balance out the difference between Mannerheim and his Russian surroundings.

One day in the autumn of 1897 Mannerheim received a summons from his former commanding officer in the Chevalier Guards, General Artur von Grünewald, now head of the imperial stables department. The General was looking for a young assistant and had recalled his favourite, the young Finnish expert on horses. Mannerheim could not resist the offer, which was made yet more tempting by the prospect of pleasant journeys abroad and fine official quarters. A happy time now began, although he had to leave 'my agreeable regiment' with its good comradeship. Now followed many interesting journeys to buy the best possible horses from famous stud farms in Germany, Austria and Hungary, and he could also count on help from his brother Johan, who had become a farmer and was a good judge of horses. On one of these journeys Mannerheim suffered a severe injury. He had previously had several minor accidents during races, but on this occasion, in Berlin, a kicking horse broke one of his knee-caps. Operations and long periods in hospital were necessary in Berlin and St Petersburg. This accident prevented him from taking part in the centenary celebrations of the Chevalier Guards and for a long time it was even doubt-ful whether he would be able to continue his army career. However, the hospitality and kindness shown him as a Guards officer by Kaiser Wilhelm II in Berlin was some consolation.

Horses, carriages and court life in St Petersburg were fascinating and magnificent, but Mannerheim was much too seriously interested in his profession to be contented with these things alone. He wanted to continue his military career, and when, after six years with the imperial stables, he received an offer which would enable him to do so, he accepted without hesitation. It came from one of the leading cavalry officers in Russia, General Aleksei Brusilov, whose name was to become widely known during the World War; he invited Mannerheim to take up an assignment of great interest to him: the command of the demonstration squadron of the Officers' Cavalry School in St Petersburg. The School had been founded by the Grand Duke Nicholas Nikolaevich the elder to improve the standard of riding and horse-breeding in the army. Those appointed to the staff were distinguished cavalry officers, attracted by rapid promotion; squadron commanders had the precedence of a colonel and could obtain a regimental command directly after leaving the School.

Mannerheim's military career was thus following a successful course, but the first years of the twentieth century were difficult ones for him personally. His marriage had gone from one crisis to another. Anastasia, who had a restless nature, had gone out as a nurse to the Russian troops in Manchuria during the Boxer Rebellion in 1900, but the task was beyond her strength, and she returned ill. Two years later she left their home in St Petersburg with her daughters for a visit to the French Riviera, and Mannerheim understood that their marriage had come to an end. Because of the dominant influence of the Orthodox Church, it was impossible for him to get a divorce in Russia, and thus he had to be content with a bachelor's life. He found compensation in friendships with some of the outstanding women of St Petersburg society – one connection in particular, with the intelligent and charming Countess Elizaveta Shuvalova (née Baryatinska), gave rise to talk.

Mannerheim did not see Anastasia again till 1936, when they met in Paris. They were able to agree that life can be full of misunderstandings, and that offence can be given and taken unnecessarily. She was already ill, and died the same year. He was happy afterwards that their meeting had sustained her, and that she understood that he had acted sincerely and with good intentions.

As for their two daughters, they ceased living with Anastasia in 1910, and contacted their father and their relatives in Finland and Sweden. Mannerheim did not like the idea of bringing them up in his military surroundings in Poland, and his sister Sophie, a prominent hospital nurse in Helsinki, managed to make a home for them. Both had difficulties in adapting themselves to their Finnish environment: Sophie eventually went to live in Paris, and Anastasia entered a Roman Catholic religious order.

On top of Mannerheim's domestic troubles in1904 came political ones. Threatening clouds had long been visible on the horizon, and for Finland these meant strong pressure from Russian nationalism and military power. Since 1809 the country had become accustomed to many benefits from its imperial protection. The Finnish Diet was summoned in 1863 for the first time since 1809, and a cautious policy of reforms then followed. But the almost idyllic conditions which developed in the nineteenth century were followed by a harsh regime aimed at the russification of the country; the institutions of the grand duchy of Finland and its autonomous position in the Russian empire were to be dismantled. Under Nikolai Bobrikov, the governor-general, the new policy began abruptly in 1899. The administration was russified, the Finnish army was disbanded, and it was ordered that young Finns were in future to perform their military service in Russia. This was answered by a strike of those due to be conscripted. Confronted by-resistance, the Governor-General was given the right, as in the empire, to send undesirable persons into exile – if necessary outside Finland. Censorship of the press was introduced.

Mannerheim, like many of his fellow-countrymen in St Petersburg, not unnaturally thought that the politicans at home in Finland were being excessively compliant and at the same time neglecting the opportunities that existed to make use of the fennophile circles in Russia. He considered that the Russian nationalist front was by no means as strong or as united as it appeared; thus there was hope for the future. We catch a glimpse of his thoughts and hopes in his letters; in 1901 he urged those in Helsinki to exploit the goodwill which many members of the imperial family felt towards Finland. Gustaf Mannerheim's first personal crisis arising from the political situation came with the exiling of his elder brother Carl in April 1903. As a lawyer in Helsinki, Carl Mannerheim had taken part in the fight for legality and thus attracted Russian disfavour. He was not alone: the politicians Leo Mechelin and Victor Magnus von Born and many other leading Finns had to keep him company on the journey to Sweden. Gustaf, who was then in Moscow, at once took his brother's part against the 'brutal' Bobrikov régime. 'I scarcely need tell you how sorry I am to see you struck by such a hard and unjust blow,' he declared to his brother Carl. However there was a ray of light in that his brother had avoided deportation to Russia; and the recognition and sympathy Carl received from all sides was to sustain his morale. Gustaf wrote that he was at his brother's disposal for any service he could do (27.4.03).

Gustaf Mannerheim viewed the immediate future with concern. 'I cannot believe', he wrote to Carl, 'that Bobrikov's desire for vengeance will be satisfied with your exile. Our boats will have to bring away one cargo of exiles after another.' In St Petersburg there had been violent censure of the expulsions from Finland, but perhaps this was from a desire to be diplomatic. In Russia it was usual for the system of government to exact great sacrifices from its subjects; for example, a blind eye was turned when 35,000 workers were sent home from Moscow before the imperial visit to the city which Mannerheim had witnessed in 1903. 'The authorities are satisfied, for the impression must be that all is going well, there is no sign of trouble and everything that was said about dissatisfaction, disorder and so on is just idle talk . . . But the people I met expressed their indignation at B's violent policies. However, public attention is more occupied by developments in Macedonia and in the Far East . . . I have not suffered personally from these sad events, but every day it becomes more and more distasteful to remain in the service.'

Carl Mannerheim's exile was soon followed by the departure to Sweden of their brother Johan to start a new life, with his Swedish wife Palaemona Treschow, as an industrialist and farmer; and during the period of political oppression, their aunt Mimmi sold Louhisaari and left for Sweden, where she spent her last years. Gustaf's life was to follow a different course from that of his brothers. Now, as both earlier and later, he put loyalty and the fulfilment of duty first. Only if this led one into degradation, subversion or downright criminality did one have the right to break free. For the time being he hoped for a brighter future. He disapproved of the Russian policy of oppression and remained loyal to his brothers Carl and Johan, but when indignation in Finland came to a head in June 1904 with the murder of Bobrikov, Gustaf Mannerheim was no more able than the respected lawyer and liberal leader Leo Mechelin to approve of such a deed: murder represented an abandonment of the ideals of a lawful struggle, with perilous consequences for a society based on the rule of law.

Work at the Cavalry School provided Gustaf Mannerheim with a new stimulus. Important reforms were in progress there in the art of riding, which had long been conventional and conservative, and Grand Duke Nicholas Nikolaevich* had arranged for the appointment of James Fillis, the internationally known English riding master, as instructor. Mannerheim was able to inform his family that he was well satisfied with his new appointment.

---

*'The younger', son of Grand Duke Nicholas Nikolaevich the elder, who died in 1891. The son, like the father, became Inspector General of the Cavalry.

III
THE RUSSO-JAPANESE WAR
1904–1905

The Russo-Japanese War broke out in the spring of 1904. Mannerheim had already reported in his letters home in 1903 the unexpected threat which had arisen in the Far East, and his astonishment at how little attention the Russians paid to it; St Petersburg was far from Vladivostok and Mukden. As rumours multiplied, the Russians trusted to negotiations with the 'yellow men' to solve the problems, but the negotiations were badly handled and the Japanese attacked without a declaration of war.

The Russians' defeat on the Yalu river showed at the start of the war what kind of difficulties confronted them in their conduct of war and policy. The decision was taken to send large military reinforcements – in which the Guards regiments were not included. Mannerheim, like some of his comrades, found it hard to remain in the calm of the capital; he was eager to gain experience of war and therefore wanted to volunteer for active service, but the oppressive Russian policy in Finland placed an obstacle in his way. When he told his relatives of his plans, they reacted strongly. His father travelled to St Petersburg to discuss the situation with his son. Both Carl and Johan had already written to him with sharp criticism and more pointed advice. Gustaf Mannerheim replied from Krasnoe Selo on 28 June 1904 in a letter addressed to Carl, whom he reminded that he was as deeply disturbed by Bobrikov's policy and his brother's exile as were the rest of the family. He had considered, at the time, leaving Russian service, but his father, brothers and sisters had quickly dissuaded him, and any thought of leaving the service now during a war was impossible. 'A year ago, when we felt extreme bitterness over your banishment, I would have regarded throwing everything up as only a justified expression of opinion. What would then have been a justified expression of opinion would assume a totally different character and name today – in other words, it is at present absolutely impracticable.'

For an officer to perform his duties, Mannerheim emphasised, does not imply that he approves of the more or less temporary measures of the prevailing political régime. He follows his profession in a state in which there are different lines of development, and he must not become isolated from the life of the state. 'Most if not all opinions are usually

14

represented within a country's army. To demand the voluntary repudiation of all opinions other than the official one only helps indirectly to strengthen a cause which does not command support. So long as you do not come into a direct conflict of loyalty, I cannot see the advantages of this principle. On the contrary, I see the most practicable course as being to try to obtain as strong a position for yourself as possible, taking an active part in all that concerns the army and to using every opportunity to try to develop your abilities and gain experience. Although not a soldier, you must easily realise that nothing corresponds to this aspiration, which in my opinion is an absolutely creditable one, so much as participation in a thoroughly serious campaign. In a foreign war the individual is not fighting for a régime but rather for the country to whose army he belongs.'

The profession of a soldier demanded practical experience. Also, Mannerheim's own personal circumstances contributed to his decision: 'You must also understand and recognise that seventeen years' service and residence in a place must form certain bonds and impose certain obligations which men of all opinions have to respect . . . Besides these purely theoretical reflections, I have several personal reasons as well. I am thirty-seven years old. Serious campaigns do not occur often, and if I do not take part in this one, there is every chance that I shall become a mere armchair soldier, who will have to keep silent while more experienced comrades make the most of their wartime impressions. After a war such as this the number of the "more experienced" will run into thousands.'

Thus Mannerheim offered himself for service on the Manchurian front. He was appointed lieutenant-colonel in the 52nd Nezhin Dragoon Regiment, which was commanded by the liberal-minded Colonel Pavel Stakhovich, and formed part of a corps commanded by General von Bilderling, Mannerheim's former commander at the Nikolaevskoe Cavalry School. Before leaving for the Far East Mannerheim went to Helsinki to see his family and friends, who had loyally accepted his decision while disapproving of his motives: why should he risk his life for an emperor and a system of government that were responsible for his brother Carl's banishment and were trying to destroy the social system of Finland? He deserved a better fate and he could have become more useful. On 15 October 1904 he left Helsinki for the front, travelling by train from St Petersburg to Moscow and thence by the long Trans-Siberian Railway. Former comrades from the Chevalier Guards accompanied him to the station in the capital, and in Moscow he was seen off by other friends.

On the train Mannerheim began to keep a diary, which with few interruptions he continued till the end of the campaign. It was a long journey to the front. The capacity of the Siberian Railway was never particularly large, and now during the war passenger traffic encountered even more difficulties than usual. From Moscow the route ran to Irkutsk, and then Lake Baikal had to be crossed by boat, because the railway line around it had still not been completed. Mannerheim crossed the lake on 31 October in a snowstorm. On 15 November he was at Harbin. The route lay through Nikol'sk Ussuriisky. He and his travelling companions availed themselves of the opportunity to make a detour to Vladivostok while awaiting the arrival of their horses by a later train; then the journey continued to Mukden,* which was finally reached on 20 November, On the journey Mannerheim had the opportunity to discuss the war and politics with his travelling companions. Some were sympathetic and 'modern', others were dyed-in-the-wool reactionaries and strong nationalists. In his writing he expressed time and again his suspicions and fears of Russian reaction. After the long journey to the front, Mannerheim arrived to a winter campaign. His regiment, the Nezhin Dragoons, were 13 miles south of Mukden, and the outpost line ran as close as 1½ miles further south. When he arrived, his new comrades gave him a good reception, but life with them was fairly trying for an energetic officer like Mannerheim. At first there was little to do, and he therefore had plenty of time to write down his experiences.

From his diary and letters home we can follow the development of a young officer faced by the realities of war. He looked at the course of events mainly from the standpoint of military efficiency; in this the Russian army commanders in the most easterly parts of the empire were open to criticism, and the young Finn did not spare them. It is well known that General Kuropatkin, commanding the land forces, was an unsatisfactory commander, and under him one reverse followed another. Partly the system itself was to blame, since commanders of different sectors not infrequently gave exaggerated reports of Japanese superiority. Some of the generals sought in this way to excuse their own failures or to give exaggerated reports of Japanese superiority to magnify their own achievements. The result could be unfortunate decisions by the high command, which had thus been given a false picture of the situation.

There was much else in the army that gave cause for criticism. Com-

---

*Mukden, the capital of the province of Manchuria, was then a Russian administrative centre, since Russia had a firm hold on this part of China. In spite of promises to Peking to evacuate it as soon as possible, the government in St Petersburg continued the occupation on various pretexts, and China was powerless to resist.

manders intrigued and struggled for power and sometimes made themselves appear ridiculous by courting popularity among their men. Defective discipline in the ranks was especially noticeable with the Cossacks; along with efficiency and bravery went actions of folly, cowardice and pillage. The reserve officer system was unsoundly based, and this was a major reason why the officers were not always able to perform adequately. Because the Cossacks did not respect the international rules of war or the property of the civilian population, the Russians found the Chinese turning against them. Mannerheim regarded unchecked drunkenness as a cancer in the army. Defective hygiene was also a severe handicap, and he tried to interest his brother-officers and his men in sport and outdoor activities at times when there was nothing else to occupy them.

Mannerheim concluded from these experiences that the troops had to be taught discipline and order, the officers also must not become slack or drink to excess, and that military law was to obeyed uncompromisingly. Commanders had to display energy and an offensive spirit. However, the war still had not made any great impact on the sector of the front where Mannerheim was posted. In his letters he was able to assert that reality did not correspond to the terrible descriptions he had become familiar with in Émile Zola's famous account of the Franco-Prussian War of 1870, *La débâcle*. Soon enough he was to experience something similar.

Mannerheim was eager to gain military experience, and thus often tried to join active operations. He succeeded at an early stage in taking part in the raid towards the coast led by General Mishchenko. This popular and well-known cavalry officer had been given the task of capturing the port of Yin-kou and cutting the railway between Port Arthur and Mukden by making a surprise attack with large cavalry forces (see Map, pp. 24–5, below). It was an important operation and great expectations were pinned on it. The raid began on 6 January 1905. The march was undertaken in three columns. The Nezhin Dragoon Regiment rode in the right column, which was commanded by General Aleksandr Samsonov (later to acquire a melancholy fame at the outbreak of the World War through the Russian defeat at the Masurian lakes). Mannerheim commanded two detached squadrons. However, the great enterprise was a failure. Mannerheim had thought that the Russian units would 'roar out like a gale'. But the advance was too slow. The troops were weighed down by excessive and over-heavy equipment. Minor operations delayed the main thrust, and the element of surprise was lost. The Japanese had time to bring up infantry, which made an attack on Yin-kou impossible. Also the railway could not be cut.

A Russian offensive against San-de-pu followed Mishchenko's raid.

This was led by a Finn, General Oskar Gripenberg, veteran of famous Russian campaigns in Turkestan, and now commander of the Second Army. He had favoured an active prosecution of the war, and criticised Kuropatkin's tactics as demoralising. But even this action at San-de-pu failed because of Kuropatkin's repeated interference. A sensational breach between the generals followed.

There now followed a Japanese offensive against Mukden. Port Arthur had fallen on 3 January 1905, thus releasing large Japanese forces for action elsewhere. The immediate Russian aim was to ascertain the enemy's movements and intentions by means of energetic reconnaissance. Mannerheim was given command of two detached squadrons of the Nezhin Dragoons, which were put under the 1st Siberian Corps commanded by General Gerngross; his operational area lay west of Mukden. The task was exacting and frequently dangerous. The Japanese had more modern equipment than the Russians, their machine-guns and also their artillery being particularly effective. The consequence was serious losses for the Russians. One of Mannerheim's reconnaissances was especially costly, and he described it briefly in a letter home: 'One day I had to carry out a reconnaissance with two light infantry detachments and three-quarters of a squadron which, thanks to the Japanese machine-guns, became very hot. In no time I had lost 15 men and about 20 horses. A young Count Kankrin, who was serving as my orderly, fell dead with a bullet in the heart at the moment when he was turning to take an order.' On one of these reconnaissances Mannerheim's beloved horse Talisman was shot under him. 'Fatally wounded, the noble animal carried me till the end of the battle to fall down and die to my deep sorrow after completing his task.'

Mannerheim's reports from these reconnaissances showed that the enemy was attempting a big enveloping operation towards Mukden, and contributed to Kuropatkin's decision to abandon the town. The order was given to retreat which, according to Mannerheim, was 'foolish' and badly executed: 'The withdrawal from Mukden was ghastly. It was decided so unexpectedly that all the baggage trains marched out at the same time as the troops, which produced an indescribable jam. The entire terrain was open to artillery cross-fire . . . I have seen troops who had fought like lions, whole regiments, crumbling in the course of a few hours into a few hundred men. I have also witnessed scenes which I cannot recall without disgust.'

During the battle Mannerheim gave proof of outstanding abilities. Dr

Faltin of the Finnish Red Cross recounted that he displayed a courage and assurance which impressed the soldiers. 'They felt instinctively that they were in the presence of a real leader and they obeyed.' A German military attaché, who witnessed the last fighting in Mukden, has described a scene at the railway station where he suddenly heard the Finnish cavalry march: the Nezhin Dragoons, with the blue collars on their uniforms, dashed up with Mannerheim at their head, and gave the infantry a badly-needed breathing space. Mannerheim himself summed up after the battle, 'How one came out unscathed is something one really cannot understand oneself.' However, during the retreat from Mukden Mannerheim fell ill, and had to ride his horse while suffering from a temperature of 104°. 'I was so weary that I was ready to lie down under artillery fire.' To have carried out his duties in that condition must have called on all his endurance and will-power. Eventually he got a place on an improvised hospital train and reached the Finnish field ambulance at Kunchu-lin, north of Mukden, where he received treatment.

New tasks awaited Mannerheim on his return to duty, mainly involving reconnaissances into Mongolia. The final phase of the war involved a remarkable mission. Mannerheim had to undertake long-range reconnaissance rides as commander of some improvised Chinese militia – in reality 'local highwaymen' who had been enlisted in the Russian service. However, it was not the long-drawn-out land battles that proved decisive for the course of the war, but the fate of the Russian Baltic fleet. Its defeat in the Sea of Japan at the battle of Tsushima was the enemy's most brilliant victory – 'above all a victory which will decide the war', Mannerheim remarked. Peace came into effect on 5 September 1905, on terms that were surprisingly mild to the Russians.

The war was over, and Mannerheim had made his first important contribution as a servant of the Russian empire. And for himself, he had gained the experience of war which he had sought. He was not slow to draw his conclusions from it, and ten years later he was able to put them to use. However, the advent of peace did not mean that he could travel home. Large masses of troops had to be transported back to Russia, a process which lasted for months and had to be supervised.

In the mean time the social structure of Russia had cracked open. The strains of the costly, badly-led campaign in the Far East had had their effect, and with the conclusion of peace the first revolution broke out. Mannerheim, who eagerly followed internal political developments, was not surprised. The ruling bureaucracy, which he mistrusted, did not in the end relinquish its hold: 'All I can understand is that they are playing a

dangerous game in St Petersburg' (3.2.05); he observed on the internal
political front 'an obstinacy which promises little good'. The imperial
manifesto promising a constitution and civil rights followed on 17 October
1905, and news of it reached Mannerheim while the troops were being
evacuated from Siberia. 'When our column reached the railway line we
were met by a newsvendor with the constitutional manifesto. I bought a
whole bundle and got an orderly to gallop off to distribute the manifesto to
the officers in all squadrons of the regiment' (12.11.05). Nevertheless, he
remained sceptical. Earlier, after the Emperor's promise to summon a
parliament, the state Duma, he had already doubted whether this would
'satisfy many elements in society. If you take account of the fact that the
revolutionary movement in recent times has obtained its strongest support
from the working people, I cannot imagine that this permanent hotbed of
disaffection has been reckoned with at all, and will be given the chance to
elect a single representative' (30.8.05). He thought himself that 'these
absolutely amazing political upheavals are of riveting interest'.

The October manifesto, pushed through by Grand Duke Nicholas
Nikolaevich the younger, saved the Emperor his throne, although revolutionary disturbances continued for a time afterwards. There were rumours
of mutiny and the murder of officers, but when these reached Carl Robert
Mannerheim he received them calmly, because 'Gustaf is on good terms
with his men, whom I have always seen him treat in a friendly way like
human beings' (19.12.05). The war also brought about revolutionary
consequences for Finland. The dictatorship eased under Bobrikov's successor, to Mannerheim's great delight, and eventually legal order was
completely restored. A new senate (or government) was formed with Leo
Mechelin as leader, and made up largely of liberal politicians who had
defended the Finnish constitutional position during the years of
oppression. A period of reform was ushered in.

Mannerheim now at last enjoyed a long leave, and returned to Helsinki;
he wanted to familiarise himself with conditions at home since the restora-
tion of legality. 'The changes which have taken place in Finland fill me
with amazement . . . The most persecuted yesterday are the most influential men in the country today. If only everything would continue on the
same auspicious course' (12.2.06). His brother Carl had already had his
banishment revoked, and he was offered a seat in Mechelin's senate, but he
declined it and stayed in Sweden. Gustaf Mannerheim had wanted on
previous occasions to take part in the Finnish Diet but had always been
prevented by his duties. Now, when the four estates of nobles, clergy,
burgesses and peasants were to meet for the last time, he had a new oppor-

tunity; he represented the baronial branch of the Mannerheim family. Before long the radical parliamentary reform was begun which resulted in a single-chamber parliament, elected by a universal franchise that applied even to women. But, as Mannerheim observed, 'strangely enough the socialist parties continue to be dissatisfied.' He began to fear that the reform had been carried out too quickly, and was made uneasy by the existence of the Red Guard, which had been formed by socialist elements during the Great Strike of 1905. The country seemed on the brink of civil war, but instead developments moved in the direction of Russian reaction. He was to see unpleasant signs of this during the journey he was soon to undertake across Russia and China to Peking: 'In our great neighbouring country reaction is lying in wait for new victims' (13.2.06).

IV

THE RIDE ACROSS ASIA
1906–1908

Mannerheim was to have no opportunity to participate in Finnish politics or social development, because at this very time his career took an entirely different direction – a result of the qualities he had shown during the Manchurian campaign. The chief of the general staff, General Palitsyn, was paying great attention to conditions on the empire's southern border adjoining China. Preparedness for a war in the future was essential; a reformed China was capable of becoming dangerously strong. What was now happening in western China regarding reforms and military policy? What was the attitude towards Peking of the non-Chinese, partly Muslim population in the western provinces? Earlier they had rebelled against the Chinese: could the Russians count on their support? Military operations might be necessary in Turkestan with its difficult mountainous terrain and desert regions. Inadequate information was available about roads and passes and their practicability for the movement of infantry, cavalry and artillery.

Palitsyn happened to think that Mannerheim, the capable rider and talented officer, with his recently-acquired experience of war in the Far East, should be suitable for a reconnaissance mission in that vast region. The general did not order Mannerheim to go, but merely offered him the assignment, which he accepted.

The mission was highly secret – in many respects it was politically sensitive, even in relation to the British in India – and it was therefore carefully disguised as a largely scientific expedition. The explorer Mannerheim was attached to a French expedition in Asia (France and Russia were staunch allies and no political misgivings were encountered in Paris); this expedition, led by the well-known archaeologist Paul Pelliot from the Sorbonne, was due to travel along the same or adjacent routes to those being taken by Mannerheim.

Mannerheim was attracted not least by the possibility of expanding the military task he had been given partly into a scientific one as well. Here at last he might achieve something independently and give his life a new direction. He could associate himself with the great traditions of his family, represented above all by the name of Adolf Erik Nordenskiöld, the navi-

22

Carl Robert Mannerheim

Gustaf Mannerheim as a cadet with his eldest
brother Carl

Helène Mannerheim, née von Julin

Fencing practice at the Nikolaevskoe Cavalry School

The coronation of Nicholas II in Moscow, 26 May 1896. Lieutenant Mannerheim
of the Chevalier Guards is on the right in front of the Emperor

Gustaf Mannerheim as commander of the 13th Vladimir Lancer
Regiment at Nowo Mińsk in 1909; the uniform was blue with
a yellow plastron

Gustaf Mannerheim in the uniform of the Chevalier Guards

Anastasia Mannerheim, née Arapov, in 1898

Anastasia and Sophy Mannerheim

The fair at Uzgenn where Mannerheim bought horses

Mannerheim measuring the height above sea level in the Chapchal Pass

The mandarin general of Aksu in 1907 with his three wives, children
and several servants

Mannerheim's caravan ascending the glacier in the Muzart Pass

Mannerheim with officers of H.M. the Emperor's Guard Lancer Regiment in
Warsaw in 1913

Mannerheim at an outdoor lunch party with Polish friends

At left: Mannerheim and Georg Scalon, the Governor-General of Poland

Below: With a hunting party on Count Potocki's Antoniny estate in Volhynia in 1913

In Odessa, 1915

In a village in the Carpathians

Mannerheim as a divisional commander with Colonel Zhukov, one of his regimental commanders

gator of the north-east passage, who had married his father's sister. The ride would pass through regions of great interest for archaeological, historical and ethnographical research. In particular the eastern part of the vast area of Turkestan had recently been found to contain fabulous treasure from antiquity. Sven Hedin had travelled here, in the 1890s, inspired by Nordenskiöld's example; Sir Aurel Stein had found great hoards of manuscripts; notable Buddhist paintings had been discovered by the Prussian ethnographer Albert von Le Coq; and Russian explorers such as N.M. Przewalski and P.K. Kozlov had also been active there. Gustaf Mannerheim's relatives were pleased that he could now cultivate pursuits superior in quality to his military ones, in which they had little interest.

Mannerheim himself arranged cooperation with Finnish, Swedish and Russian scholars. Senator Otto Donner was a valuable supporter in Helsinki and provided contact with the Finno-Ugrian Society. The Antell Committee contributed a sum for the purchase of objects for the collections of the National Museum of Finland. Ethnographic expertise was contributed by Mannerheim's cousin Erland Nordenskiöld in Stockholm, a scholar specialising in the study of South American Indians.

The expedition offered yet another advantage in that it would remove Mannerheim from political events and from the feared Russian reactionary policy. His own reflection was that it was wonderful not to have to take part in punitive expeditions in the countryside and to be able to turn his back on Russia and its problems. During the first stage of the journey, down the River Volga, the passengers had the opportunity to acquaint themselves with violent reactionary propaganda in the Russian provincial press. Turkestan, which he reached next, had been governed by a liberal Russian official, Subbotich, whom Mannerheim liked, but to his regret this good administrator soon fell victim to reaction. Mannerheim thus found it 'wonderful in these volcanic times to plunge into the silence of the grave'.

The importance of the long ride prompted Mannerheim to make detailed notes and to take numerous photographs. His diaries with their extensive detail and route maps could not, however, be utilised by his Russian patrons till after his return. He therefore wrote long letters throughout the journey addressed to his father in Helsinki, who was to copy out the parts of the letters of interest to General Palitsyn (called 'Fedya' in the correspondence) and send them on to him in St Petersburg. Thus we have a voluminous series of fresh and vivid descriptions in Mannerheim's own hand as well as his diary.

At the end of the long ride Mannerheim also wrote a detailed report,

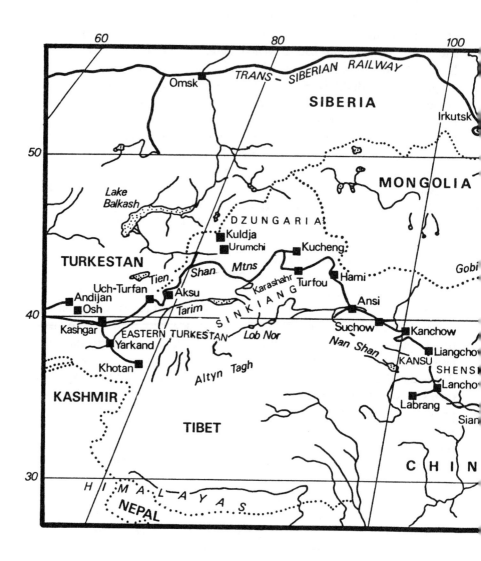

The ride across Asia.   *Inset, top right:* Manchuria, 1904–5.

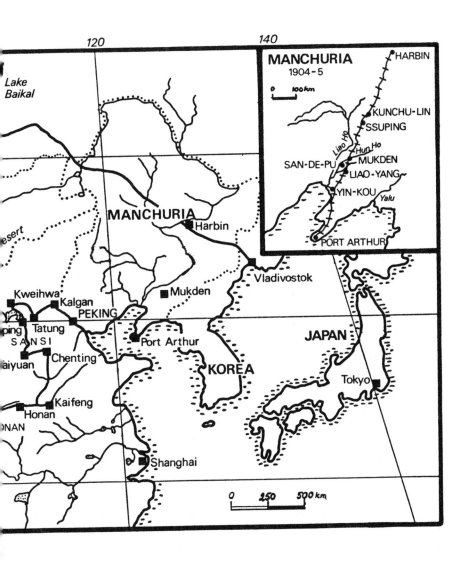

which was the most important document he prepared for the general staff. On the other hand he kept as his own property the considerably more comprehensive diaries and photographs, which were subsequently edited and published. He was unable to carry out the final work on them himself; this was entrusted by the Finno-Ugrian Society in 1937 to Professor Kaarlo Hildén, and the English edition of the work was published in 1940.

From Moscow the journey ran south to the Caspian Sea, first by train to Nizhni Novgorod and then by boat down the Volga to Astrakhan. This journey was of great interest, taking five days and passing through great varieties of scenery, and ending at Krasnovodsk. Mannerheim continued by train to Tashkent, where he met the then Colonel Kornilov, who later became famous in the drama of 1917. In Samarkand he was joined by two Cossacks who had been attached to the expedition, but in the end the hardships of the journey proved too much for them, and they had to be replaced by others.

The ride began at the town of Osh, where Mannerheim joined Pelliot's large company. They continued towards the frontier between Russia and China, which divided Turkestan in half. At the frontier Mannerheim saw evidence of the vast difference between the two empires: both, he thought, had been autocratically-ruled bureaucratic states for a long period, with a different social character from that of Finland. But whereas Western Turkestan lived under the protection of an ordered, Russian society and was a flourishing country, Eastern Turkestan was under Chinese administration and its people, although of the same origin as those on the western side, had sunk into apathy and poverty. They had been incapable of freeing themselves from Chinese oppression, despite lengthy struggles and insurrections. This, if nothing else, was a proof of Chinese military power.

Mannerheim was now to travel in Eastern Turkestan for more than a year exploring roads and passes; he was occupied principally with map-making. He entered the country through the high Taldyk pass, and then followed the ancient Silk Road to China, which had been known since Marco Polo's journey to Kublai Khan in 1271. The road led first to the big town of Kashgar where it divided into two branches, a northern and a southern. In Kashgar Mannerheim separated from his French companions. The idea was that they should meet later at Urumchi in Sinkiang, but this plan could not be realised. Contact with the French was maintained by letter. Mannerheim had now to reconnoitre the area around Kashgar. A month's stay there was followed by a six weeks' reconnaissance along the southern branch of the Silk Road towards India – obviously a link in the Russians' preparations for a possible conflict with the British. The first stage ended in Yarkand, which he found beautiful, and where he met a Swedish missionary and explorer, Gösta Raquette, who was to become his life-long friend and correspondent. From Yarkand the journey went through a desert region to Khotan, in the neighbourhood of which Aurel Stein had just carried out his successful investigations. This was the end point of the ride south.

After this southern detour, Mannerheim returned to Kashgar in order to continue from there along the northern branch of the Silk Road. The road went northwards along the edge of the great Takla Makan desert in the centre of Eastern Turkestan. His objective was the province of Ili, which had been occupied by the Russians thirty years previously, and his task there involved reconnaissance of the routes which might be used in the event of a new Russian operation into Chinese territory from the north. The journey went up into the huge mountain chains of the Tien Shan range, ever nearer to the Russian frontier. Mannerheim was to pay particular attention to the oasis of Aksu which was of military significance. After spending two weeks there, devoted to map-making, he had to cross the great and famous Muzart pass; part of the route was across a glacier, and the going was difficult. A source of pleasure here – as frequently elsewhere – was the magnificent scenery, which Mannerheim never tired of describing. This marked the beginning of a life-long interest in the Alpine world.

After the Muzart pass he reached the region of Ili and Kuldja, the most northerly point of his long journey, and an area in which the Russian military command was especially interested. The Chinese, too, had a clear appreciation of its military importance. The rivers and streams, which flowed south-eastwards, opened up routes into China which were worth new and detailed investigation. Estimates had to be made of their suitability for the movement of troops of different arms.

Mannerheim attempted in his politico-strategic deliberations to answer the question whether the non-Chinese population would be of assistance to the Russians if war were to break out. Only a few decades previously, large military operations had taken place there in the course of the struggle of the people for their political freedom against Chinese forces. However, Mannerheim did not think that insurrection by the non-Chinese, Turkic language-speaking population of Eastern Turkestan or by the Muslims of Western China could now be of any great significance to Russia; the Chinese had succeeded in suppressing their longing for freedom. His advice was to try a policy of infiltration.

The journey now continued first southwards to the valley of the River

Tekes and then through the Yuldus valley to Karashahr and Urumchi. These parts of the ride were also extremely strenuous. 'Everyone who loves the beautiful and magnificent in nature must enjoy this.' He had to endure 'the exertions accompanying a sporting life in the Alps'. In accordance with his instructions he steered his course for the inhospitable Yuldus valley with its harsh climate and rough roads.

When Mannerheim reached Urumchi he encountered the reforms and military-strategic planning of the new China, but these were still unimpressive. The town was an important administrative centre and commanded a major road network; if the Russians could succeed in capturing it, that would be of decisive importance on this sector of the front. In his report to the general staff Mannerheim outlined how such an operation could be carried out and indicated a suitable time of the year. But he warned against a more extensive operation into central China from such a very narrow base. The principal theatre of war ought once more to be in Manchuria.

Mannerheim's work now changed in character. In Eastern Turkestan his job had been to reconnoitre roads and terrain and obtain an idea of the political attitude of the non-Chinese population. In China proper his task was to gain an impression of the results of the recently initiated reforms. From Urumchi he rode through Kucheng to Turfan, an important place on the edge of the great Gobi desert. The desert was crossed after a ride of several weeks and he then reached the Great Wall of China at a little fortified town. 'When you go to bed in the evening in your grimy hovel at the foot of the walls of the fortress and hear shots and trumpet blasts proclaim that the five iron-bound gates are closing, you are struck by a solemn feeling of being at last within the Central Empire.'

After a ride of a year and a half in Turkestan and among the rugged mountain tracks of Sinkiang, a journey of 2,500 miles to Peking lay ahead of him. But he had now entered a cultivated landscape and a plain in contrast to the tremendous Tien Shan mountain range. His ride continued towards Lanchow – one of the most important objectives of his whole reconnaissance, for this town could serve as a base for a Russian offensive against the interior of China. Lanchow was of immediate interest as the centre of Chinese reform policy in Kansu and Sinkiang; and Shen, the powerful viceroy who ruled there, represented a new era. He had earlier served for a time at the Chinese legation in St Petersburg, and arranged a large dinner party for Mannerheim and the Europeans in the town. The guests wore evening dress with decorations, but when Mannerheim's father received a picture of this notable entertainment, he commented that his son 'in his travelling coat looks like a tramp'. The process of reform in western China did not impress the Finnish guest, since Shen plainly lacked sufficient strength to direct it.

On the way east Mannerheim halted at the monastery town of Labrang to look at a number of famous Buddhist temples – a visit which was disturbed by demonstrations by fanatical believers. At last he reached Sianfu, the capital of Shensi province. Here he received for the first time an impression of Chinese reforms of real importance, impressions which became more pronounced the nearer he approached to Peking. Greater progress had been made along the path of reform in Shensi than in Lanchow.

On 29 May 1908 Mannerheim heard again with unalloyed delight 'the melodious whistling of a locomotive'. He travelled by train first to Kaifengfu, the capital of Honan, and then to Taiyuan, capital of Shansi, where he again met the sole Cossack remaining in his company, Lukanin, with the expedition's horses and baggage. Here he sold the majority of his equipment and sent the Cossack with the remainder to Peking. He himself mounted his faithful Philip for a last ride in China. This was to Utaishan where the Dalai Lama, the Tibetan incarnation of the deity, was living in exile. The Dalai Lama eagerly received the emissary of the Russian Emperor, expecting a message. He was interested in politics and clearly took Russian support into account when making his calculations. His disappointment was evident when he found that Mannerheim had brought no letter with him. The journey on horseback ended on 20 July in Kalgan, where Mannerheim finally dismounted. He was soon in Peking.

His time there was mainly taken up with the preparation of a detailed account of the long ride and its results. But Mannerheim also made several interesting accquaintances during his stay; he met Kornilov again, whom he had last seen in Tashkent, and among the foreign diplomats were several with whom he was later to have dealings in post-war Europe. Before his return journey to St Petersburg, Mannerheim availed himself of the opportunity to pay a short visit to Japan. The country and the people – the doughty enemies of the war three years before – interested him.

The long ride across Asia was undoubtedly a success, but Mannerheim had to pay a heavy price with a deterioration in his health. For long afterwards he was to suffer from lumbago. At first he doubted whether he would be able to continue an active military career, but after a while his condition improved. In any case, after returning home he had to remind the authorities, who would now have to decide his future, of his existence. The high point, as after the Russo-Japanese War, was an audience with the

Emperor, who had to be informed of the results of the journey. Nicholas was so interested that he listened for an hour and twenty minutes – far in excess of the allotted time – as Mannerheim gave his account. After the audience the Emperor asked Mannerheim about his future plans: these were to obtain command of a regiment.

V

IN POLAND
1909–1914

Where would appointment as a regimental commander take Mannerheim? Throughout the vast Russian empire, there were many regiments, of variable quality – some of them were élite units, while others offered less agreeable conditions. Eventually he was appointed to take over the 13th Vladimir Lancer Regiment at Nowo Mińsk, east of Warsaw. During the Russo-Japanese War this regiment had belonged to the home forces and nobody there had any experience of war; however, with great energy Mannerheim set about the task of modernising its training to take account of what the war had taught the Russians. The results of his work were good, and after a close inspection by the Grand Duke Nicholas Nikolaevich, promotion to an élite unit, H.M. the Emperor's Guard Lancer Regiment in Warsaw, followed – thus demonstrating the confidence of the authorities in Mannerheim and his outstanding organising ability.

Mannerheim was now a major-general – the commanders of guards regiments held general's rank – and he had official quarters near the barracks in the neighbourhood of the beautiful Lazienki Park. Two years later he was appointed to the command of a brigade – comprising the Lancers, the Grodno Guard Hussar Regiment and a battery of horse artillery. Mannerheim took the field in the World War in 1914 with this Independent Guards Cavalry Brigade.

Gustaf Mannerheim's transfer to Poland in 1909 pushed the Russian empire's nationality problem once more into the forefront of his attention. Unlike Finland, Poland had come into armed conflict with Russia – in 1830 and 1863. Polish autonomy had then been smashed, and a rigorous russification policy had followed. Mannerheim was naturally very conscious of his position as a Russian officer in Polish eyes. Twenty years earlier he had turned down the idea of the Grodno Hussars when considering his choice of regiment at the Nikolaevskoe Cavalry School; in spite of being a distinguished Guards regiment it was stationed in Warsaw, where the population looked askance at Russian officers. However, now that he had finally come to Poland he succeeded – thanks to his personality, his tact and his interest in sport – in earning widespread goodwill. He could not understand the wisdom of the Russian oppressive policy. 'So long as

31

Russia does not manage to solve the Polish question successfully, it will always have millions of opponents among the Slavs themselves,' he wrote to his father. Among many new friends were some of the country's most able men, such as Prince Zdzislaw Lubomirksi, who became a members of the Council of Regency after the end of the war in 1918, and Counts Maurice and Adam Zamoyski, who played important roles in Polish life, the former becoming independent Poland's first ambassador in Paris, and the latter, like Mannerheim, chairman of his country's Red Cross. They all had progressive inclinations and were eager for reforms in education and health care. Lubomirksi's wife Marie was a talented woman with political and social interests; during the World War she maintained an interesting correspondence with Mannerheim, the Finnish general fighting the Central Powers on the plains of Poland.

The insights which Mannerheim gained into Polish and Russian politics during his years in Warsaw were of special interest to him. The Poles were confronted by the same problem as his own compatriots: to maintain their national character against Russian nationalism. They had failed earlier in their attempt to regain their independence by force of arms. Finland, after a century of quiet development, had at last reached a similar position to that of Poland. In the conditions of power politics then prevailing both peoples lacked the possibility of conducting a successful policy of radical opposition. In Finland thoughts of gaining complete independence were still impossible. Was it possible to attain a tolerable coexistence with Russia? Mannerheim was no exporter of a policy of unlimited compliance for Finland, but he did not support a hopeless struggle either. Were other courses open? Developments in Poland might perhaps provide an answer to the question.

The disturbances of world politics soon made themselves felt again. The struggle of the great powers in the Balkans, and Italy's attack on Turkey in 1911 in its attempt to seize Tripolitania, were factors ushering in dangerous developments. The Balkan War followed in 1912, with the eager attempt of the five small Balkan countries to seize what remained of Turkey's European possessions and divide them among themselves. Time after time a great power conflict seemed close. Developments were naturally followed attentively in Warsaw, which would be in the front line if war came.

Mannerheim thought over the risks and the prospects. Would St Petersburg really dare to enter a major conflict? Was the army actually prepared for one? Were the Panslavist aspirations in the Balkans sufficient grounds for such a venture?

The shots in Sarajevo on 28 June 1914 finally provoked a crisis, the depth and extent of which scarcely anyone could have conceived at the time. Up to the last moment hopes were pinned on a compromise. But Austria declared war on Serbia on 28 July. While Mannerheim was having dinner at his club in Warsaw on 29 July he was brought a fateful order; in reply to Austria's move St Petersburg had began mobilisation. This was the measure which soon precipitated the First World War. Berlin considered it could not allow the Russians to gain the advantage of an already completed deployment without attacking. Germany declared war on 1 August, the Austrian declaration following on 6 August. Thus Russia was once more at war but now in alliance with the Entente. As enemies the country had not only Austria-Hungary but also Germany, the strongest military power in Europe.

Mannerheim, personally, faced the same problem as in 1904: loyalty to the empire or the hope that a Russian defeat would bring a better future for Finland. It was clear that opinion in Finland was divided. Before long many began to seek support in Sweden and later in Germany for the liberation of the country. After failing to obtain the help they wanted in Sweden, Finnish volunteers went secretly to Germany to obtain military training. This operation became known as the *Jäger* movement, because those men were eventually organised into a Prussian *Jäger* (light infantry) battalion.

VI

THE FIRST WORLD WAR

1914–1917

During the first year of the war Mannerheim was convinced that the Allied powers would win a speedy victory. 'Britain's fighting forces will grow unceasingly and in neither Russia, France nor Britain will famine break out.' He considered the cause of the Entente morally superior to that of the Central Powers: the Germans, whom he admired for their industry and order, had shown to his disappointment and sorrow an unprecedented contempt for international law and an outrageous brutality and arrogance. It was therefore better to fight for a victorious conclusion to the war rather than to a compromise which would only mean a pause. The great conflict in Europe could not possibly last long.

However, belief in the striking power of the Russian army took a number of knocks. As early as the autumn of 1914 Mannerheim got to hear of shortages in the supply of ammunition and subsequently of other serious defects. But although at times the great successes of the Germans dejected him, he did not doubt that the Allies would ultimately win. Even after Russia's collapse in 1917 he retained that conviction – which, naturally enough, formed the basis of his views about the future of Finland and the correct policy to be followed there. His sympathies and those of his brothers and sisters were with the western Allies. It seemed to him wisest now, as in Russia's earlier wars, for Finland to try to gain Russian confidence by displaying an attitude of loyalty.

Mannerheim gave expression to these thoughts on several occasions in the first year of the war. He approved when Grand Duke Nicholas Nikolaevich, as commander-in-chief, issued a proclamation in 1914 promising greater freedom for the Poles; it was only a pity that it had not come earlier, before Russia's military situation had become so difficult. Should one not now show solidarity with the empire as it fought for its very existence? New thoughts arose in consequence. When Nicholas II visited Helsinki in May 1915, Mannerheim considered that the chairman of the city council, J.A. Norrmén, had been altogether too guarded in his speech of welcome. 'It would have been so easy in a few words to touch on some of the matters which the World War has made into burning questions, and to demonstrate that the people of Finland, or rather the citizens of Helsinki, are fully behind the aspirations of the empire' – such was his critical comment to Sophie Mannerheim in a letter (23.4.15). Others in Finland shared that opinion. Mannerheim also developed these views in a talk about his experiences in the war given to his former comrades from Hamina in the course of a prolonged visit to Helsinki at the beginning of 1916. However, it was clear he was not well informed of the climate of opinion then predominating in Finland. After his talk he was given a hint of the real situation by his old friends Birger Åkerman and Hannes Ignatius, both later to become generals, and on another occasion by Heikki Renvall, who became a member of the senate in 1917. Mannerheim himself was able to sum up cautiously that he had encountered differing opinions in Finland.

On the eve of the war the Guards Cavalry Brigade was given six hours' warning to march towards Lublin in southern Poland – and the troops' readiness to depart showed the excellent state of their training. 'In pouring rain we left Warsaw six hours after receiving the order to mobilise.' Nevertheless, when war broke out a few days later, the Russian mobilisation was far from complete. The army found itself in a dangerous situation, with the enemy well prepared to attack. Formations already mobilised had to protect the continuing Russian deployment.

The Guards Cavalry Brigade, south of Lublin, became part of General Tumanov's cavalry detachment (the general was a Caucasian, whom Mannerheim had known since the Russo-Japanese War, and who had become a friend to him and his daughters). The cavalry had been concentrated near the town of Krasnik, an important junction for the roads towards southern Poland. In mid-August it could be seen that enemy troops were advancing on a broad front. These were Austrian *Landwehr* formations, in great strength with cavalry and artillery, and far superior in numbers to the Russian defence.

Tumanov gave Mannerheim orders to take up a defensive position south of Krasnik immediately. This had to be held at all costs. The task was difficult, since the Austrians were trying to envelop the left flank of the defence and break through. Mannerheim could now put the lessons he had learned from the Russo-Japanese War into practice. Later he proudly contrasted his tactics at Krasnik with Kuropatkin's 'tactics of patience and defence'. He gave an offensive character to a defensive battle by deploying a third of his force for an attack in the enemy's rear. This became a successful outflanking movement. He led the action himself in the most forward positions with complete fearlessness. 'Constantly

Theatres of war, 1914–17.

composed and calm, he followed the development of the action and gave his orders,' recalled his chief of staff, Jeletski.

The battle at Krasnik ended in an Austrian defeat, which had a strategic significance far exceeding its actual scale. The dangerous enemy attack was halted, while the Russian deployment behind the front could continue. Mannerheim was rewarded with the sword of St George, a rare honour. However, after a short while Austrian troops were able to proceed to a new offensive towards Lublin. They drove forward again through Krasnik towards the Russian front which now curved round as far as the Vistula, and thus threatening the Russian lines of communication. Mannerheim received orders to drive the enemy back across the Chodel and retake the river crossings. He succeeded, thanks mainly to a surprise flank attack.

Up to now Mannerheim had encountered Austrian troops. In October 1914 a German offensive threatened Warsaw and the centre of the Russian western front. Following victories at Tannenberg and the Masurian lakes, General Hindenburg was able to go over to the offensive in the east with large forces. The Russian headquarters were forced to carry out extensive transfers of troops. The Guards Cavalry Brigade, which also comprised some rifle units, was now incorporated into a light formation to protect the Ninth Army on the Russians' left flank. The formation's task was to hold the small western Polish town of Opatów, 15½ miles north-west of Sandomierz. The Germans were quite close. 'We are again on the point of a great battle in which the Germans will certainly apply all their strength and vigour,' Mannerheim wrote to his father on 2 October. 'It is always with a sense of wonder that one sees these great battles emerge from the haze which for so long enshrouds the advance of an army and gradually assume a more distinct form.'

However, the attack was carried out by Austrian formations. The battle began on 3 October, and the enemy tried to outflank the Russian defence. The following day the rifles found themselves in a tight corner after their line of retreat was cut; they had to fight their way out with heavy losses. Mannerheim, on the other hand, succeeded in the course of fiercely fought actions in checking the enemy advance south of Opatów, But by then the battle was already lost and his troops too had to withdraw. During the retreat across the Vistula his brigade was in difficulties because all the bridges had already been destroyed; however, thanks to his presence of mind and vigour his forces made the crossing intact. For his achievement Mannerheim now received the Order of St George 4th class, the Russian order for valour. Sophie was told of her brother's pleasure: 'At

our age we are already fairly indifferent towards vanity and conceit. . .
Nevertheless I must confess that it was a happy moment for me when in
the middle of the night my chief of staff woke me with a telegram saying
that I had been decorated with the Order of St George.' The order
conferred not only prestige but also a small pension.

The German offensive rolled on. 'The third chapter of the war is
beginning for us. Everything gives us reason to believe that it will be much
more serious than the two preceding ones . . . At the moment the Germans are aiming at striking us a severe blow' (8.10.14). But developments
moved in a more favourable direction than had been feared. The commander-in-chief, Grand Duke Nicholas Nikolaevich, succeeded by means
of a finely planned counter-offensive in compelling Hindenburg to make
new dispositions, and thus saved Warsaw for the time being from falling
to the Germans. The Guards Cavalry Brigade took part in the offensive,
and this brought it close to Cracow, then a strongly fortified Austrian
town. But the Russian Ninth Army, to which the brigade belonged, halted
there. They had to spend Christmas at Kielce, in a beautiful part of the
Carpathians. Here Mannerheim met his friend Tumanov, 'whose cheerful
disposition and humour are always a great asset'.

From western Galicia, where the fortress of Cracow held out against the
Russians, the Guards Cavalry Brigade was moved to eastern Galicia where
a new offensive was planned. The commander of this was General
Brusilov, 'an old acquaintance . . . commandant of the Officers' Cavalry
School at the time I belonged to the School's permanent staff' (to Sophie
Mannerheim, 18.2.15). 'It will be interesting to ride through such natu-
rally beautiful regions, especially later in the spring' (to Louis Sparre,
10.2.15).

Mannerheim did not serve as commander of the Guards Cavalry Brigade
for more than half a year. On 2 March 1915 he was given command of the
12th Cavalry Division, whose regular commander had been wounded.
The regiments over which Mannerheim was now placed were, as he
emphasised, first-rate. Of the four cavalry regiments of the division the
Akhtyr Hussars were richest in tradition; they had fought the armies of
Frederick the Great and their origins went back to the seventeenth century. The Hussars' dolmans were chocolate-brown with gold braid, in
commemoration of a campaign during which the men had tried to warm
their frozen limbs with the brown habits of Capuchin friars, and their
horses had all to be of *café-au-lait* colour. The colonel-in-chief of the
regiment at that time was the Emperor's sister, Grand Duchess Olga
Aleksandrovna. The Starodubov Dragoons and the Belgorod Lancers also

had a distinguished past. The fourth cavalry regiment was the 3rd Orenburg Cossacks. A Russian cavalry division also·included an excellent artillery brigade and a sapper unit.

The divisional staff were experienced, hard-working and high-spirited, but somewhat unconventional – in a letter to Marie Lubomirska he described them with some humour. The senior was a Polish general, a true diplomat whose weary eye saw exactly what needed to be done. The senior medical officer, also a Pole, was a talented man, interested in everything except medical matters; he would happily have taken over command. However, the most important thing was 'that none of them idles about when we are in a tight spot'. 'Nothing makes responsibility easier than to be surrounded by young and dashing people,' Sophie was told.

When Mannerheim took over the 12th Cavalry Division its task was to delay the advance of Austrian troops towards the Dniestr. The battles, which were successful, were a stage in a Russian advance towards Stanisławów. Afterwards the division was moved east and during the following months was to operate on the great plains between the Dniestr and the Prut, with battles at Zaleszczyki, Uście Biskupie and Horodenka. 'We have carried out a fine advance,' he was able to inform Marie Lubomirska on 17 May, 'forcing the Dniestr and reaching the Prut.' However, the great breakthrough by the Central Powers at Gorlice-Tarnów happened at this time: their forces rolled eastwards. Mannerheim was shaken but after some reflection did not consider the enemy's success of decisive importance in relation to the war as a whole. However, the Russian armies were compelled to withdraw, and on 5 August 1915 German troops were able to enter Warsaw, where they remained until the end of the war.

The retreat was grim. The commander-in-chief, Grand Duke Nicholas, ordered a scorched earth policy, hoping by this means – following the precedent of the war against Napoleon – to stop the enemy's advance. Mannerheim regretted having to carry out these orders and thus be forced to contribute to the country's melancholy fate. 'All along our way fires, pillage and nameless suffering. I am ashamed and disgusted by the profession which I follow,' he wrote on 7 July 1915 to Marie Lubomirska. The consequences were destitution and terror.

During the summer of 1915 the division fought along the upper reaches of the Dniestr to delay the enemy's advance and protect the Russian withdrawal. There were long and tough battles on the Gnila Lipa and again at Zaleszczyki. Eventually the front stabilised along a line between the rivers Stryj and Strypa.

After half a year as commander of the 12th Cavalry Division Mannerheim had to report sick; the lumbago which he contracted in Manchuria and Turkestan had grown worse: 'I am suffering from severe rheumatic or neuralgic pains in the back and kidney region.' The doctors prescribed a course of baths, to be taken at Odessa on the Black Sea where there were warm springs. During his stay there Mannerheim received welcome company; his sister Sophie undertook the journey from Helsinki and he received news of the general state of affairs and opinion in Finland. Sophie for her part found that the war had changed her brother's previously light-hearted and humorous nature. 'The kind of experience they have over there turn them into serious people. They will never really forget what has happened to them,' was her comment. Gustaf spoke of 'his hard and rough exterior', but thought that underneath there could still be found 'a little feeling in spite of all the atrophy brought about by the war'.

After returning to his division, tough battles were fought on the Dniestr and its tributaries, and the Russians now succeeded in checking the enemy offensive to the east. He was commended for a successful cavalry attack at Haiworonka. There followed a calmer period, which Mannerheim used for a month's visit to his sister and friends in Helsinki. His father had died in the autumn of 1914 and his brother Carl a year later. He had not been to Finland since the summer of 1913 and was anxious to understand attitudes and conditions there correctly.

He met former comrades from Hamina and from his schooldays in Helsinki. Many of them were now pro-German – like Ignatius and Åkerman – while the political opinions of others, like Georg Schauman, chief librarian of the University of Helsinki and for many years his friend and admirer, were completely different. Opinion was sharply divided even within the family. He received ample information from Mikael Gripenberg (husband of his half-sister Marguerite) and his brother Johan, who came over from Sweden. What he told of the reality of the war and the demands of his military calling made a deep impression. Sophie summed up her feelings: 'Poor brother, it is frightful enough that good and kind men should be exposed to all the atrocious things that a war involves, especially if they belong among those who have to order others to come under fire.'

In the late winter of 1916 Mannerheim was back with his division. The spring was quiet. 'My regiments are rested,' he reported. What happened next formed part of the Brusilov offensive, which began on 4 June and was successful, though at a fateful cost. The 12th Division now formed part of the Eighth Army, which achieved a great breakthrough at Łuck. It was able to continue its advance as far as the neighbourhood of Wladimir-Wolyńsk. However, the offensive was now approaching its concluding phase. German troops, who had been transferred from the Western Front, checked the Russians and saved the Austrians from a catastrophe. In the course of these battles the 12th Division gained excellent results: 'Many mounted attacks, not only during daylight but also at night bold reconnaissances,' as Mannerheim briefly described what they achieved. Then followed defensive battles and trench warfare. The great Russian offensive of 1916 attained notable results: it compelled the Germans to redeploy troops from the Western Front, and appreciably weakened the military strength of the Austrians. Mannerheim saw in these results a confirmation of the lessons he had learned and digested from the Russo-Japanese War. 'You see from the summer's operations the value of taking the initiative in war,' he proudly explained to Sophie.

The Russian successes had repercussions on foreign policy, which were to affect Mannerheim closely. Bulgaria had earlier joined the Central Powers, whereas the Rumanian government took up arms on the side of the Entente. A long internal power struggle was thus decided with a diplomatic victory for the Entente. But soon afterwards there was a severe military reverse. At first Mannerheim was pleased at Rumania's decision to join the Allies, but became deeply disappointed by its subsequent fate, which he considered a cautionary example of the misfortunes that could befall a small country taking part in grand politics on the side of a great power. He believed that the Russians should have advanced with strong forces through Bulgaria to the Bosphorus. The Balkans might have become the decisive theatre of war, but instead the Germans and Austrians under Mackensen's command crushed Rumania's armed forces and occupied most of the country. The 12th Cavalry Division had been ordered to proceed to the Rumanian front as part of a large Russian relief operation to prevent the complete collapse of the Rumanian forces and a German incursion into southern Russia. There was no railway available for transport down to the front, so from their trenches on the banks of the River Stochod the troops had to ride some 265 miles to Suczava in the Carpathians, which took them three weeks. Here Mannerheim was to spend his third war-time Christmas, far from 'his loved ones . . . But of all the miseries prevailing in the world, perhaps this is the least.'

Mannerheim's task was now to take command of a sizeable battle group – named Wrancza – consisting of his own 12th Division and a Rumanian infantry brigade, augmented by other Russian and Rumanian units. The group could be used to delay the enemy until their attacks ceased. The results won the recognition of the Rumanian command. For Mannerheim this demanding task of leading a large battle group composed of troops of different nationalities was instructive, and he saw too how difficult it was for a small nation to assert itself against a great power. The haughty attitude shown by many Russians towards the Rumanian people in their misfortune aroused his indignation. He understood how important it was for the leaders of a small country to behave in a way that won them respect. These were experiences which he was to put to good use before long.

From the front in northern Rumania the 12th Division was moved into reserve in Bessarabia, and Mannerheim thus obtained a long-awaited chance to visit Finland again. On his way through St Petersburg, in accordance with the regulations, he waited on the Emperor, who happened to be in the city; usually he was at the headquarters in Mogilev, having taken over the supreme command from Grand Duke Nicholas in 1915. Mannerheim observed that the Emperor's mind seemed distracted; anxiety was plainly weighing on him.

When Mannerheim returned to the front everything had changed. The empire had been overthrown; the era of the second Russian Revolution had begun. He had left Helsinki on 9 March 1917, and the next day in Petrograd he encountered the outbreak of the Revolution, caused by high prices and food shortages in the city. Rumours of disturbances had circulated in Helsinki, but the authorities still seemed in control. Mannerheim stayed as usual at the Hotel d'Europe and went the following evening to see a ballet performance at the Opera. During the day troops had been used against the demonstrators in the central areas of the city on orders from the Emperor in Mogilev – a fateful error. Shots had been fired and many were killed. When he left the Opera the city was deserted. A brother-officer from the Chevalier Guards had a car and drove him to his hotel. There Mannerheim met Emanuel Nobel, his good friend of many years' standing. They walked to a club, but found it empty and returned home. The next day the Revolution broke out. The troops refused to fire. The government was helpless. As in 1905, extremist elements resorted to terrorism and murder.

As a senior officer Mannerheim was at once in danger. The revolutionaries began a hunt for officers, whom they often murdered. As he attempted, by peering from his hotel window, to follow how events were developing he noticed that soldiers and armed workers in the street had spotted him – he was, of course, wearing general's uniform. The hotel porter came up and advised him to leave the building by a rear exit, and by back streets he reached Nobel's apartment. He was able to borrow civilian clothes, but they had been made for a shorter and stouter man. The trousers only came half-way down his calves.

Hazards did not end there. A Finn whom he knew gave him a refuge.

He met there his brother-in-law Mikael Gripenberg who by chance was on a visit to the imperial capital. When the revolutionaries began house searches the next day, he was almost discovered.

However, the situation calmed down to some extent and Mannerheim was able to continue his journey via Moscow to the front. The troops were now committed to operations in the mountain regions of Rumania, and the 12th Cavalry Division was now in reserve in Bessarabia. When he reached Kishinev he was met by brilliantly sunny weather, and the magnificent scenery caused thoughts of the Revolution to sink into the background – 'A great deal of it reminds me of my rides in the mountain labyrinths of Central Asia.'

The Emperor's authority had rapidly collapsed and on 15 March he was persuaded to abdicate. His powers devolved upon a provisional government under Prince Lvov, which thus acquired a legal basis. In Finland the hated governor-general Seyn was dismissed; his succeessor, Mikhail Stakhovich, was a benevolent liberal politician, whose brother had commanded the Nezhin Dragoons in 1904–5. The representative of Finland in Petrograd was now Carl Enckell – a son of the director of the Cadet Corps at Hamina in Mannerheim's time there. Finns who had been in Russia as prisoners or deportees came home – among them Pehr Evind Svinhufvud, the speaker of the reformed Finnish parliament who had been exiled to Siberia in 1914 for his resistance activities, was greeted with special honour.

Mannerheim had already experienced the Revolution of 1905, then he had hoped that a more auspicious era would dawn for the many peoples of the Russian empire. Then the revolutionary frenzy had quickly calmed down after Nicholas II was induced to make concessions. Therefore, after the events of March 1917, Mannerheim was not completely depressed, but he quickly realised that the circumstances this time were more difficult. Many forces threatened a development towards the freer Russia of which he dreamed. What he experienced of the revolutionary days in Petrograd had made him wary: 'If you look a little deeper, what you see causes great concern for the future, particularly the immediate future.' But he was not completely negative; the national constituent assembly might take more sensible decisions than the utopian resolutions on freedom, justice and equality with which all meetings now ended. 'How events will move later on, how social and political conditions will be arranged, and who will finally have power are open to very considerable doubt, although I admit that the world will in many ways look very different from how it has been up to now' (27.5.17 to Sophie Mannerheim). As matters were developing, they were unlikely to see 'this country of freedom, justice and equality which clever agitators dangle before the masses', but 'perhaps the gloom which veils the future will increase people's interest in the years that lie ahead'. Some weeks later he was even more pessimistic.

At this point – in June 1917 – Mannerheim received a new and more senior command. He became commander of the VIth Cavalry Corps, which comprised three divisions, including the 12th. At the same time he was promoted lieutenant-general. The summer passed fairly quietly for Mannerheim and his corps; it was certainly intended to take part in the offensive which the war minister Kerensky planned with troops that had become completely demoralised, but in the event it was never drawn into that catastrophic undertaking or the ignominious retreat that followed. Mannerheim was later able to assert that the officers had, by gradual stages, been able to arrive at tolerably satisfactory conditions, in spite of 'the commitees and other demented organisations with which the recent months have favoured us'. Lenin's attempted coup in Petrograd in July failed, after which the position of the Provisional Government seemed more secure.

But in September came a new catastrophe: Kornilov, the new commander-in-chief whom Mannerheim had met long before during his ride across Asia, attempted to seize power by a military coup against Kerensky. This proved a disastrous failure, and had the effect of breaking off progress towards more settled conditions and driving Kerensky into the arms of more radical elements. 'To crown misfortune came Kornilov's revolt,' wrote Mannerheim, 'the inevitable consequences of which were to deprive the more senior commanders and the officers as a whole of what little authority they had succeeded in saving.' He anticipated the final dissolution of social discipline. Conduct of the war would cease and be followed by political conflicts of which it was impossible to foretell the outcome. The soliders would be led by dishonest agitators and rush towards objectives which would never be more than dreams, at least for the present generation. It was therefore time for Mannerheim to review his position in the Russian army, where he had served so long. To begin with he took advantage of a knee injury, caused by a fall from his horse, to apply for sick leave and travel to Odessa.

Already before this Mannerheim had wondered whether the right place for him was not at home in Finland. In the course of several meetings with another Finn, Colonel Martin Wetzer, he had raised the question of their country's future: how was it to be saved from being swallowed up by revolutionary Russia?

On 22 September 1917 the last Russian commander-in-chief of the old school, General Dukhonin – an acquaintance from his time in Warsaw –

transferred Mannerheim to the reserve. The reason given in the notification of this was that his opinions were not in accord with those then prevailing. After Mannerheim learned of this decision he made up his mind to return to Finland. Before his departure the officers and men of the 12th Division decided to arrange a farewell party for their popular and admired general. This proved a melancholy occasion, since there was a universal premonition that it would be for life. However, it took some time before he could begin the journey; first he wanted to obtain civilian clothes and get his documents in order.

During his involuntary stay in Odessa conditions in Russia became even more chaotic. On 7 November Lenin attempted another coup in Petrograd, and this time succeeded. This was the Great October Revolution, which was shortly followed not only by a more general seizure of power in the larger Russian cities but also by three years of civil war.

On 3 December 1917 Mannerheim at last set out on his journey home. It proved a dramatic expedition. He had with him as ADC a Finn, Martin Franck, who had served in his division as a volunteer, and his Russian soldier-servant Karpatëv. After due consideration, Mannerheim decided to wear his uniform and decorations in order to get through the disturbed districts more easily. At Mogilev he saw where Dukhonin had just been murdered. It was at the railway station where he was to have met his Bolshevik successor Krylenko there were still pools of blood on the platform. While the train was halted at another station revolutionary soldiers threatened to drag him out, but his resolute bearing and the assistance of Franck averted the danger.

Gustaf Mannerheim was now leaving Russia after thirty years' service in the army of the empire. The wild youth from the Cadet Corps at Hamina had evolved into a military leader with a high sense of responsibility, who had thoroughly learned his profession and was aware of his ability to perform difficult tasks. At the same time he had shown a lively interest in politics; he was fascinated by the social problems of Russia, and by the difficulties of Finland and Poland and their important ramifications. In Asia and on Russia's western front he had taken part in great events, but both his activity and his interests had extended into fields other than purely military ones; he had developed into an interested amateur of the natural sciences and archaeology, and in St Petersburg and Warsaw he had kept up a rich cultural life. And from his years in Russia he had acquired extensive international connections which were to stand him in particularly good stead in the years to come.

VII
IN FINLAND AGAIN;
THE WAR OF INDEPENDENCE
1918

The general who returned to Helsinki in December 1917 was practically unknown to the Finnish public. Mannerheim himself had certainly been particular about maintaining lively contacts with Finland and about following developments there; but this had been achieved through visits and correspondence with relatives and acquaintances from his youth.

Developments in Finland had taken an increasingly disquieting course. The powers of the senate (or government) formed after the abdication of Nicholas II in 1917 were not clearly defined. The authority of the Emperor as Grand Duke of Finland had been transferred to the Provisional Government in Petrograd but this too had not been defined with any precision. The majority in parliament after the elections of 1916 – at which there had been a low turn-out – was held by the Social Democrats, and the senate was controlled by the socialists. However, parliament was not thought to represent prevailing opinion accurately, and new elections were considered justified both in Helsinki and in Petrograd. Kerensky's government, which had assumed the authority of the Grand Duke, declared new elections on 1–2 October 1917, but when these elections resulted in a non-socialist majority, the socialists were deeply disappointed. They claimed that the election was illegal, and there were soon demands for the recall of the old parliament which had been dissolved.

In accordance with the election result, a new non-socialist senate was formed, eventually with P.E. Svinhufvud as chairman (or prime minister). In the course of the autumn, animosities within the country increased sharply; socialist Red Guards obtained weapons and other assistance from Russian troops still in Finland, and acts of terrorism took place, especially in factory communities. In some areas Civil Guard units were formed for the maintenance of law and order; all citizens were eligible to join them. However, it became ever clearer that the powerful left wing within the Social Democrats was aiming at a revolution – a class conflict with the establishment of a dictatorship. As the position of the Bolsheviks in Russia became stronger after the October Revolution, so developments in Finland became more radical. On 10 November the Red Guard formed in

46

October was mobilised. Many in the national trade union federation, supported by the more violent element in the Red Guard, urged revolution, but the more moderate hesitated and launched instead a general strike to force through their extreme political demands, known as the *Me vaadimme* ('We demand') programme. Bolshevik emissaries – Stalin among them – urged a revolution, which at this moment could easily have been carried out with the help of Russian troops. The general strike proved a far from bloodless prelude to 1918; surprisingly, however, it was called off after ten days. But this won only a short respite.

The animosities within society emerged clearly when the senate issued the declaration of Finland's independence on 6 December 1917. The bonds that had tied the Grand Duchy to the Empire had to be broken, but in the political situation prevailing in the late autumn of 1917 parliament could not even achieve unanimity on this vital question: the Social Democratic party voted against independence.

The most immediate task of the political leadership was to try to win the Russian government's assent to independence. This was granted as early as 8 January 1918, according in theory with Lenin's nationality policy as applied to Russia. He regarded the oppression of nationalities during the imperial era as a bourgeois error, such a policy being alien to a socialist society. However, the documents show that in fact Lenin's idea was that the Finnish proletariat would destroy bourgeois society and unite itself with the newly-formed Russian state of the future. The recognition of Svinhufvud's Finland was therefore a gesture with a significance other than that which appeared at the time. On 9 January 1918 the senate reported to parliament Russia's recognition and that of Sweden and France which had followed it. Gustaf Mannerheim, who watched the session from the public gallery, was among those who rejoiced. But during the following weeks there was a further sharpening of internal political antagonisms, with fears of a coup on Russian lines by the Red Guard.

Finland's newly-won independence was thus threatened from many sides. The government of the country had scarcely any armed forces at its disposal, but appreciable numbers of Russian troops still remained in the country, part under communist control, and part still not clearly revolutionary. These troops were gradually to be sent back to Russia, but this proved to be a slow process.

The senate delayed for a long time over organising a Finnish military force. Finland was thus divided and in turmoil when Mannerheim returned on 18 December 1917. He was welcomed by Sophie and her circle, and through them and through his other relatives, the friends of his youth and his Cadet Corps comrades from a now distant past he quickly found his bearings. Georg Schauman was one of his principal informants, and his cousin Jacob von Julin, now a leading industrialist, put him in touch with a group which had been preparing itself for the situation when Finnish independence could at last be declared. This chiefly involved the so-called Military Committee, composed of a number of officers from the Finnish army that had been disbanded as a result of Bobrikov's policy at the beginning of the century. Its most active member was the retired cavalry captain Hannes Ignatius, a junior comrade of Mannerheim at Hamina. Several at first mistrusted the general who had returned home from the Russian army, but after a number of conversations they became convinced of his patriotism and determination to defend the country's independence. They were naturally conscious that he was no supporter of a pro-German policy.

At the beginning of January 1918 Mannerheim was made a member of the Military Committee, which was shortly afterwards declared an official organisation; this decision was an element in the senate's attempt at long last to create an armed force. He found the committee ill-organised and amateurish, and after a few meetings he announced his decision not to attend any longer. To the dismayed questions of the members as to what he proposed, he gave a peremptory answer: 'If you gentlemen can travel north on the overnight train this evening, you should do so.'

Mannerheim's view was that military units should be organised and an administrative centre set up away from Helsinki. His experience in Russia had taught him that the senate in the capital would run the risk of being put out of action by revolutionary forces which it would be unable to hold in check. For this alternative centre he proposed Vaasa in the farming region of Ostrobothnia, which had close communications with Sweden and the rest of Europe. The Committee heeded Mannerheim's advice: Lieutenant-General Claes Charpentier, who had been chairman, resigned and – with Svinhufvud's consent – Mannerheim was elected as his successor on 14 January. He was thus intended to be the future commander-in-chief, becoming so in fact sooner than had been expected. The members of the Military Committee at once recognised that they had acquired an energetic, experienced and self-confident leader. The same day, 14 January, parliament had decided to raise military forces. Two days later Svinhufvud called on Mannerheim; he wanted to hear the General's views on the prospects of defending the country's independence if it were attacked. They met in the senate chamber. Assured by Mannerheim of his conviction that Finland could be defended, Svinhufvud gave him the task of organising an army.

On 18 January 1918 Mannerheim took the night train from Helsinki, accompanied among others by four members of the Military Committee and some senators. The journey was dangerous. Red Guards and Russian soldiers guarded communications, hunting for Russian officers and 'white' Finns. Major-General Ernst Löfström (who used the name Toll to protect his family in Petrograd) came from another direction at Mannerheim's summons to join his group in Vaasa.

Mannerheim himself travelled with a passport in the name of Gustaf Malmberg, a commercial traveller. Several times he came close to getting into trouble; Russian military patrols searched the compartments, and while the train was waiting at Tampere the travellers were examined by Russian soldiers who were unwilling to accept Gustaf Malmberg's identity papers. At the last moment a young Finnish railwayman intervened by stating that they were in order, and the journey proceeded.

The man who had now emerged as the country's military leader was unknown. A former Russian general was viewed with mistrust even if he could claim Svinhufvud's commission; therefore it was a remarkable achievement for the chosen commander-in-chief of a virtually non-existent army to win the confidence of the Ostrobothnians. This success was due, as often before in his career, to his natural quality of leadership, calm bearing and psychological insight.

During the preceding week unrest in the country had been growing, and there were clear signs that revolutionary coups could be expected. In Viipuri Russian troops intervened in support of the Red Guard, and now – at the last moment – the senate took a number of measures to prepare the country's defence. The Civil Guard were declared to be government troops. It was an important step when, on 27 January, Mannerheim was appointed Supreme Commander in Northern Finland, and a telegram to that effect reached him in Vaasa via Sweden. This appointment was properly regarded as covering the whole of Finland – even though at that moment the authority of the senate did not extend outside the north. Action against the Russian garrisons seemed more and more desirable; however, Svinhufvud wavered between the hope that it would be possible to come to an agreement with the Russians, thus preventing a revolutionary coup in Finland, and the realisation that armed intervention against the Russian troops and the Red Guard was essential. In consequence orders and counter-orders reached Vaasa. For Mannerheim

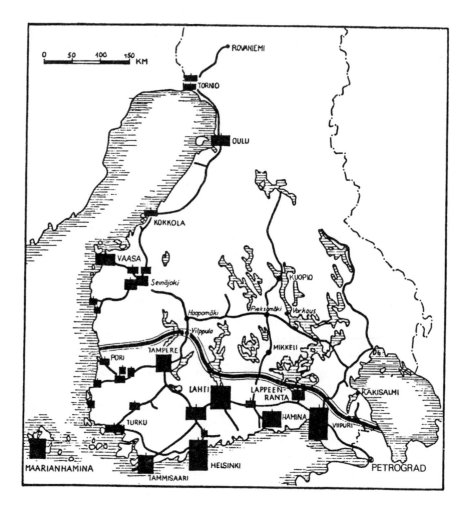

The War of Independence, 1918.

The front from the beginning of February to mid-March

The black squares show the biggest Russian garrisons in Finland at the beginning of the War of Independence. The size of the squares corresponds approximately to the strength of the garrisons: in Helsinki and Viipuri about 10,000 men; Lahti 8,000; Tampere 5,000, and so on. These strengths were altered significantly by various troop movements during the winter and spring.

it was desirable to gain time to continue the work of organising his forces, but the crisis developed so quickly that delay became ever more dangerous.

Not surprisingly, the Civil Guard were eager to attack the Russian garrisons in Ostrobothnia as soon as possible, and keeping up the men's morale meanwhile was not easy. Mannerheim had difficulty in inducing the Civil Guard to obey an order from Helsinki to postpone an attack planned for 23 January. He prevailed on their leader at Lapua, Matti Laurila, who had once served as a non-commissioned officer in the Finnish army, to accept a delay by appealing to him as a fellow-soldier who would understand that it was sometimes necessary to give orders which the men could only accept unwillingly.

Events in eastern Finland were the principal reason why Mannerheim was forced to move more quickly than purely military reasons required. The Civil Guard there had gone into action with broad popular support and achieved significant successes. But threatening reports arrived that Russian reinforcements were on their way from Petrograd which could completely alter the situation both there and in Ostrobothnia. The senate admitted that it lacked the means to stop Russian troop trains. If the Russians reached Vaasa, the senate there would be in a hopeless situation.

On 25 January Mannerheim had a new plan of action ready. First he summoned a council of war but then, against the advice of General Löfstrom but with the support of the others, he took his decision. On 27 January they were ready to attack Russian troops in Vaasa, Lapua and other places the following morning, and when these actions took place, all without exception were successful. The garrisons were disarmed and interned. In a carefully worded proclamation to the Russian units, Mannerheim explained the reasons for the Civil Guard's action.

To Mannerheim the fight that had now begun was directed primarily against the Russian garrisons in Finland. These presented a latent danger through their cooperation with the local units and the central leadership of the Red Guards. The operations against the Russians were a realisation of the dream of liberating the country, of independence and freedom. The limitation of Mannerheim's plan was evident from the directives he issued at that time to the local Civil Guard to disarm the Russian garrisons in specific places. News of these successes was immediately cabled to Svinhufvud.

On 27 January the Red Guard in Helsinki – unaware of Mannerheim's plans in Ostrobothnia – began their concentration and the next day deposed the senate and appointed a council of people's commissars in its place. In many parts of the country the Red Guard followed orders from

Helsinki to seize power and remove the officials answerable to the senate. The senate in Helsinki had ceased to function.

The operations of the Red Guard in the capital and the larger industrial centres gave the action of the Civil Guard a completely different direction from that previously intended. They were now a defence not merely against the Russian troops and their Finnish sympathisers but against a *coup d'état*. The Red Guard were aiming at a social revolution to be carried out against the rest of the country's population. On the question of revolution the Social Democratic party split into three groups. Väinö Tanner and his group on the right were absolutely against it; Edvard Gylling and O.W. Kuusinen and several others were hesitant; and Yrjö Sirola and an extremist group forced the pace. The radicals within the Red Guard and the party were behind the decision to seize power. When the Social Democrat parliamentary group had to decide on their position towards this plan, the majority voted against it; only later did they join the revolutionaries out of loyalty to the workers' movement.

Against the background of the profound division within the workers' movement which were thus revealed, it cannot be convincingly argued that the rebellion was a necessary consequence of social evils in Finland. Inequalities existed and had grown worse during Russian rule. However, a period of great reforms had already begun in 1917 and could have continued. Over the decision to start a revolution in Helsinki the influence of communist Russia was crucial; shortly before the coup Lenin had dispersed the elected national constituent assembly in Moscow.

The Red coup in Helsinki had deposed the remaining members of the senate and their officials from office. Three senators, Renvall, Frey and Pehkonen, had travelled to join Mannerheim on 26 January, with Senator Arajärvi arriving later. Eventually Svinhufvud, the senate chairman, succeeded in escaping from Helsinki and with several companions seized an icebreaker which took them to Tallinn. They subsequently reached Vaasa on 24 March by way of Germany. By these means the commander-in-chief obtained a representative government at his side.

Throughout central and northern Finland newly-formed Civil Guards and small regular units were able to secure the authority of the lawful government, and the great majority of the population took the government's side. Country people on the whole did not follow the Red slogans, but on the other hand existing antipathies led to tougher battles in some industrial centres, such as Oulu and Tornio. On 8 February Mannerheim was able to transfer his headquarters to the important railway junction of Seinäjoki. In southern Finland the Red Guards from the industrial centres got the upper hand, with the Russian garrison in Viipuri supplying arms and instructors. Helsinki was controlled by the Russian fleet.

Before long a front line was drawn between White and Red Finland, running from Pori, north of Tampere, down towards Viipuri. However, White units held out in various places south of the front, in Western Uusimaa, in Porvoo and in the countryside. Throughout February, Red forces directed repeated attacks against the front line, culminating at the end of the month in a powerful offensive aimed at Haapamäki with the objective of breaking the Whites' communications between eastern and western Finland. The White front held, but the forces at Mannerheim's disposal were still too weak to be able to take the offensive. As an experienced soldier he had to restrain the eagerness of those wanting an immediate battle, gain time, and work at organising and expanding the army. 'We shall gradually get everything organised so as to be able to think of bringing help to the suffering south. Everybody is burning with impatience and I perhaps not the least, but I must restrain them, nothing can be risked in this struggle in which everything is at stake.' This was the outline of Mannerheim's plans in February.

At first resources were weak indeed. The war now being fought was improvised. The Finnish army had been disbanded by the Russians at the beginning of the century, and the military service law of 1878 had not been reactivated. The units at present available were chiefly Civil Guards formed during the autumn. They were not tightly organised, and both their weapons and their training were generally inadequate. Later Mannerheim was to recall 'what ridiculously small forces were at my disposal in Vaasa at the time of the coup'.

The men were volunteers, and at first the commanders did not know how many soldiers they could count on. No operations of a demanding nature could be undertaken with forces such as these; they had to be, in Mannerheim's phrase, 'threaded together like pearls on a string in order to form a continuous front'. It was therefore essential to strengthen organisation and recruitment. First the Civil Guard were organised. The country was divided into Civil Guard districts under separate commanders, and the troops were divided into units with a clearly defined system of command. At the beginning of April there were ten Civil Guard regiments, a distinction being made between active service units and the lines of communication and training organisation. Next, voluntary enlistment was also tried, initially with Mannerheim support. Against the alternative of reactivating the military service law he pointed out the difficulties which the insurrection could cause; conflicts of conscience could arise over fighting the forces south of the front, particularly within the Social Democrat party. But Mannerheim was eventually induced to give conscription his approval. There were thus many delicate questions to be decided which were especially difficult in a conflict which was also a civil war. The commander-in-chief therefore approved the idea of a consultative body to facilitate cooperation between himself and the public. This was a wise move.

Mannerheim's most difficult problem was weapons. 'Shall we be forced to strike at the enemy with knives and cudgels?' he asked in a letter to his brother Johan in Sweden, and later he wrote: 'Only a fraction of these budding civil guards had rifles.' He estimated that the number of rifles available was about 1,500 – ranged against the well-equipped units of the army of a great power! Hopes of obtaining arms were pinned on the Western powers and on Sweden.

Also, not enough trained officers were available. There were a number of officers prepared to help who, like the commander-in-chief, had returned home from the Russian army: for example, Major-General Ernst Lofström and Colonels Martin Wetzer and Karl Fredrik Wilkman. But these were far from being enough, and it was therefore a great help when a number of officers came from Sweden to take part in the War of Independence. During the early days Mannerheim often went to meet the train from the north in the hope of obtaining new helpers from Finland's former mother-country. Among the first who came was a friend from his youth, also an esteemed fellow-horseman: the Finnish-born Lieutenant-Colonel Ernst Linder from Stockholm. He was followed by other trained officers: Henry Peyron (cavalry), Archibald Douglas and Gösta Törngren (infantry), and Axel Rappe and Adolf Hamilton (artillery).

The headquarters was organised using Finnish personnel assisted by the Swedish officers. The personality and leadership qualities of the commander-in-chief made an impression everywhere, and gained the devotion and admiration of his new collaborators. 'He seemed always to be equally calm, considerate and friendly, his whole noble personality impressed all who came into contact with him', was how a Finn described him at headquarters. The Swedes were equally captivated and impressed, and he made life-long friends among them.

The Finnish *Jägers* made a very valuable contribution – the German authorities had agreed that they could return home after resigning from German service. On 25 February the last and biggest contingent of them reached Vaasa, and received a jubilant welcome. They made a very good impression on Mannerheim, who greeted them in Finnish and Swedish

The Commander-in-Chief during the battle for Tampere in 1918. Painting
by Eero Järnefelt

Mannerheim and Svinhufvud in Senate Square, 16 May 1918

16 May 1918. Mannerheim receives a tribute from a national organisation

The march into Helsinki on 16 May 1918

Mannerheim speaking in Senate Square, 16 May 1918

The Commander-in-Chief decorating a wounded young Civil Guard. In the background is the Swedish Colonel G. M. Törngren, head of the Operations Section at Headquarters

The White General

The Regent at a Civil Guard parade in Helsinki, 16 March 1919

The Regent at his desk

Mannerheim with his aides-de-camp in 1919. Akseli Gallen-Kallela, the
artist, is to the left of Mannerheim

Departure from Helsinki, 17 September 1919

Mannerheim and G. A. Gripenberg; on
leaving Helsinki, 17 September 1919

King Gustav V welcomes the Regent to
Stockholm, 11 February 1919

Return home, 2 July 1920

Mannerheim watching Civil Guard sports, 1922

Mannerheim watching the first car race in Finland in 1920

Mannerheim on the steps of the
Seurahuone Hotel in Loviisa,
1922

Tiger shoot in Nepal, 1937

In Nepal, 1937

Mannerheim during a hunt in Austria

Mannerheim greeted by children outside his villa in Kaivopuisto, 4 June 1937

The Field Marshal as guest of Svinhufvud, 1933

Field Marshal Mannerheim. Picture by Apollo

Mannerheim at a café run by the Lotta auxiliary defence organisation for the parade on 16 May 1932

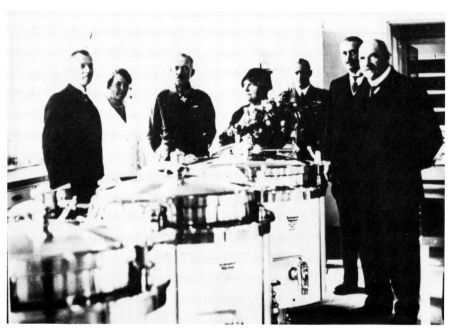

Opening of the Red Cross Hospital. Included in the picture are President and Mrs Svinhufvud, Lieutenant-General Oesch and Simo Brofelt, the chief medical officer

after a parade in the market square. However, a conflict soon broke out over the future duties of the *Jägers* and their role in the war; the *Jägers* wanted to fight at the front as soon as possible in a single unit, but Mannerheim intended to use them at first as instructors for his troops. After much difficulty, the essence of his scheme was eventually carried out.

Building up an army was a difficult task in any case, made all the more so by all kinds of political and personal antipathies. After a time at headquarters, Mannerheim's close collaborator Gösta Törngren pointed out the problems: 'In this free country, with its spoilt people who have no understanding of military things, split apart by the language struggle [between Finnish and Swedish] . . . in circumstances in which attention is paid to thousands of generally completely superfluous matters . . . the task has not been easy' (5.3.18). As in many armies, the commander-in-chief also met with opposition from within in the form of intrigues and power struggles. There was an especially high risk of this in an improvised army lacking established traditions.

It was clear to Mannerheim that he had to crack down on arbitrary and undisciplined conduct, what – as he wrote later – could 'undermine respect for the authority of the higher levels of command, which in the conditions then prevailing was not easy to uphold'. But his natural disposition and earlier experiences prevented him from making the mistakes which a more bureaucratic and authoritarian leader might easily have fallen into. He recognised the need for sympathy with human weaknesses and ambitions in the present situation. He also showed deftness in his handling of the Ostrobothnian yeoman farmers at the start of the war. He could not risk losing the support of those who would help him, and patience and a tolerant outlook had to be shown.

However, the intrigues grew worse than ever towards the end of the war as enemy pressure lessened. Strongly pro-German politicians and solidiers opposed the commander-in-chief with the clear aim of having him dismissed; and there were numerous people who now gave free expression to their antipathy towards anyone who had served in the empire. In addition there were people who wanted – and expected – to wield influence in the new Finland being created. These were an important element during the time of momentous political decisions which soon followed, in which Mannerheim played a central role.

In Russia Mannerheim had, indeed, sometimes seen nationalism manifest itself in a disagreeable from. However, in the imperial army there had still been an inherited tolerance towards other national groups within the great empire, even though Great Russian sentiments also came to be asserted there during the latter decades. He was thus not always able to understand the antipathies that were now evident, mostly between the younger Finns and those who had served in the empire, any more than those between the pro-Germans and others. He remained indifferent himself to the calumny and malevolent gossip to which he was not infrequently exposed at this time.

During the World War many Finns, expecting a Russian defeat or a revolution, had attempted to prepare the ground abroad for assistance to their country. At first thoughts had turned to Sweden, but in many ways the Swedish government's policy made Finland's struggle for independence more difficult. That government was composed of a coalition of Liberals and Social Democrats, and in 1918 its policy was determined principally by the misconceptions of the radical Social Democrats who regarded the coup in Helsinki as a link in what, according to Marxist theory, was the inevitable class struggle against the ever harsher oppression of capitalism. To them the Red insurrection represented the struggle of the working class for liberation and ought to be supported by the proletariat in other countries. They were untroubled by the fact that the leaders of the rebellion had espoused dictatorship and treated democracy with contempt. These Swedes were equally unwilling to note the connection between the Finnish insurrection and simultaneous developments in Russia. Admittedly Hjalmar Branting, the leader of the Swedish Social Democrats, declared that he put democracy above the working-class movement, but even so he did not dare to oppose the more radical members of the party, Thorsson, Wigforss and Undén.

This was why for a long time the majority of the Swedish government did not want even to supply arms to its neighbours in their fateful struggle. However, the foreign minister Johannes Hellner held completely different views, for which he eventually gained support. Assistance to Finland on a larger scale was ruled out by reference to the risk that Sweden might be drawn into the World War on the German side – a risk which Mannerheim was convinced did not exist. He regarded this merely as an excuse.

In addition the Swedish government caused Mannerheim and Finland great disappointment by its intervention in the Åland islands, which formed part of Finland, and where in February 1918 Russian troops still remained. On 10 February a Finnish unit consisting of Civil Guards from Uusikaupunki, who had been forced to leave their own district by Red troops, reached Åland over the ice. At first this force went some way towards attaining its objective by disarming part of the Russian forces; then negotiations began for the evacuation of the Russians. Mannerheim for his part prepared to send the Guards weapons from the mainland, but he now received information that Sweden planned to intervene in the fighting, with the aim of inducing the Uusikaupunki guards to leave the island. To this his reaction was that 'nobody but ourselves may fit out expeditions to Åland' (17.2.18, to Johan Mannerheim).

Rumours had been spread in Stockholm of outrages against the inhabitants of the Åland islands, and these served to justify the sending of a humanitarian expedition. The Swedish Customs even intervened to prevent arms from reaching the Uusikaupunki Guards from the mainland of Sweden. The Swedish government tried by every means at its disposal to compel the Guards to give up their fight and leave Åland. Mannerheim was outraged, and instructed the Finnish legation in Stockholm to present his view of the matter; he considered Swedish conduct to be 'a distinctly unfriendly action'. Åland in the hands of the Finnish authorities was of great military importance, and the Civil Guard there were under his command. However, the Swedish authorities, led by the navy minister Erik Palmstierna, even interfered with his communications with the Guards; his messages were either not forwarded at all or were sent in a grossly distorted form. By such methods and by strong pressure on Alexis Gripenberg, the Finnish minister in Stockholm, the Swedes succeeded in inducing the commander of the Guards to accept a disadvantageous agreement with the Russians and to allow themselves to be evacuated, without their weapons, to Sweden. Mannerheim commented: 'I am indignant that in spite of my protest the Swedes mounted an expedition to the Åland islands which in the most serious way has now complicated my operations there.'

The Swedes seemed to have gained a free hand in the Åland islands, but the result of their policy turned out quite differently. A German action against the islands quickly followed which forced the Swedes out. Time was to pass before Stockholm could again revive the Åland question, openly demanding the annexation of the islands with the support of public opinion among the islanders. The most serious immediate consequence was that the Finnish leadership were driven into the German camp. Mannerheim was sure that their increasing inclination to seek support from Germany was connected with the intervention in Åland by Sweden. He repeatedly told his Swedish collaborator, Gösta Törngren, that he was afraid a completely pro-German policy would came about. This he had hitherto succeeded in preventing, having worked for an orientation towards Scandinavia. Now many of those who had supported him in this work had become pro-German, including Senator Renvall. These state-

ments were corroborated by the reports of the Swedish representative in
Vaasa, whom Renvall had told that hopes of a common Nordic policy
would now have to be abandoned.

Thus at a moment when Finland was fighting to win back its freedom,
the Edén-Branting government in Sweden had succeeded by its policy in
severely worsening Finnish-Swedish relations, with after-effects that were
to be felt for decades to the injury of both countries. It was now Germany
and not Sweden which gave military help to the Finnish government, a
development Mannerheim had consistently opposed. Before travelling to
Vaasa he had asked Svinhufvud for a promise not to approach Berlin – a
promise he believed he had obtained. However, the Russian policy of
oppression in Finland had changed the political orientation of the Finns in
the years immediately before the World War. There were now extensive
circles, both Finnish- and Swedish-speaking, who harboured a strong
hatred of Russia and advocated cooperation with Germany. Naturally
Mannerheim had understood the connection that existed between the
struggle of White Finland and the German eastern front. In so far as the
Germans penetrated towards the Gulf of Finland and Petrograd, pressure
on the Finnish front would ease. Mannerheim's principal objective was
nevertheless cooperation with Scandinavia, first and foremost with
Sweden. A pro-German policy would limit Finland's freedom of movement and be a dangerous handicap in the future. An independent Finland
was also obliged to cooperate in the future with its great eastern neighbour. By intervention against the Bolsheviks it would be possible to gain
goodwill in a future democratic Russia. But Finland must not become a
German vassal-state.

On 21 February Mannerheim could still conceive of continuing his
march towards Petrograd, plainly to forestall the Germans (letter to Johan
Mannerheim). Finland also had its own interests to watch over in Eastern
Karelia, where the future of the Finnish population was a matter of
pressing concern. Lenin in a proclamation had promised this region, his-
torically Russian, to Red Finland, and on 23 February Mannerheim replied
with a 'Karelian' order of the day (which was to have a successor in 1941).
The aspirations of the Karelians were widely supported in Finland and
were of immediate interest throughout 1918.

During the first months of the war the senate shared Mannerheim's
view on relations with Germany. The initiative towards a pro-German
policy was not taken in Vaasa, but came rather from Berlin where Edvard
Hjelt, a former rector of the University of Helsinki and a leader of the
Jäger movement, had been living for some time. His advocacy of German

support in the fight against the insurrection received immediate approval in Germany itself, a reaction which was connected with German policy in the east. Peace negotiations between Berlin and Moscow had been broken off on 10 February, the armistice then in force was repudiated on 18 February, and a German offensive was set in motion. This offensive met only slight resistance, reached Tallinn and threatened Petrograd. It was in connection with this that the German High Command, and above all Ludendorff, made plans to help Finland which would facilitate a German attack on Petrograd.

News that the senate had asked for German military assistance reached Mannerheim on 2 March 1918 and came as a shock; in so doing the senate seemed to him to have broken its promise, and to be entering upon a dangerous policy. The idea, so promising for the future, that Finland had fought its fight to a victorious conclusion with its own forces had been spoiled. What would happen to Finland if the Central Powers lost the war?

Mannerheim's first reaction was to fight for his own policy, and in this he succeeded. At a meeting with the senators, he shook their resolve, arguing that it was important for the people of Finland to fight their battle to a conclusion themselves, even for the sake of overcoming the internal consequences of the rebellion. When asked if the lawful government could win, he answered that he was 'absolutely convinced of it'. However, there was a soldier who made a diametrically opposite assertion and who eventually persuaded the senate once more to change its mind; this was Wilhelm Thesleff, a lieutenant-colonel in the Russian army who had gone over to the Germans and accompanied the *Jägers* to Vaasa. Unlike Mannerheim, he had an unshaken belief in a German victory in the World War. He pointed out the losses which southern Finland might suffer if it had to be liberated from the north; the revolutionary forces could grow faster than those of the government. The occupation of the Åland islands by the Swedes was one argument in favour of a German intervention, and the large Russian fleet at Helsinki was another. Moreover, Mannerheim's troops had so far had no opportunity to show what they were capable of.

Mannerheim's chief weapon against the hard-pressed senators had been his threat to resign if German help was accepted. Who could replace him? Who else had his skill and authority? But Thesleff wrested this weapon from his hands by offering himself as successor.

When Mannerheim was informed of the senate's changed decision 'he was almost apoplectic with rage', according to a witness. But he eventually felt the necessity to accept it with as good a grace as possible. It would be more dangerous for Finland and the army if he abandoned his command and gave the Germans a free hand. But Renvall complained to Hjelt that German assistance breached the solidarity of the Scandinavian countries; the liberation struggle had been robbed of its exalted nature. However, Mannerheim made conditions for staying on as commander-in-chief. The German troops who would come to Finland could help to free the country, but not participate in resisting the insurrection; they should also come under his command. These requests were accepted. At the same time the senate appointed him general of cavalry, which meant that he was assured of a higher military rank than that of any likely commander of the German expeditionary corps.

By the middle of March the formation of the army had made such progress that Mannerheim considered the time had arrived for a decisive offensive. He wrote in a private letter on 11 March: 'We have behind us some hard organising work, and I think we are not so far from the day when we can at last bring help to the south.' A particular reason for seeking an immediate decision was the expected arrival of the Germans. Before they arrived, the country's own army ought to have demonstrated its capability. The immediate objective was Tampere, where strong Red forces and Russian troops, backed by artillery, were to be encircled. During the campaigns in Poland and the Ukraine, Mannerheim had carried out several successful operations of this sort. It was especially important that the enemy should not be allowed to withdraw from their present position and hasten away to the south. The attack had to be coordinated from the north, west and east. The warning order was given on 5 March.

But it could not be overlooked that such a large operation entailed great risks. Ernst Linder, who was spokesman for this viewpoint, warned Mannerheim against premature operations; what he had seen in the course of his inspections induced doubts. The troops, who were inexperienced and moreover insufficient in numbers, were incapable of undertaking a major offensive.

Mannerheim now called a council of war at Kauhajoki on 8 March. In spite of the misgivings that were expressed there, he decided to start offensive operations on 15 March. There were strong reasons for doing so quickly, not least because the enemy were clearly preparing their own offensive northwards. The White troops were to advance from the line Kuru-Ruovesi-Vilppula-Mänttä-Jämsä towards Orivesi; then, in a second phase, Tampere was to be encircled and captured.

At first there were appreciable successes, especially by the group commanded by Wilkman, which reached Orivesi. But the great victory, which had seemed to be in sight, was not achieved. The other formations did not carry out their operations with sufficient vigour, with the result that most of the enemy forces were able to escape from the planned encirclement and reach Tampere. This was a severe disappointment to Mannerheim; the town now had to be invested and captured – a hazardous task for a newly-formed army, especially as the enemy had the advantage in all types of weapons. The task was pressing because there were repeated alarming reports from the eastern front in Karelia to the effect that the Civil Guard were short of ammunition. Their commanders feared attack by superior forces. In this threatening situation Mannerheim wanted the prospective German expeditionary corps to arrive as soon as possible.

The second phase of the Tampere offensive began on 20 March. Initially, the situation was that the groups commanded by Linder, Hjalmarson and Wetzer – from west to east – were on a line north of Tampere, with Wilkman east of the town. Mannerheim ordered Wilkman to move towards the south-west to cut the town's communications with the south and prevent Red units from joining up with the enemy in southern Finland. This objective was attained on 24 March. The encirclement was completed during the following days by Linder's troops cutting the last railway link with Pori. At headquarters they now hoped for a capitulation, and there was panic in the town. But fanatics among the Reds and the Russian command forced its defenders to continue with the hopeless struggle. Thus the attack had to be continued. Mannerheim hoped to take the town on 25 March, but the fighting was unexpectedly tough, and he was forced to commit larger forces, the strategic reserve which he had not wanted to sacrifice. The attacking troops had to recover their strength, and there was a pause in the fighting for five days; then on 3 April they made the final assault, and two days later the battle was largely over. The town's defenders surrendered.

Before the final battle Mannerheim reminded his troops of the rules of war and the requirements of honour and international law: 'On the capture of Tampere it is to be observed most strictly that enemy who surrender are to be treated as prisoners of war and that there will be no actions to sully the honour of Finland.' The opposing side made no pretence of not being rebels, and in 1918 they were not protected by international law as combatants. But Mannerheim did not hesitate to apply the same humanitarian rules as would apply in regular war.

The cost of victory was high, but it had important consequences, as Mannerheim subsequently pointed out: 'The way to Finland's freedom lay open. The Finnish people had recovered a belief in their own strength . . .

broken an opponent in whose ranks their countrymen, blinded by alien doctrines, fought with disregard for mortal danger and true Finnish tenacity.' The victorious troops had been inadequately trained and equipped, and both the attackers and the defenders had to pay the price for this with heavy losses. Mannerheim had unhesitatingly borne the responsibility for this difficult and dangerous operation; he had considered it essential from both the military and political points of view, and without his experience and resolve a success would not have been possible.

The way to Viipuri was now open. Mannerheim had already left for Karelia before the capitulation of Tampere, and found new tasks awaiting him. He organised an Eastern Army for the operations which were obviously soon to take place there, and appointed Ernst Löfström as its commander; because of this choice, Mannerheim was soon criticised for favouring Russian brother-officers at the expense of the *Jägers*. This was a typical intrigue at that time, and the commander-in-chief refused to let it influence him. Two weeks passed before the Eastern Army was ready to attack, during which the Western Army under the command of Martin Wetzer was able to take Pori and continue southwards.

On the same day that the battle for Tampere reached its turning-point, a German expeditionary force commanded by Major-General Count Rüdiger von der Goltz landed at Hanko. It met with no resistance, and was able to advance quickly on Helsinki, which was liberated on 13 April. A second German force under the command of Colonel von Brandenstein landed at Loviisa. Both these German formations were able to provide valuable assistance to the continuing operations of the Western Army, which involved the encirclement of Red forces in the region of Lahti. After Tampere these forces had withdrawn to the south, and were trying to resume the fight in the south-eastern part of the country or make their way to Russia. However, after a desperate struggle they ceased fighting on 4 May. The most difficult operations involved Viipuri and the Karelian isthmus with their fortified positions and close communications with Petrograd. At headquarters there were differing opinions as to how the problem should be solved.

Mannerheim hoped to be able to capture Viipuri without heavy fighting by using the element of surprise and by good planning, but as with the capture of Tampere these hopes were not to be realised. There was stubborn fighting around the town, but after an assault lasting several days complete success was achieved. The leaders of the insurrection were in the town but most thought it best to flee to Petrograd by sea. Only the commissar for finance Dr E. Gylling – later head of the Karelian Soviet

Republic and eventually a victim of Stalin's purges – stayed in the town and tried to negotiate surrender terms. 'Today Viipuri fell after an operation that has been successful in all respects,' Mannerheim delightedly wrote to his brother Johan on 29 April. 'With this the War of Independence is as good as over. Kouvola and Hamina remain, and some backwaters of the insurrection here and there, of varying strength.'

During these operations Mannerheim had been close to the frontier between Finland and Russia. His companion Colonel Gösta Törngren attempted to follow his thoughts: 'Someone who has seen Russian power in all its brilliance and grandeur, reaching its highest peak of might during the World War and then falling apart, to reach its greatest depth of degradation when a small, hitherto oppressed nation crosses its frontiers with a newly-raised army, must find this a deeply moving occurrence.' The War of Independence came to a halt at the Russian frontier. There could be no action against Petrograd or in Eastern Karelia. German policy imposed an absolute obstacle to this after the peace concluded at Brest-Litovsk between Germany and Bolshevik Russia on 3 March 1918.

The short but hard struggle was over. It had developed from a war of independence into a civil war, mainly because of the misguided coup on 28 January. It had been brutal; and upholding international law had been difficult. Ever since the Russo-Japanese War, Mannerheim had vigorously denounced the plundering of the civilian population, the ill-treatment and murder of prisoners, and cruelty of all kinds, and now in Finland he was coming up against lawless behaviour once more. Before the insurrection there had been local acts of terrorism, motivated either by Marxist slogans or of a purely criminal nature. The Red terror provoked a White terror. In successive proclamations he called attention to the laws and usage of war which he wanted to see applied, and experienced shock when his orders were not obeyed. In a letter to Hannes Ignatius he later recalled: 'I have never sanctioned the execution of Reds without trial, and I think you can state with confidence that I not only never consented to the executions at Varkaus [where numerous prisoners were shot in February] but did not even know about them.' But rumours alleging that the commander-in-chief himself had been responsible for such brutality were in circulation; for the defeated side Mannerheim now came to symbolise the illegal tyranny of the bourgeois 'butchers'. This grieved him greatly.

The prison camps established in different parts of the country were the most difficult immediate consequence of the War of Independence. The idea behind them was primarily legalistic; the insurrection had been illegal, and therefore the participants should be tried and convicted according to process of law. Many had committed more serious offences as well. However, the judicial machinery could not work quickly enough to cope with all the cases. The prisoners' families were now deprived of support, and food became increasingly scarce throughout the country and thus in the prison camps as well. The tragic consequence was that many prisoners died of hunger and disease. Undoubtedly the prison camps deepened antagonisms and increased bitterness which had started with the fighting. However, they were not Mannerheim's responsibility; he looked at the problem as a soldier with a practical approach and long experience; a number of those guilty of serious offences should be punished and the remainder let off. But circumstances soon removed him from influence over developments.

Soon Mannerheim's foremost endeavour – and one beset with difficulties – was to overcome the evil consequences of the Civil War. There were too many on both sides of the front line who remained irreconcilable. The Finland-Swedish writer Bertel Gripenberg was for a long time one of those on the White side who wanted to preserve, in the form of poetry, the gulf between 'loyal men in Finland and raging Red gangs', a gulf never to be bridged. A similar spirit of irreconcilability existed on the Red side, and this also found notable expression in poetry and prose. Here too were those who wanted to maintain the 'gulf'. Mannerheim's sister Sophie expressed his contrary aim when she wrote to their elderly aunt Hanna Lovén in Stockholm that victory ought not to be followed by reaction. The 'White General' wanted, both then and always in the future, to work for national unity rather than destructive internal strife.

After the end of hostilities Mannerheim wanted a victory parade in the capital, as a demonstration of particular national significance. The German troops had celebrated their entry into the capital in April; now it was the turn of Finland's army to be presented to the government and people. In this the senate had supported him at its last meeting in Vaasa, from where soon afterwards it was able to move back to its proper home, the senate building in Senate Square, Helsinki. Preparations were complete on 16 May. With Mannerheim leading, the victory parade began in the suburb of Töölö and moved towards the centre of the capital. The day was eloquently described by Jarl Hemmer in his novel about 1918 *En man och hans samvete*, translated into English as *A Fool of Faith*. The general was mounted on Neptune, his beautiful new acquisition from the stud of his brother Johan. The parade proceeded along the streets which now form the thoroughfare that is named after Mannerheim, and the mayor of the city met him at the spot where his equestrian statue now stands. The procession continued to Senate Square, where the senate received Mannerheim and next greeted the army. After a religious service, the commander-in-chief took the salute at the march-past of the troops by the statute of Finland's national poet Johan Ludvig Runeberg on the Esplanade. Now, five months after its declaration of independence, the country had an army. Few events have made such a powerful impression on the Finnish public as those of 16 May, and the day was commemorated with a parade for the next twenty-one years. After the Winter War Mannerheim was to command, for the sake of national unity, that this parade should be replaced by a day given over to the memory of the fallen.

In creating the new armed forces, Mannerheim and his helpers had performed a difficult task, made all the more so by various political and personal antipathies which he had nevertheless succeeded in overcoming so long as the fighting continued. The army and its commander-in-chief enjoyed a unique degree of confidence, but the government now faced an uncertain future and great dangers. How should defence be organised? How was a new insurrection to be forestalled, or a Russian attempt to recover Finland defeated? Already at the end of April Mannerheim had explained to Johan that it was necessary 'to set to work to organise the country's young army, the force which will secure and defend the fruits of our victories in the future. The majority considered him the natural choice for the task, but he was not willing to take it on unconditionally. 'The immediate future will show whether I take on this extra work. I will do it only if I really find that I enjoy the complete confidence of the whole country and can carry it out with the full authority which is necessary for its success. If this should not be the case, I prefer to leave the responsibility to others.'

In the event Mannerheim did not obtain that authority. At his meeting with the senate on 16 May in the chamber of the senate building he resolutely made his attitude clear ('I did not talk trivialities to the senate'). He stated his view of the role of the armed forces in society, and recalled dramatically the last occasion when he had had discussions in the same place – with Svinhufvud, chairman of the senate, on 16 January 1918. He had then received command of an army which did not exist: 'It had to be created with funds subscribed voluntarily and with weapons that had to be bought or captured from the enemy.' Now, once more, he was in the senate building 'at the head of Finland's young, victorious army. It has been granted to us after battle and toil . . . to break a powerful enemy and create for the government and people the power and strength which are necessary for building the country up again for the future . . . The solution of these great tasks is in the hands of the same government which last autumn pronounced the proud words proclaiming Finland a sovereign state, but which . . . was forced to remain powerless against pillage and violence and watch helplessly as Finnish citizens were murdered until the last shadow of power was taken from it and its members were compelled to flee or go into hiding.' The army now required guarantees against a repetition of these events; it wanted the helm of the state to be in steady hands. The dead demanded that their sacrifice should not have been in vain.

Two weeks after telling the senate these home truths, Mannerheim chose to resign rather than serve the senate further. There were many different reasons why he was set aside, the principal one being the orientation towards Germany which had existed in various quarters before the war but which grew stronger during the insurrection, particularly after the arrival of German military assistance. To the population living to the south of the front line, it was easy for German help to seem the decisive factor that saved them from chaos – and Mannerheim was known to be an opponent of German influence. The fact that Swedish was his mother-tongue and that his previous career had been in the empire could easily be utilised in propaganda against him in the strongly nationalistic and anti-Russian mood of Finland in the spring of 1918. Svinhufvud and the majority of the senate were also counting on a German victory in Europe, leading to future German protection against the Russian menace. They were prepared to elect a German prince as king if a monarchy could be established in Finland.

The *Jägers* are generally believed to have been pro-German, but the majority were loyal to the commander-in-chief. However two men connected with them worked explicitly against him. These were V.O. Sivén, a doctor, and Wilhelm Thesleff, who saw in Mannerheim's leadership a serious threat to their political programme and their own influence. The senate on the whole was certainly prepared to defend Mannerheim against such opposition – indeed Svinhufvud and most of the senators admired him greatly – but the decisive question was in fact quite different, namely the organisation and future role of the Finnish armed forces. Mannerheim reluctantly accepted various demands for German instructors, as well as for training and organisation along German lines, but the German military command in Finland were not content with that alone: the Finnish army must be organised on the German pattern, exclusively with German instructors, and should be completely subordinate to 'the German general in Finland'. The shaping of Finnish foreign and military policy would thus inevitably have to conform with the eastern policy of the government in Berlin.

A member of the Vaasa senate fairly close to Mannerheim, Alexander Frey, stated the attitude of the senators in May as follows. They 'were scarcely able to grasp the grandeur in General Mannerheim's scheme to create a Finnish army with an independent Finnish military organisation unconnected with the Germans in spite of their presence in the country. This was for him a question of national pride, just as the waging of the War of Independence with our own forces had been. But to us his stand-point seemed . . . scarcely feasible in terms of practical politics.'

Instead the Finnish political leaders – with Svinhufvud and Paasikivi at their head – came to an agreement with the Germans in accordance with the latter's wishes. Already for some time Svinhufvud had been negotiating with von der Goltz behind Mannerheim's back concerning the organisation of the army and relations with Germany. As the result, Mannerheim lost the right of freely choosing instructors, who were now to be exclusively German. A German general staff officer was to work alongside him to work out requisite proposals which he was to sign. To Mannerheim this programme was impossible. In no circumstances was he willing to act as the subordinate of a foreign commander. In his opinion the agreement was dangerous for Finland, since it implied that the senate was putting the country's independence at risk. He learned fully what had happened only in the course of a fairly long meeting with the senate on 30 May. Mannerheim's answer was to resign immediately: 'I have only to add that I will lay down my command this evening and go abroad tomorrow.' 'None of the senators had anything to say to me', he later recounted, 'nobody even rose to shake me by the hand.' The breach was final.

On 2 June, under the light night sky, Mannerheim boarded the boat for Stockholm in Turku harbour. Only his sister Sophie saw him off as he left the country which, only a short time before, he had saved from ruin and given national freedom and a free, constitutional social system. The Finnish officers at headquarters and the Swedish officers in Finland resigned with him.

VIII
REGENT OF FINLAND
1918–1919

Mannerheim had gone to live in Stockholm until conditions in Finland should change. The summer of 1918 was partly taken up by political activity. He was received by King Gustaf who conferred on him the Grand Cross of the Order of the Sword in recognition of what the Finnish War of Independence had meant for Sweden. He sought contacts with the British and American ministers Sir Esmé Howard and Ira Morris. They held him in high regard for his service in the Russian army, which had also served the cause of the Entente, and for his opposition to the growing German influence in Finland.

Mannerheim's conversations with the ministers were mainly concerned with Finland's orientation towards Germany. What risks lay in Germany's ever-increasing influence? What would be the situation after Germany's defeat, which was now generally expected? Various measures for gaining goodwill for the Entente and counteracting German demands in Helsinki were discussed. What the Finns wanted chiefly were food imports, a port on the Arctic Ocean and support for their aspirations in the territory of Eastern Karelia, which was controlled by British troops as far south as Petrozavodsk. However, it was impossible at that time to obtain the support of the Entente governments for these aims, and Mannerheim's efforts were not understood in Stockholm. But he had made a good impression and made valuable contacts with the representatives of Western governments.

During the autumn of 1918 it became ever plainer that Germany's military defeat was imminent. Mannerheim now became a considerable diplomatic asset to Finland, perhaps the only one it had, since he was untainted by the government's unsuccessful policy with regard to Germany. The senate summoned him to Helsinki, and he went there on 8 October. After discussions with Svinhufvud, Paasikivi the prime minister, and Stenroth the foreign minister, he was asked to go to London and Paris to try and make contact with the governments of the Western powers. Realisation had dawned in Finland of the seriousness of the situation. Mannerheim was willing to undertake the mission but only in a private capacity. There was a delay while all the permits to make the hazardous journey across the North Sea to London were obtained, and he became ever more alarmed at the seriousness of the situation, as he wrote to Sophie.

In the meantime the pro-Germans in Helsinki had continued their work. A German prince was elected king of Finland, and the monarchists tried to get him to come to Finland as soon as possible. Mannerheim feared that the Western powers would interpret this as a new provocation, but the prince never arrived. Finally everything was arranged for Mannerheim's journey, and he was free to leave, in company with his brother-in-law Mikael Gripenberg. On 10 November he landed at Aberdeen, and the next day the armistice between the belligerents was announced, ending the World War after more than four years of fighting.

When Mannerheim reached London it became clear that his task was going to be harder than he had anticipated. 'It was necessary', he said afterwards, 'to try to influence a public opinion that was not particularly well disposed towards Finland. It was necessary not only to secure French agreement to the resumption of relations with Finland [which had been ruptured because of its pro-German policy] but also to induce France to urge England to assent to a joint recognition of Finland before the peace conference.' In the British *de facto* assistant foreign secretary Lord Robert Cecil and in the foreign secretary Arthur Balfour he had difficult opponents. His conversations with them and other leading members of the cabinet, with Sir Henry Wilson, the Chief of the Imperial General Staff, and with the principal Foreign Office officials were arduous since he had not only to overcome the suspicions provoked by the Senate's former policy, but also take account of the concern felt by Britain for Russia's interest in preserving an influence on Finland. However, his time in Russia had given him a number of good contacts which he could now put to good use, especially with Englishmen who – like Lord Hardinge of Penshurst (British ambassador in St Petersburg in 1904–6 and Permanent Under-Secretary at the Foreign Office in 1906–10 and 1916–20) – had been diplomats there, or whom he had met during the war. He concentrated his attention on obtaining food supplies for Finland and on getting the country's independence recognised. He emphasised that the country might be thrown into serious internal conflicts if the people were to go short of food.

While he was in London, the news reached Mannerheim that parliament intended to elect him Regent, in accordance with a provision of the Form of Government introduced by King Gustaf III of Sweden in 1772 and still part of Finnish constitutional law. Svinhufvud wanted to resign his position as head of state and worked for Mannerheim's appointment as his successor; he had never ceased to admire and have confidence in the General. It was felt that the Western powers now had an additional reason for supporting him and thus recognising Finnish independence immediately. But the British government was still not prepared – least of all on its own – to take up a position on Finnish questions. Mannerheim therefore decided to cross to Paris. At first he met resistance there – he lacked the right contacts – but he did succeed in winning French confidence. 'He captivates everyone by his charming personality and by his superb intelligence and his keen political eye,' records a Finn who was then acting as an unofficial envoy. The help he received from his Polish friends from Warsaw – especially Adam Zamoyski – who enjoyed considerable goodwill among the French, contributed to his success. Thus he secured from Pichon, the foreign minister, a promise to work for recognition and for the sending of food supplies.

However, Paris demanded certain conditions for recognising Finland. In Helsinki Svinhufvud had already formed a new senate under the leadership of Lauri Ingman, subsequently the Lutheran archbishop, with Carl Enckell as foreign minister and Rudolf Walden as minister for war – two men who enjoyed Mannerheim's confidence and were to remain with him to the very end of his career. But the senate contained two other names which the French government disapproved of. The Regent consequently found himself in a delicate situation, but decided not to give in to the French on this point, believing that to do so would jeopardise Finland's honour. The Entente powers further demanded new parliamentary elections as soon as possible as a guarantee of democracy. Finally they demanded that all German soldiers should leave the country. Mannerheim acceded to both these demands.

On returning to London, Mannerheim was able to play off the favourable attitude of the French against the British. 'I considered that I could not travel home until I had obtained from Mr Arthur Balfour the express promise that England would join France in the recognition of Finland's independence.' But recognition was delayed. Intrigues of all kinds – in the Foreign Office and at home – caused the British to postpone the final decision until after the Finnish parliamentary election in March. But Mannerheim won an important success in the matter of food supplies. In spite of the prevailing blockade, he obtained permission to import grain into his starving country, and at the same time Sweden and Denmark promised to lend sufficient grain for an initial shipment of wheat. This shipment had already arrived by the time Mannerheim returned to Turku.

Bread could now at last be baked – it was popularly known as 'Mannerheim's loaves'.

Mannerheim set out for home on 15 December, arriving in Stockholm on 19 December and at Turku on 22 December. It was clear that in the course of this journey to Western Europe he had succeeded in every significant respect, despite the difficulties caused by the intrigues of untrustworthy Finns, among them Rudolf Holsti, the political envoy in London who eventually became foreign minister. Swedish diplomats had also worked against him, alarmed by the fact that while in Western Europe he would have many opportunities to defend Finland's case over the question of the Åland islands. While passing through Stockholm on his journey home, he learned that that question was once again exercising the government in Stockholm.

During only seven short months the new head of state made his mark on the country in several ways. At the beginning of 1919 the situation seemed practically hopeless. There were the many serious problems left behind by the war; the unexpected Swedish claim to the Åland islands had caused mutual animosity in place of understanding, and new attacks were threatened from Russia. A mood of anxiety and uncertainty was widespread. It was necessary as a first step to bridge the serious antipathies within society, and in his speech to the senate on 23 December 1918 Mannerheim called for a policy with that in view. An honest attempt had to be made to treat all social classes justly and, as far as possible, to remove existing injustices. He urged reconciliation and unity; clearing up the sad legacy of the insurrection was the central task. He began with a limited amnesty and called for a speedy general amnesty – which was postponed, against his will, until 17 July 1919 when the new constitution came into force.

On the first anniversary of the outbreak of the War of Independence Mannerheim donated a considerable sum of his own money to assist children whose fathers had been killed in the war, irrespective of the side on which they had fought. This marked the beginning of a policy of reconciliation which, in time, was to bear fruit.

The possibility of a renewed rising, with Russian support, could not be ruled out, and we now know that the fear of it which prevailed at the time was justified. A defence against this danger was the Civil Guard organisation, created in 1918 and based on voluntary support. Originally apolitical and open to all, this organisation had acquired as the result of the insurrection an anti-socialist character, which only became less conspicuous with the passing of time, and which had the unfortunate consequence that for a long time it was distrusted by the left. Mannerheim's idea in 1919 was that the defence of the country could largely be based on the Civil Guard, while the organisation of the regular army could be more circumscribed. One of the reasons for this approach was financial: the costs to the state would be limited if defence were essentially based on private self-sacrifice. Mannerheim was therefore anxious to enlarge the Civil Guard organisation. He not only valued it highly from the standpoint of national defence, but was also aware of the need to provide legally-based conditions for its organisation and activity. This was how the decree of 14 February 1919 on the Civil Guard came about; it was signed by Mannerheim and countersigned by Rudolf Walden – the same names as appeared on the law which marked the end of the Civil Guard, enforced by the Soviet Union, twenty-six years later. The decree of 1919 gave the organisation a significant degree of independence from the army but at the same time subordinated it to the President as commander-in-chief of the armed forces and obliged it to follow government directions. The Civil Guard districts were organised on a broad-minded application of democratic principles. This shocked many professional soldiers at the time, but produced good results.

Much of the Regent's strenuous activity was directed towards defence and foreign affairs. After the armed forces were freed from German influence, he was able to return to the plans he had made in the spring of 1918 and utilise several of the collaborators he enlisted then. Hannes Ignatius once again became chief of the general staff and Ernst Linder inspector of cavalry, but they left these posts after Mannerheim's departure. Among the many valuable initiatives now taken was the foundation of the Finnish Cadet School for the training of officers. Several senior officers were sent to staff colleges in France and Sweden. In the administration of foreign affairs Mannerheim was especially concerned with the selection of personnel, convinced as he always was of how important diplomacy was for a small country.

In March 1919 the new parliamentary elections were to be held which would confirm that Finland was a democracy. Parliament had been obliged to function with only two socialist members remaining, the rest having more or less willingly joined the rebellion. New elections would restore normality, but many believed they were a gamble; too short a time had elapsed since the war and its aftermath. However, for reasons of foreign and domestic policy they had to go ahead.

It scarcely came as a surprise when a non-socialist majority was returned again. The Social Democrats took 80 seats out of 200 and became the largest party. In radical quarters in Finland and certain circles in Sweden and England, there were hopes of cooperation between the centre parties and the socialists which would force Mannerheim to resign, but mutual antagonisms were still too strong for that. The Agrarians (the Finnish-language peasant party) had had enough of the political game – of attempted co-operation with the socialists – which they had played in 1917.

After the elections the conservative senate led by Ingman had to resign. The newly-appointed Regent had been presented with a *fait accompli* on its formation, but now as head of state he had the chance to take part in the political game involved with the forming of a new government. This proved troublesome because the Agrarians and the Young Finns (a Finnish-language liberal party) refused at first to participate in a non-socialist coalition, and proposed conditions which the other non-socialist parties could not accept. Eventually, however, Senator Kaarlo Castrén succeeded in forming a government which was significantly less conservative than Ingman's, but was nevertheless prepared to support Mannerheim. Rudolf Walden remained a member. Rudolf Holsti now became foreign minister, and quickly showed himself to be disloyal to the Regent in many ways.

In foreign policy, two difficult problems came to dominate the period of Mannerheim's regency: the Åland islands question and plans for an action against Petrograd. The latter had a decisive influence on the outcome of the presidential election and the Regent's position.

Mannerheim was particularly anxious to strengthen Finland's Scandinavian contacts. In this he received considerable assistance from King Gustaf V of Sweden, who had a high opinion of him, and personally arranged for him to be invited on a state visit – an example followed by the Kings of Denmark and Norway. On 12 February 1919 the Regent arrived in Stockholm with his suite and was hospitably received, although the friendliness of the reception was marred by extreme left-wing demonstrations. The goodwill visit continued to Copenhagen, where Mannerheim gained a friend and admirer in Christian X. However, the visit to Christiania (Oslo) was cancelled when Mannerheim realised that leftists there would make difficulties for King Haakon and the government.

It quickly became apparent in Stockholm that the Åland islands would be the central topic of discussion during Mannerheim's visit. Shortly after the German collapse in November, the Swedish government had again raised the matter. It was no longer simply a question of an alleged humanitarian action to protect the population, but Sweden was openly claiming the islands on the basis of the inhabitants' wishes and military considerations.

It wanted a plebiscite in the islands and demanded their demilitarisation.

Mannerheim had adopted the view that Finland should endeavour to give due attention to Swedish security requirements as well as to Nordic cooperation. But he refused absolutely to abandon Finland's right to the Åland islands, and considered that the principle of nationality was not applicable there because the Swedish population in Finland was considerably more numerous than the Ålanders and the country was bilingual. He tried to reach a compromise, but political opinion in Sweden was so inflexible that a compromise would scarcely get a hearing. Instead Mannerheim was subjected to diatribes, some of a malicious character.

Gustaf V and the government leaders raised the Åland island question on the day of Mannerheim's arrival. In his diary Enckell, the Finnish foreign minister, recorded his indignation that the King had brought up the question 'immediately after Mannerheim had managed to swallow his last mouthful at the King's welcoming lunch'. In fact Gustaf V had done so even before they sat down at table. In the ensuing conversation with the Swedish premier and foreign minister, it was in vain that Mannerheim put forward compromise proposals acknowledging Sweden's right to fortify certain points in the archipelago.

Towards the end of the regency the Russian question became ever more urgent. It had occupied Mannerheim's thoughts from the very beginning of the War of Independence. He had explained to Sir Esmé Howard and Ira Morris in the summer of 1918 that he would have wanted to occupy Petrograd if it had been possible for him maintain his position in Finland; the aim was to 'help Russia to recover its equilibrium' and to ensure Finland's security, also to influence the Civil War in Russia to the advantage of the White armies. On the other hand, most of his fellow-countrymen had a decidedly negative attitude towards their eastern neighbour – resulting from its policy of oppression during the immediately preceding decades – and were not prepared to exert themselves on its behalf.

Mannerheim saw the problem in the east differently. His motives were both political and humanitarian. Like many in Western Europe, even including some Social Democrats, he regarded Bolshevism and the dictatorship of the proletariat as a serious danger for the future, frightening in its dogmatism and fanaticism, its oppression and terror. Finland was well aware of the dreadful calamities which had befallen Russia. Above all Mannerheim wanted to see a free Russia with a liberal social system and a federal constitutional structure. Only thus would the numerous non-Russian peoples of the empire be able to lead tolerable lives. Decades of experience and political thinking lay behind this vision of the future.

At first leading Western states rejected the idea of intervention in Russia, the United States President Woodrow Wilson and the British prime minister Lloyd George being the decisive influences in this, but with Winston Churchill the mood soon changed. Even many on the Social Democrat side advocated intervention, including Hjalmar Branting in Sweden, who hoped for an intervention in the name of democracy. When the White Russian armies won great successes in the spring of 1919 under Kolchak and Denikin, the idea of intervention gathered support.

Attention, naturally enough, also turned to Finland, where a body of opinion undoubtedly existed in favour of an operation against Petrograd provided that the White Russian leaders recognised Finnish independence. Here crucial obstacles were encountered. Russian soldiers and civil servants who had grown up in the nationalistic atmosphere of the Russian empire were, understandably, unwilling to concede independence to the 'border peoples', and wanted to refer the matter to a future Russian constituent assembly, but from the standpoint of practical politics in 1919 this attitude was misguided. Kolchak and Denikin vigorously rebuffed all Mannerheim's demands for concessions until it was too late. These experiences provoked Mannerheim into saying that he did not know who were the worse, the Red or the White Russian leaders.

In the spring of 1919 the British and French governments had decided to intervene in Russia – Britain took charge of the Baltic region and North Russia, France of the southern fronts – and it was of great concern to Finland whether it would become involved in a thrust against Petrograd. But it was soon clear that the British and French had completely different views on this subject; Paris favoured action by Finland, whereas London did not. The British were influenced by the White Russian leaders who were opposed to a Finnish operation against their former capital; it was important to them that the city should be liberated by Russian troops alone. When a British military mission arrived in Helsinki at the end of May 1919 to coordinate policy and strategy in the Baltic region, its head, General Sir Hubert Gough, had instructions to prevent Finnish participation in operations; Petrograd was to be captured by Russian troops based in Estonia.

However, the most important question in Helsinki was still whether Kolchak – now the most important leader on the White Russian side – could be induced to recognise Finnish independence; the prospect of a new Russian regime that had not made any promise to Finland was unpalatable. On the other hand General Yudenich, who was organising the White

Russian army in Estonia, was in Helsinki seeking Finnish help. The game became even more complicated.

Mannerheim was still willing to assist in the victory of the White Russian forces over Bolshevism, notably by means of an operation against the former imperial capital, but he was less willing to conduct a policy designed only to incorporate the Finnish region of Eastern Karelia into Finland, which for the time being was a dangerous task. He did not want Finnish troops engaged in Eastern Karelia, although he allowed the region to be invaded by a Finnish volunteer force. He hoped for British help in a march on Petrograd, the success of which he now considered possible, especially in view of the strong dissatisfaction in Russia with Bolshevik rule. He tried to persuade the British and French governments and above all Gough in Helsinki to support his scheme – at first unsuccessfully (27 May 1919). At that time he was still opposed by Kolchak, although Yudenich in Helsinki was prepared to come to an agreement on Mannerheim's conditions. A proposed agreement was drawn up and submitted to Kolchak's government in Omsk. Kolchak became more compliant only after suffering serious military reverses in mid-June in Siberia and North-West Russia, although he was still unwilling to approve of Yudenich's draft agreement. He nevertheless appealed to Finland at a fateful moment when Petrograd was at stake, and the Western powers supported his appeal. In this situation the question of intervention took on a new urgency in Helsinki. Dramatic discussions followed in the government and with the British, but since clearly neither Kolchak nor the British would accept all the political, military and economic conditions put forward by Mannerheim, no unanimous and affirmative decision could be reached. The Regent was unwilling to act without the requisite support from the government and from parliament.

However, other plans were being hammered out in more activist Finnish circles, where it was considered that a turning-point lay ahead, perhaps of importance for the whole of world history. There were fears, too, of a Russian attack on Finland, which made it preferable for Finland to act. Mannerheim was urged, before it was too late, to force through the march on Petrograd on his own responsibility, after manoeuvres had taken place which resembled a *coup d'état*; he was first to confirm the new constitution, then dissolve parliament and, while new elections were pending, march on Petrograd. A war cabinet would be formed if Castrén's government resigned. At first Mannerheim showed interest in this plan. but on reflection he found it far too hazardous. After some days of hesitation he overcame the temptation which the activists' proposal undoubtedly presented to him. His character and political upbringing would not allow him to lead his country in such a dangerous direction.

How the Russian question would be decided was thus now connected with the new constitution, the confirmation of which would be the crucial moment. The country's future constitution had been under discussion since 1917, but by 1919 it was clear that Finland would become a republic with a president as head of state. Parliament had been composed since 1906 of a single chamber, elected by universal and equal suffrage including women; the parliamentary principle was now to be written into the constitution. However, a political conflict had grown up around the role of the president. The Social Democrats wanted the President to be weak, whereas Mannerheim had striven for the opposite. Eventually the head of state was granted certain important powers – the right to dissolve parliament and appoint officials; the position of commander-in-chief which, however, might be transfered to another person in war-time; and the direction of foreign policy. So as to have an independent position, the President was to be elected by the people through a college of electors, although in fact the first presidential election was to lie with parliament. Such was the compromise accepted by the Regent, fully conscious of the risks it presented to his own candidacy. The constitution also contained far-reaching provisions on civil rights.

On 17 July 1919 Mannerheim confirmed the constitution, and the first presidential election had to be held immediately afterwards. He of course stood as a candidate, but in the end was supported only by the Conservative Party (an amalgamation of two nationalistic conservative groups within the Finnish-speaking population) and the Swedish People's Party (representing the interests of the country's Swedish-speakers). What was finally decisive was the refusal of the large Social Democratic group to support the 'White General' as head of state. To avoid a split, the centre parties – where Mannerheim had numerous supporters – chose as their candidate Professor K.J. Ståhlberg, a former senator. He was acceptable to the Social Democratic members of parliament, and attained the requisite majority on 25 July 1919. With that, plans for an intervention in Russia became unrealisable.

There was a sequel to the presidential election of which it is not easy to obtain a clear picture. Mannerheim distrusted Ståhlberg and many of the politicians who surrounded him, and feared that their policy of compliance with the left would lead them too far; he felt that their commitment to national defence was not to be relied on. Ståhlberg and Castrén offered Mannerheim command of the army, but he was not disposed to accept it without further consideration and requested answers to certain important questions about his future position. These concerned the extent of the commander's authority, his independence in relation to the government and the civil service, and his right to prepare for an attack on Petrograd at a favourable moment. It was also pointed out that a state of war prevailed between Finland and Russia; an intervention in Russia thus formed part of the conduct of war, which was the responsibility of the commander. Mannerheim never received an answer but it was made to appear that he had refused the offer; he himself doubted if it had ever been made sincerely.

After seven months the period of the regency was over. The country had been freed from its heavy dependence on Germany, the defence forces had been consolidated, many of the most serious consequences of the insurrection had been overcome, a new parliament had been elected according to the constitution, an amnesty had been promulgated, and finally a new republican constitution had been confirmed. For Mannerheim the outcome of the presidential election was a disappointment. Much of what he had wanted to accomplish remained undone, and many plans had been pushed aside. How was national defence to be built up now and a reasonable relationship with Russia brought about? He regretted extremely that he had been deprived of the opportunity to carry out his social policy.

Mannerheim was inclined to regard the future with apprehension. He mentioned to his sister Eva Sparre (19.7.19) the characteristics of contemporary Finnish political life which he found inauspicious, 'the need to put party before public interest' and 'the prevalent inexplicable weakness'. Nevertheless he viewed the situation and his own role in a balanced way: 'I hope I am exaggerating the gloom of the situation. There is always a tendency to believe that your own ideas are the only efficacious ones, and yet many roads lead to Rome.'

Mannerheim stayed in Finland for a few months after the election, and then left to travel around Europe to familiarise himself with the current political situation. Events in Russia engrossed his attention; he still hoped that Lenin's dictatorship would collapse under the pressure from internal political difficulties and from the White armies which were fighting their way towards Moscow from different directions. He still considered Bolshevism a severe threat, not only to the social ideals in which he believed but also to the states on Russia's borders and to Europe in general.

He visited France first, and it was during his stay in Paris that he heard that Yudenich's army from Estonia had begun its march on Petrograd. At the same time the White armies in the south of Russia achieved notable successes, and were on the march to Moscow. According to the information he obtained in Paris, their strength was growing while that of the Bolsheviks was on the decline. It was generally believed in the West that the collapse of the Bolsheviks was imminent. He now saw the prospect of a victorious White Russia, dominated by groups in which the old nationalist aspirations would find fruitful soil. However, Finland was in danger of being confronted by a greatly strengthened Russia, backed by the Western powers. The government in Helsinki had not done much to deserve the favour of the future White Russian leaders, and the opportunity to do so would soon be past. Such reasoning led Mannerheim to propose most fervently that Finland should at long last support the army led by Yudenich which was advancing on Petrograd.

On 2 November 1919 the Finnish press published, in the form of an open letter from Mannerheim to the President, a skilfully worded justification for the active policy which Mannerheim had long advocated. He again pointed out the importance of Finland making a contribution to the decisive struggle 'against the most cruel despotism the world has known' in order 'to secure our freedom and show the world that the unrestricted sovereignty of the Finnish state, based on law, is a matter of general European interest'. Mannerheim's appeal did not lead to action by Ståhlberg's Finland. The government had been divided; several of its members, like Mannerheim, had wanted to give active support to Yudenich.

It was not long before the situation on the Russian front altered radically to the disadvantage of the White Russian troops. Lenin had indeed given up Petrograd for lost, but its defence had been organised in time under the vigorous leadership of Trotsky. Already on 23 October Yudenich's corps suffered a serious reverse on the outskirts of Petrograd and soon had to return to Tallinn. Denikin was defeated on the central front at the end of October, and in Siberia shortly afterwards Kolchak's armies collapsed. Mannerheim considered that the eventual defeat of the White troops was due to psychological factors, weariness and disillusionment, and to military miscalculations, but above all to the absence of a programme of social and agrarian reforms. His advice on these matters remained unheeded until it was too late.

The Civil War in Russia continued for two more years, and parallel with it battles were going on between Soviet armies, Ukrainian forces and the Poles, with alternating fortunes. In the autumn of 1919 Mannerheim tried to follow developments in Poland, and discussed the situation there with Pilsudski, the Polish head of state. The Polish armies were at that time advancing into Russia, having experienced the same difficulties with the White Russian leaders as Mannerheim had done himself. In 1920 Soviet cavalry (commanded by Budenny, once a non-commissioned officer at the Officers' Cavalry School where Mannerheim had served during the years immediately before the Russo-Japanese War) were able to drive the Polish army out of Kiev and the Ukraine, and advance to the very outskirts of Warsaw, but with French help and under the command of General Weygand the Poles inflicted a sharp defeat on the Russians, who had to withdraw rapidly eastwards. Mannerheim followed these events eagerly.

The outcome of the long Civil War in Russia changed the situation of Eastern Europe and of Finland. In the course of time the Bolshevik regime became consolidated. Moscow accepted peace treaties with the new countries on its western frontier; peace was concluded with Finland at Tartu in October 1920. This treaty secured for Finland the Petsamo region in the north, but put an end to hopes of incorporating in the republic the Finnish-speaking region of Eastern Karelia.

IX
PRIVATE CITIZEN
1919–1931

The political climate in Finland had become uncomfortable. For a time Mannerheim frankly doubted whether he ought to settle there at all, but he quickly overcame those feelings. 'Politics here,' he reflected, 'led as they are by defeatists and compromisers, have nothing pleasant to offer.' He feared that the Civil Guard would be disbanded and the army's strength reduced. After that the communists could take over Finland by peaceful means.

However, he received repeated proofs from his homeland of the esteem in which he was held and of gratitude for what he had accomplished. The principal demonstration of this came with the substantial national gift presented to him in 1920, the proceeds of a collection made the previous year. It was accompanied by a national address saying that the gift was an expression of gratitude to the man who was 'an exalting and uplifting example', and who 'expressed noble thoughts to the whole people, and impressed upon their minds the demands of moral obligation, chivalry and patriotism raised far above party politics'. The gift, on which Mannerheim was to enjoy the interest for life, freed him for the first time of the financial worries that had dogged him since his youth.

However, Mannerheim's relations with President Ståhlberg and the constantly changing governments were poor. It can be said that the President entertained an unjustified suspicion (fomented by his wife) of the 'White General'; he had never been able to grasp that his opponent was far removed from any lust for power and nurtured no plans for a *coup d'état*. Mannerheim found this suspicion deeply insulting, and his response was to keep consistently at a distance.

There were several occasions for sharp conflicts. An especially serious one occurred in 1921 between the leadership of the Civil Guard, the President and the government. At issue was whether the government had the right to remove a meritorious and capable commander in the Civil Guard for reasons of foreign policy. This commander, Major-General Paul von Gerich, had made various statements in a letter to a newspaper which gave rise to protests from the governments of the Baltic states. The government considered that the crisis which followed could only be resolved if von Gerich were dismissed, and the defence minister therefore instructed the head of the Civil Guard, Colonel Didrik von Essen, to dismiss him. However, von Essen refused on the grounds that there was insufficient justification for such a step. The government chose to remove von Essen but then found itself without a commander of the Civil Guard. Meanwhile the order to dismiss von Gerich was given to a former defence minister, Major-General K.E. Berg, then chief of staff to the commander-in-chief. Berg carried out the order but recognised that he was in an intolerable position, and committed suicide during the night of 22 June 1921.

The government now faced a difficult issue in the appointment of a new head of the Civil Guard. The latter considered that they had the right to make the nomination, which should be of someone who enjoyed their confidence. On 16 September they proposed Mannerheim for the appointment, but Ståhlberg refused to confirm their choice for fear that the General, as head of the Civil Guard and thus commander of forces larger than those of the regular army, would be in possession of too much power. In consequence there were pro-Mannerheim demonstrations. The President solved the problem by appointing a comparatively junior officer, Lieutenant-Colonel (subsequently Major-General) Lauri Malmberg, as commander of the Civil Guard.

As the result of his sharp antagonism to Ståhlberg and his immediate associates, Mannerheim was continually cold-shouldered by the government, the civil service and the defence establishment. On the other hand it was all too clear that his indisputable abilities and great energy were not being utilised to the benefit of the country, and the government was frequently criticised for this. For Rabbe Wrede, an eminent lawyer and politican, this pointed to the weakness of the democratic social system.

Clearly, for someone as constantly active and industrious as Mannerheim, the lack of demanding work was now a problem. He tried to occupy his time with self-imposed tasks, and partly succeeded, but those who knew him well understood that the easier existence he was enjoying was hard to endure. This went so far that at one time he considered trying to enter the service of a European great power – France – to maintain and deepen his professional knowledge.

Mannerheim had no significant political contacts in Finland during these years, nor was he anxious to acquire any. He was not interested in Finnish party politics and was reluctant to become caught up 'in the acrimony which Finnish internal politics is devoted to engendering'. He refused an invitation to stand as the candidate of the Swedish People's Party in the presidential election of 1925, when Lauri Relander was elected as Ståhlberg's successor; he considered it quite wrong that the party now appeared with a separate candidate. The 'White General' nevertheless enjoyed such prestige and such wide popularity that, despite everything, he was able to exercise an appreciable influence. He used it in the first instance for the benefit of the defence forces and especially the Civil Guard.

Free from public employment, Mannerheim was able to take on other tasks in the decade that followed. Much time was given to ceremonial functions of all kinds, and he was frequently invited to participate in and speak at commemorative ceremonies and gatherings. He devoted a lot of time and interest to the villa in the elegant Kaivopuisto district of Helsinki which a few years later became his final residence, and to his summer home at Hanko – both their furnishing and the layout of their gardens interested him. He also gave a great deal of time and attention to his personal friends in Finland and abroad. Since the time of the War of Independence he had been close to the Finnish artist Axel Gallén-Kallela, who at one time served as his aide-de-camp, followed his work with interest, and twice arranged commissions for him to paint his portrait. With his great fondness for music Mannerheim was happy, too, in his friendship with Sibelius, who played a role in the War of Independence by composing the *Jäger March*, heard for the first time when the *Jäger* battalion arrived in Vaasa. Mannerheim's home became a meeting place for various groups whom he happily gathered round him, and to the diplomatic corps in Helsinki he was a liberal host and a valued guest.

Mannerheim wanted to arrange and publish the results of his journey of exploration in Asia. Above all he was eager to foster medical care and humanitarian social work. In the autumn of 1920 he took the initiative in the foundation of a child welfare association. Undoubtedly he was inspired to do so by his sister Sophie and her friends, among whom Erik Mandelin had already been a faithful helper in his political activity before the War of Independence and now helped also in his social work. While training as a nurse in England during the Boer War, Sophie had been appalled by the poor physical condition of many British Army recruits; in Britain this state of affairs prompted various measures to improve health care among the young. During the Red uprising Sophie herself created a special hospital for children, known as the 'Children's Castle', to help small children during the difficult conditions of those times.

Gustaf Mannerheim shared her interests. As a soldier he could easily see the connection between health and social care, on the one hand, and the physical wellbeing which was essential for the defence forces. Social work, he thought, could also promote a more equal society, which was particularly desirable in Finland after the devastation of the Civil War. In the autumn of 1920 he was able to inform Marie Lubomirska, with satisfaction, that he had just started 'a big association for child welfare in Finland', which came to be known as 'General Mannerheim's Child Welfare Association'. Before society had embarked on such activities (when it did so later, the Association altered its programme somewhat), it concerned itself with infant mortality, the care of orphans, the health of the people, and education. Through his prestige and his many connections Mannerheim was able to persuade many people to help. He obtained an expert helper and valuable support in the paediatrician Professor Arvo Ylppö.

In 1922 Mannerheim was elected to the chairmanship of the Finnish Red Cross. He had come into contact with its work in Manchuria in 1904–5 and later during the First World War, so that he was conversant with its aims. Here too it was necessary to enlist voluntary helpers, and with the assistance of writers and artists – notably his friends Sibelius and Gallén-Kallela – he was able to organise profitable fund-raising events and collections. He pressed on with the development of the Red Cross, promoted the building of its hospital in Helsinki, and stimulated work on allergies and rheumatic illness, areas which especially interested him. He was able to devote time and interest also to the International Red Cross.

During these years of private life Mannerheim travelled extensively. His interest in foreign countries had been aroused early; now 'I want to see as much of the world as possible, before age compels me to stay put in the cottage corner.' He travelled for various reasons – for relaxation and recreation, to hunt and out of interest in nature, but most of all to learn, to maintain old contacts and to acquire new ones. He wanted to meet leading politicians and soldiers and gain for himself 'an opinion about the world situation – my own, even if it is superficial' (19 January 1932 to A.H. Saastamoinen, a Finnish businessman and diplomat). It is clear that this experience of travel and study enlarged his knowledge of European politics and diplomacy. The Swedish defence minister P.E. Sköld declared, after a meeting with Mannerheim in the late summer of 1939, that nobody else in Scandinavia had such a grasp of the situation. The British minister in Helsinki could ask on another occasion if Mannerheim possessed 'a seer's eye', his judgements were so often to the point. It is clear, too, that he was glad not to be concerned with the sometimes vexing party struggles and other conflicts of Finland. Personally unassuming, he preferred to avoid appearing at great official occasions if there were not special considerations that prompted his participation.

In 1923 he planned a long journey by car to French North Africa. 'Sated as much with wrangling as with gala dinners in Helsinki, I am on my way to Algeria and Morocco to find rest, sun and refreshment on the great highway from Algiers to Marrakech.' But he had only gone a little way beyond Algiers when he broke his leg badly in a road accident and was forced to stay a month in hospital.

Four years later he realised a long-cherished plan to visit India. His ride across Asia in 1906–8 had passed north of the British Indian empire; now he wanted to get to the know country itself. In December 1927 he began the two-week steamer voyage to Bombay, which gave him time to read books on Indian history, 'about the land of dreams and wisdom, with its tigers, elephants, temples and flowers'. His journey took him first to Lucknow where hunting was on hand. In Delhi he met his English friend General Sir Walter Kirke, who had served as military adviser in Helsinki some years before. Kirke introduced him to the Viceroy, Lord Irwin (later Viscount Halifax and British foreign secretary during the first year of the Second World War), and numerous senior Indian Army officers.

A hunting trip in the jungle was arranged by British officer friends. 'I am at Seoni and hunted yesterday and today around the same jungle pond where the animals held their council in Kipling's description of the jungle,' he wrote with obvious delight. From Delhi he travelled up to the mountains in the north, to Sikkim. He did not reach Nepal, but memories of the mountain world of Turkestan enticed him into new experiences of beauty. At Gangtok he could see 'the snow-capped mountains' of Tibet 'forming a magnificent background to the beautiful alpine landscape and with a bewitching, attractive force luring one in deeper. . . . It was a release to be in the Himalayas where the petty difficulties over which men stumble and tumble disappear from view.'

In Sikkim Mannerheim got to know an interesting Englishman, Colonel Eric Bailey, who was well-versed in the problems of India and Asia. In the 1900s Bailey had been British agent at Gyantse in Tibet and intelligence chief in the north. He was an expert authority on the flora, animals and insects of the alpine world, and a keen hunter. A life-long friendship began with Bailey and his wife. They corresponded right up till Mannerheim's death, and often visited each other. On the advice of English friends Mannerheim went on to Burma to see some unusual wildlife; however, his most notable experience on that trip was a visit to the beautiful pagoda city of Mandalay.

In March 1928 Mannerheim left for home. He had not really wanted to appear at the celebrations of the tenth anniversary of 16 May 1918, but he understood in the end that people hoped he would be present. He did not want, by not appearing, to disappoint the many who had served in the army in 1918.

His great Indian adventure had so captivated him that in 1936 – in a changed political situation – he decided to make a return trip. Eric Bailey was now British Resident in Nepal and enticed him with the prospect of hunting there. After landing in Bombay he went south to Madras, Mysore and Hyderabad. This time the high point of the visit was a fairly long stay in Nepal with some dramatic tiger shoots: '2–3 days with the Maharajah and his 200–300 elephants. The shoots have been exciting. We shot 3 tigers, of which I got 2. I am enjoying the freedom and the life in the jungle' (28.1.37 to Karin Ramsay, a friend active in the Finnish Red Cross).

Mannerheim's love of travel was not sated with this second journey to British India, but political developments in Europe forced him to abandon plans for further travelling. A hunting trip to Alaska presented an exciting prospect – an American friend from India had interested him in this and in a visit to the United States – and a congress of the International Red Cross offered him a renewed opportunity to visit Japan and familiarise himself with developments there. However, he considered it imprudent, having regard to Finland's fragile relations with the Soviet Union, to travel to a great power which clearly might become its enemy; his visit would be regarded in Moscow with disfavour.

As a lover of the open air and a devotee of hunting, he devoted time to the game that was available in Finland, and became a popular member of various hunting associations. He also rented some fairly large shoots in the Tirol. In the worst case hare shooting could offer an acceptable diversion, but Emperor Franz Joseph's old favourite shoot provided interesting game, and the Alps enchanted him. 'My God, what beauty the people of Tirol and Steiermark have,' he exclaimed. His thoughts returned to Turkestan.

A visit to Louhisaari, 8 August 1935. On the left is Oskar Hannus, the owner at that time; on the right is Mannerheim's nephew, Carl-Erik Mannerheim

At a world championship shooting match in 1937. Svinhufvud is urging his successor Kallio to take part

Flowers strewn in Mannerheim's path outside his villa in Kaivopuisto, 4 June 1937

Mannerheim inspects the parade of the Helsinki Civil Guard, 4 June 1937

Parade in the Stadium to mark the twentieth anniversary of the War of
Independence, 1938

Mannerheim on the Svir, 10 September 1941

The Field Marshal with foreign nurses

A morning ride on Andermann

Mannerheim, Colonel Pajari and Generals Nenonen and Linder at Rätykylä, 12
August 1941

Mannerheim and General Nenonen

Mannerheim with his ADC, Major Ragnar Grönvall, on the way to the officers' mess

A visit to the front

At the front

The Field Marshal at Headquarters, Summer 1941. Picture by Laux

The Marshal of Finland examines the portrait medal struck by the government to mark his 75th birthday

Crown Prince Gustav Adolf of Sweden invests Mannerheim with the sword of the Grand Cross of the Order of the Sword at Headquarters, 17 March 1942. On the left is K. J. Westman, the Swedish Minister in Helsinki

Mannerheim with his personal physician, Major Kalaja, at Mikkeli during
the Continuation War.

Mannerheim and General Rudolf Walden, 4 June 1942

Mannerheim, Hitler and Ryti, 4 June 1942

Mannerheim at the sauna door of the hunting cabin given him by soldiers

X
RETURN TO PUBLIC SERVICE
1931–1939

For Europe the 1920s were a period of recovery after the unprecedented devastation of the First World War. However, the end of the decade saw the beginning of developments which were to lead to the Second World War. These began with the American economic crisis of 1929, soon to influence the continent of Europe. The consequences were unemployment, depression, unrest and bitter internal strife. At the end of 1931 Mannerheim summed up for his brother Johan his impression after a period on the continent. The new year 'begins with signs presaging a storm. May they prove incorrect. Since the World War the nations have not opposed each other as they do at present, and there have never been deeper conflicts. Will there be a catastrophic explosion, or will there be agreement resulting from greater understanding based on solidarity in the face of the world's problems?' In 1932 he wrote to Ignatius from Paris that he was beginning 'to be quite disturbed by the development of the world situation. One sees storm signals from almost everywhere, as well as complete inability to attain real understanding on any point.'

The international crisis soon brought about reactions in Finland. As usual at this period, Mannerheim spent part of the autumn of 1929 in Austria making use of his shoot there. Returning to Finland in 1930, he quickly encountered a 'national' awakening in the form of the Lapua movement. This Ostrobothnian popular movement had as its object the eradication of communism in Finland and was named after the town in that region where young communists had been beaten up at a provocative rally in November 1929. At first Mannerheim regarded it only as a reaction against dangerous disintegrating tendencies, not as anti-democratic or as a danger to the social system, and thus, like his faithful friend Rudolf Walden, he had some sympathy for it – an attitude formed by his earlier experiences of the Ostrobothnian yeoman farmers and his own fears of communist infiltration. He developed his views in a letter to Johan: 'A remarkable feature of this movement is the strong contribution made by the pietists, those devout men who went off to the War of Independence singing hymns and who now regard bolshevism with its anti-religious struggle as a manifestation of the devil on earth. One cannot know the

87

Ostrobothnians and their deeply-rooted democratic attitude and consider this movement anti-democratic.'

The Lapua movement reached its high-point with a farmers' march in Helsinki in July 1930 to demand national unity. Mannerheim stated his sympathy for the movement's patriotic aims and repeated this in a statement before the parliamentary elections in the autumn of that year. It has been said that if he had been seeking power then, it would have fallen into his lap; but his thoughts were not running on those lines. Instead, when the Lapua movement adopted methods he regarded as repugnant, he quickly distanced himself from it. Abductions and other acts of terrorism, and finally in the spring of 1932 an actual attempt at revolution, showed that irresponsible elements were in charge and the movement had degenerated.

Political developments in Finland thus proceeded in the 1930s in a different and more benign direction than on the continent. The climate slowly changed so that democracy was increasingly secured; at the same time a sharp vigilance was maintained against subversive propaganda. When P.E. Svinhufvud – a prominent figure in the country since the struggle for legality in the early years of the century and head of state in 1918 – once again became prime minister in the autumn of 1930 and was elected President the following year, this was partly a consequence of the original Lapua movement. Now recalled to political influence, he held fast to the principle of legality for which he had fought during the years of Russian oppression. With his election the preconditions had been created for Mannerheim again to be used in the service of the state; differences between the two men from the time of the War of Independence had been settled, and Svinhufvud had never ceased to admire the 'White General' and former Regent. On the whole there came to be trusting collaboration between them, facilitated by T.M. Kivimäki, the professor of law who was prime minister during most of Svinhufvud's presidency.

Svinhufvud invited Mannerheim to take command of the armed forces, but the offer was declined. He did not want to push aside the then commander Hugo Österman, nor at his age did he feel inclined for such a heavy task. Instead it was agreed to appoint him chairman of the Defence Council, at the same time designating him commander-in-chief of the armed forces in the event of war. Österman, who had hitherto occupied the chairmanship, recommended this himself and was willing to remain a member of the Council. The Council at that time had several members who were clearly loyal to Mannerheim, such as Lennart Oesch, chief of the general staff, and above all Rudolf Walden. The chairman's opportunity to make a significant contribution depended on his authority in general and the weight and objectivity of his arguments. His position became strength-ened further during the 1930s, when his earnest efforts won wide approval, and it became ever clearer that he stood above parties and party interests, that he was a symbol of encouragement to the nation – such a symbol was clearly needed.

His 'symbolic' position was given added emphasis when in 1933 Svinhufvud, supported by the officer corps, promoted him Field-Marshal, a rank now introduced into the army list for the first time. The idea of bestowing this rank, long unused in the small Scandinavian countries, on Mannerheim was not new. It had already been proposed in 1928, with the support of Svinhufvud among others, but the then President Relander, who at first supported the proposal, backed off when it seemed likely to arouse political controversy. There was no denying Mannerheim's delight. As he wrote to his brother Johan on 28 May, it was 'a complete surprise to me. It really is a handsome recognition of the historical significance of our War of Independence and a splendid title breathing as it does historical glamour and the clash of arms . . . In a little ultra-democratic country it may seem rather pretentious. . . .' But one good thing was that 'the marshal does not cost the state anything.' In his thanks to the President, Mannerheim emphasised that the appointment was to be considered as a recognition of the fight of the army and of the whole nation for its Western social system and culture.

Mannerheim was now used to carry out various ceremonial duties which could also have political significance and provide important infor-mation. The first time this happened was in 1932 when Sweden and Finland took part in cemmemorating the three-hundredth anniversary of the battle of Lützen and the death of Gustavus II Adolphus. Mannerheim appeared on this occasion beside the Swedish Crown Prince. In January 1936 he represented his country at the funeral of George V in London, an international occasion offering even greater opportunities for political activity. During this visit to England he had a meeting with Winston Churchill, then out of office, which his friends in the Donner family had been anxious to arrange. Ossian Donner, a former Finnish minister in London, had continued to live there, and his son Patrick was now a member of the British parliament and close to Churchill. They gave a dinner party at which Mannerheim and Churchill were able to exchange views on the dangerous situation in Europe, Hitler's threatening activity and Bolshevik Russia. Churchill was impressed by Mannerheim, whom he thought firm as a rock.

In 1937 a new President, the Agrarian politician Kyösti Kallio, was elected, with whom Mannerheim had good relations. Kallio's election brought about a changed political situation which was marked by a new government under Professor A.K. Cajander, based on a green-red coalition between the Agrarians and the Social Democrats. With the minister of defence – an Agrarian from Karelia, Juho Niukkanen – Mannerheim did not always find cooperation easy, and the foreign minister was Rudolf Holsti, who had long worked against him. The leader of the Social Democrats, Väinö Tanner, became minister of finance. Mannerheim's work for the defence forces was ultimately based on Kallio's support. If the other principal candidate in the election, Ståhlberg, had once again become President, Mannerheim would have resigned. His seventieth birthday was celebrated in 1937 and the twentieth anniversary of 1918 the next year, two events which caused a rallying to him as un undisputed national leader.

Mannerheim's work in the 1930s had to be seen against the background of the political developments on the continent from which severe international crises followed. He reacted negatively as, one after another, dictatorial regimes were established in Europe; he could not reconcile them with the ideals of society and the rule of law which he had espoused since his youth – hence his attitude to developments in Russia, the dictatorship of the proletariat and the harsh sway of Stalin. His long experience of European politics had certainly modified the doctrinaire liberal outlook he shared with his family; the revolutions he had experienced had not fulfilled their promises of improving the living conditions of the people. His views had undoubtedly moved in a more conservative direction; rapid change and radical reforms were risky. But he remained a convinced opponent of oppression and dictatorship. Thus he had disapproved of Josef Pilsudski's coup in Warsaw in 1926: 'Shouting "Attention!" to the people gives one no right to shoot down and injure hundreds of peaceful citizens' (to Hannes Ignatius).

Some time passed following the National Socialist take-over of power in Germany in January 1933 before Mannerheim fully appreciated the dangers of Hitler's system. Like many people between the World Wars, he had regarded Germany's lack of external power and its internal antagonisms as a misfortune, and perhaps now, in spite of the alarming features of the régime, Germany had found a leadership which would be able to unite the nation and carry it towards greater achievements; perhaps the obvious disadvantages could be overcome. He was still able to view the reintroduction of compulsory military service in 1935 with approval, saying that he expected Germany soon to be treated with greater respect. However, it was not long before he fully understood the danger threatening Europe and the world. He was vividly reminded of experiences from the period immediately before 1914 and during the First World War. The German coup in Vienna in 1934, when the Austrian Federal Chancellor Dollfuss was murdered, recalled the fateful shots at Sarajevo which started the war.

Against this background he watched with disappointment and concern as the system of collective security and the policy of disarmament collapsed. 'We are really going through a tense time. If they do not come from some other country, Hitler will see to it that sensational effects follow each other in rapid succession. And in the midst of this unrest the disarmament conference will sit like a Buddha undisturbed in its meditation and decide on the limitation for the weak and peaceful nations of arms and equipment such as the pugnacious will use to put an end to them!' (to G.A. Gripenberg, a Finnish diplomat and personal friend, 21.3.33). He could easily imagine what the consequence would be if the European balance again began to waver: a new great war. During the summer and autumn of 1935 the signs could be discerned of a new period of violent international politics. Mussolini's attack on Abyssinia, flouting treaties and the security system of the League of Nations, now aroused concern. There was surprise when Mannerheim, in conversation and in letters, expressed his indignation; perhaps a different attitude was expected from an old soldier from the age of imperialism. Where Mannerheim's sympathies lay appears clearly from his letter of 9 October 1935 to the wife of Eric Bailey, his friend in India: 'This Italian war is very unpopular among us in Scandinavia. One can well understand that it is tempting for a nation which has a big army, supplied with the most modern military equipment, to attack a brave but badly equipped people. As far as I am concerned all my sympathies are with the Abyssinians but feelings are not the same as politics.'

After Mussolini's Abyssinian war, events moved on rapidly towards the catastrophe of the Second World War. In July 1936 the Spanish Civil War broke out, and in the following year Austria's position again became critical. Mannerheim regularly spent time there. In the autumn of 1937 he observed growing enthusiasm for the Führer in Franz Joseph's former shoot where, suddenly, many Hitler moustaches were to be found. In February 1938 followed the incorporation of Austria into the German Third Reich in the manner of a coup.

In the summer of 1938 Hitler threatened Czechoslovakia, but at the last moment war was averted by the Western powers making concessions at Munich. However, in March 1939 Hitler was already prepared to break his word and incorporate the Czechs in the Great German Reich. 'Up here in

Scandinavia we have every reason to begin to feel alarmed,' wrote Mannerheim candidly to his sister Eva. 'It amounts quite simply to transforming the people of Europe into white negroes in the service of the Third Reich . . . The end of the world is nigh.' Mannerheim was indignant at the callous violence of the dictators. When Italy occupied Albania in the spring of 1939 it was the coup-like methods which revolted him. 'The gallant Italians' heroic attack on the threatening Albanians seems to have provoked gloom here,' he informed Rudolf Walden. Even the hitherto pro-German Hannes Ignatius now began to have doubts. 'It was obvious that Hannes was also painfully affected by the policy of surprise and *Blitzkrieg*' (to Rudolf Walden, 10.4.39). These were baleful omens of what the small Nordic countries, ill-equipped since the illusory policies and disarmament of the 1920s, could expect. Mannerheim predicted that the dictators' ambitions could lead to a new great war in which Finland would inevitably be very much at risk. 'I think that events are continually moving in a very alarming direction, especially worrying for small weak countries, which in the great powers' game are of feather weight and can easily be used as small change' (to his sister-in-law Palaemona Mannerheim, 13.5.35).

The manifest collapse of the League of Nations security system increased the risks to the small countries. On 27 October 1935 Mannerheim wrote in this connection to Rafael Erich, a Finnish expert on international law, that confidence in the ability of the League of Nations to preserve peace and protect the small countries was waning. In consequence of this, perhaps, willingness to defend the country would increase, especially in quarters 'where people readily put their trust in illusions'. Finland thus had to put its own house in order and prepare for all eventualities. Naturally Mannerheim considered an improved system of defence to be the most urgent task, but it was not the only one. In internal politics it was necessary to strive for consolidation and unity, and, as a priority, to overcome the divisions dating from 1918. In foreign policy his plan of action was aimed at the settlement of all disagreements with neighbouring countries and at a Scandinavian orientation as a link in a policy of neutrality.

Mannerheim's work on defence was undertaken primarily within the framework of the Defence Council, although its organisation and standing were not clearly defined, nor were they appropriate. The Council could not exercise a proper direction of the defence effort, nor were thoroughgoing reform or development possible; it did not even have any full-time staff, but only two secretaries who also had other duties in the general staff. The Defence Council's field of action had at first been strictly limited; it was a body to which matters were referred by the council of state (i.e. the government), but which was not empowered to make initiatives of its own. It was only granted this power when Mannerheim was appointed chairman in 1931. The presence of an energetic chairman undoubtedly offered certain opportunities, but the Council still could not take any officially binding decisions, had no significant funds at its disposal, could not undertake purchases and was without staff of its own. When the period of peace came to an end, this situation and the chairman's position had totally changed – the result of almost ten years of unremitting work on the part of Mannerheim.

And at first the Defence Council had no way of directing military training or influencing defence planning. It could issue directives. As chairman, Mannerheim had admittedly been chosen to lead the defence forces as commander-in-chief in the event of war, but this gave him no controlling authority; such opportunities for action as he had depended on his personal influence and the confidence he inspired. Mannerheim's military competence and his experience were derived essentially from the World War and the time of the War of Independence, more than ten years previously, yet they were an enormous asset such as nobody else in Finland possessed to a comparable degree. In the years after 1918 he had also followed military developments with interest, not least technical ones. In general he sought to widen and deepen his knowledge, and he could receive advice and information without feeling any loss of face, the reliability of what he learned being his only serious consideration. He was greatly interested in improving his knowledge of Finnish, which was rather poor after thirty years' absence from the country: naturally this was important if he was to use his position to the best effect. Here a natural gift for languages, combined with his varied experience, helped him.

In 1933 Svinhufvud agreed that Mannerheim should have increased authority, and from that time he had the right to give the commander of the armed forces 'directives concerning operational preparations for time of war and for planning and organisational tasks leading to the improvement of defence preparedness'. Later organisational difficulties over the control of defence prompted a reform which further improved the position of the Defence Council and its chairman. This was in fact part of a broader train of events in which the principal aim of the then minister of defence, Niukkanen, was to ensure the greatest possible influence for his own ministry. With the help of Walden Mannerheim succeeded in maintaining the interests of the Defence Council. Nevertheless there still remained a weakness in the Council's position, in that there was no guarantee that government decisions would actually take account of its pronouncements. Eventually in May 1939 Mannerheim addressed a sharply worded proposal to the President on this subject, resulting in a guarantee that attention would be paid to the military expertise of the Defence Council.

When war broke out soon afterwards, Finland was inadequately equipped. This was not the fault of Mannerheim or the Defence Council, since he had repeatedly warned of the dangers and justified the Council's demands for appropriations. Mannerheim described the shortages of defence equipment in plain words. From his own experience he well knew the strength of the Russian artillery, which was to be one of the key factors in both the Winter War and the Continuation War: 'Russia's artillery has a considerably longer range than ours, Russia's aircraft are greatly superior to ours, we are almost entirely lacking in tanks, anti-tank guns and anti-aircraft guns.' He pointed this out repeatedly.

His attempts to improve the equipment of the defence forces were tenaciously opposed by many politicians right up to the Winter War. In the general economic depression the government set up a committee to make economies with J.K. Paasikivi, Risto Ryti and Väinö Tanner as members, and the defence vote was to be cut as the result: Mannerheim visited Paasikivi, who had been prime minister in 1918 and was a conservative banker, and who promised support for defence, but he found Ryti, the chairman of the Bank of Finland and a liberal politician, a convinced supporter of disarmament. In Finland people still lived in a state of self-delusion. 'What is the point of rearmament when there will never be a war?' Ryti asked at the end of the conversation in which Mannerheim appealed for aid. These were not the only arguments used: many, like Tanner the powerful Social Democrat leader, wanted to give expenditure on social reforms priority over a strong defence.

Thus it was natural that Mannerheim was alarmed about the future, and exasperated by politicians who seemed to him reckless. He wondered whether it would be possible to save for the defence forces 'the more than modest extraordinary votes which the last parliament approved in principle for 1932 and which are now threatened with an appreciable cut. A five-year defence plan has been built up around these extraordinary votes, and it would be more than reckless – it would be irresponsible as neighbours of the hostile Soviet Union, which is armed to the teeth, to extend this already over-protracted plan' (to Palaemona Mannerheim, 4.3.31). In spite of Mannerheim's efforts, the small arms ammunition factory was never expanded as planned, and field manoeuvres were cancelled. Later he proposed that the state should raise a defence loan that would make defence independent of conflicts in the political arena, but in vain. The situation was still troublesome. 'The hesitation appearing in certain quarters, when what is needed is the execution of decisions already taken in principle, is often absolutely inexplicable but it is all-pervasive . . . There is nothing to be done except wait and accept everything with philosophical calm. When once hesitation and indecision get into the blood, one just has to be ready for them' (to G.A. Gripenberg, 18.4.33).

After some years in the Defence Council Mannerheim decided to appeal to the wider public about increasing defence appropriations. In August 1934 he summoned leading politicians and journalists to a conference at which Colonel Aladár Paasonen explained the military resources of the Soviet Union, and he himself recounted the deficiencies in Finland's defence forces. This appeal made an impression. The same autumn, parliament granted a supplementary vote for defence of 116 million marks (approximately £510,000 or US$2,572,000 at the rates of exchange then prevailing). But in the defence budget for 1935 the figure considered by the Defence Council to be the absolute minimum was again severely reduced. When, at a conference that year, Mannerheim urged a defence policy oriented towards Scandinavia – mainly because of the need to procure weapons and supplies from and through Sweden in the event of war – he was nevertheless able to thank those present for their increased interest in defence and its needs. The defence budget was increased by degrees as the economic situation improved, but the increases were still far from what was required to achieve a state of preparedness.

The more political tensions in Europe rose, the more Mannerheim urged the government and the authorities to make provision for defence. As he pointed out to Walden after the Munich crisis in 1938, it was necessary to take notice of 'the new alarm signals which from day to day are conveying an ever plainer message. Unfortunately these clouds, which move ever more darkly across the political sky, cannot discharge themselves in rain, and the world – not excepting ourselves – must prepare itself as fast as possible to withstand the greatest storm humanity has ever known. Let those in the ministry not sleep through the brief ''period of grace'' which has been granted to us. It is necessary to arm with the same full intensity as is demanded by war *when it has already broken out,* for it is at such a speed that Germany has armed and is continuing to arm.'

When it appeared difficult to get the necessary sums into the budget, Mannerheim proposed a foreign loan for the financing of defence expenditure. As late as the summer of 1939 there was still a possibility of raising a public loan in the United States to buy armaments. The new Finnish minister in Washington, Hjalmar J. Procopé, pursued this with enthusiasm, but in Helsinki the proposal was opposed by both Tanner and Ryti, then head of the Bank of Finland. The prime minister, Cajander, followed their line. Kallio, who was kept informed of developments, expressed satisfaction that Ryti had opposed Mannerheim's plan because he had great respect for Ryti's judgement; only Paasikivi approved of the proposal to raise a foreign loan. The government only changed its attitude to the loan question when the acquisition of arms from abroad had become difficult after the outbreak of the war in Europe.

When neither Niukkanen nor Cajander (acting for Kallio, then on sick leave) would consider his demands, Mannerheim asked in a letter dated 16 June 1939 to be relieved of the chairmanship of the Defence Council; he could not, as he explained, be responsible for the defence of the country as long as the existing circumstances continued. He pointed out to the President what the prevailing military and political situation required; the needs of defence were often the most imperative needs of all, but they had remained neglected or, at best, only partly met. 'It is the undeniable right of every Finnish citizen that our army, in its quality, training and equipment, should be completely on a par with any potential adversary; strong and unswerving measures are needed for us to attain this end, notwithstanding the fact that the country will now have to bear an appreciably greater economic burden than if we had proceeded with them in time.' Mannerheim considered that he could now 'no longer carry responsibility for the preparedness of the country, and because if I stay on as chairman of the Defence Council this could give the public the idea that I too approve of the inadequate measures that have been taken, an idea which would lull many into an unjustified sense of security, I have the honour most respectfully to request my discharge from my appointment as chairman of the Defence Council.'

Cajander began already to look for a successor, while Niukkanen tried to persuade the Field-Marshal to withdraw his resignation – in which he succeeded only after a dramatic intervention by Kallio, who did not want to risk Mannerheim's departure from the direction of defence, and brought about a compromise. Kallio considered Mannerheim practically indispensable, and feared great difficulties if he had to reorganise the army command. Tanner, on the other hand, had been so annoyed by Mannerheim's demands for money that he would have been pleased to see him leave the stage. In a letter to Kallio on 23 July 1939, and in another to Paasikivi on 26 July, he claimed that Mannerheim was too old and had lost his balance because with every fresh crisis abroad he came up with a new set of demands; a well-known person (Ryti) had said that Mannerheim was following the example of Russian generals in that he always tried to protect himself in difficult situations by finding scapegoats. But Paasikivi reacted with alarm, and replied that they ought on the contrary to try by all means possible to keep Mannerheim at his post. 'It is a piece of great good fortune that Mannerheim still has the strength to lead the defence forces. What other officers do we have? Absolutely nobody capable of major tasks. I know this as well as any of you. You say that Mannerheim has lost his nerve, but on all important questions he is following the same policy as both of us.'

Within the Defence Council Mannerheim was able to make an important contribution in procuring equipment and developing the armament industry. This was often hard work, which might have produced more results if the political opposition had not been so strong. His aim was first to build up the domestic armament industry, principally in the areas of artillery, armour and aircraft, and in 1934 he took the initiative over a survey of its capacity. 'The production of our young war industry must be increased significantly,' as he pointed out to the government. At the same time there should be cooperation between this industry and the private-sector metal industry which Finland already possessed; thus significant cost savings could be achieved and the ground laid even for an export industry. But vexatious objections were raised against Mannerheim's basic views; there were frequent proposals that state enterprises should be favoured on political grounds, and there was a desire to take account of local interests when the arms industry was being planned.

Mannerheim wanted to build up a fruitful cooperation with the Swedish arms industry, but even this endeavour was thwarted within the government. He initiated links with Bofors over gun manufacture, and while travelling through Sweden on a visit to England in 1935–6 visited their factory with Walden and Ryti, and made an agreement with them on cooperation. He would have liked to let Bofors handle the manufacture of guns within Finland, but the minister of defence A.A. Oksala forced through the construction of a state factory at Jyväskylä which was to work under licence, a decision which spelt a fateful delay since production had scarcely begun before the Winter War. In addition Mannerheim caused a factory to be constructed in Finland for aero engines, but when the plan was carried out, the factory was to be located in the industrial city of Tampere, a likely target for attack, to which he was strenuously opposed. He advised on other occasions against the location of important industries in the Vuoksi valley, which seemed to him much too close to the Soviet frontier.

Parallel with work for arms production at home went efforts to ensure imports from Sweden, which would be extremely important in the event of war. But in this he encountered lack of interest not only among Finnish politicians – especially Rudolf Holsti – but also from Sweden. The Swedish prime minister, Hansson, urged caution so that the Finns should have no exaggerated expectations, thus expressing Sweden's typically negative attitude towards the question of Finnish defence and its reluctance to incur any commitments in that area. The attempts of Mannerheim, with the help of Tanner and Swedish politicians and diplomats with an interest in Finland, to increase Swedish sympathy towards cooperation in this field were virtually useless. The fateful consequences became apparent during the Winter War.

Mannerheim did not lack either knowledge of, or interest in, the new defence systems comprising aircraft and tanks and the weapons to counter them – anti-aircraft guns and anti-tank guns – , but because the economic resources allocated to defence were so small, there was inadequate readiness for war when it came. As for the air arm, Mannerheim was able to develop an initiative by Svinhufvud as the newly-elected President to plan a modern air force with its own separate commander. Mannerheim tried at first to get Paavo Talvela, a retired officer of proven ability, to accept this appointment, but in vain. Eventually Colonel (later Lieutenant-General) Jarl Lundqvist was selected.

Differing opinions had been published as to what organisation and roles would be appropriate for the air arm. One notable book which both Mannerheim and Walden had studied was *The Command of the Air* by the Italian Giulio Douhet, who argued in favour of an independent air force to be used offensively. This presupposed that on the whole the country should acquire bombers, but there was another school of thought which advised fighters, which were mainly to be used in defence, at least by smaller countries. When later it became necessary to acquire suitable bombers and fighters, Mannerheim, with his customary energy, wanted to familiarise himself with what types were obtainable, their advantages and disadvantages. With this in view, he undertook journeys to England, France and Germany in 1934, when the defence vote had grown, and continued his studies the following year.

The immediate cause of the journey to England was an invitation to visit an air display at Hendon where the latest types produced by the British aircraft industry could be seen. Mannerheim took with him the Finnish military attaché in Berlin, Colonel Aarne Snellman, who had earlier dealt with air force matters in the defence ministry. Impressed and interested by what he had seen, he gave his views in a newspaper interview on returning home: the aeroplane, he declared, would come to exert an absolutely revolutionary influence on the conduct of war, both strategically and tactically. Finland had to keep up with developments to the greatest extent that its financial constraints allowed. Visiting Paris in the autumn of 1934, he was able to discuss the problem of the air arm with air force general Victor Denain and others, and learn about plans for differing combinations of bomber and fighter aircraft. The French, on the whole, championed bombers. However, his impression of French industrial capacity and French designs was unfavourable. From Paris the journey went on to Berlin; despite the stipulations of the Versailles Treaty, the German aircraft industry had advanced a long way towards the manufacture of military aircraft. Mannerheim met Göring, his permanent secretary Milch, and several other prominent officers. They too were influenced by Douhet's theories. Milch emphasised the importance of the offensive bomber aircraft, whereas Göring, as a former fighter pilot, supported the single-seater fighter for light combat. Milch declared to Mannerheim that rearmament in the air was a military necessity and a matter of honour; without an adequate air force every mark spent on defence by land and sea would be wasted. The war minister, General von Blomberg, also pointed out the great value of the bomber. Altogether the Germans showed great consideration towards Finland, and were willing to supply modern equipment on a continuing basis. Göring emphasised that the air defence of Finland was a German interest, but since Germany's own rearmament would take up production capacity for the next year or eighteen months, the Finns could not count on much being delivered before that period had elapsed.

After Mannerheim returned from his familiarisation journeys on 17 February 1936, the last round began in the tough tug-of-war over the choice of aircraft and the country of purchase; this continued for six months. Mannerheim recommended purchase from Germany, not for political reasons but because he was convinced of the superiority of the German planes and also of the greater capacity of the German aircraft industry to deliver. On the other hand, the air force commander Colonel Lundqvist was a keen advocate of the British aircraft and behaved rather disloyally towards the chairman of the Defence Council, whom he suspected of favouring German aircraft because his vanity had been flattered by the reception he had been given by the Germans. After the elimination of the British Handley Page and the German Heinkel aircraft, which had been considered previously, the choice lay between the Bristol Blenheim and the Junkers machines. Mannerheim was more interested in the latter, about which new and better test evaluations had been received, but finally refrained from implementing his wishes – as he really could have done in this instance. Thus the Defence Council decided at its meeting on 28 February 1937 to buy Bristol Blenheim bombers, of which eighteen were ordered and delivered in 1937–8. Their merits, which Mannerheim willingly acknowledged, were their great speed and certain tactical advantages. With these eighteen bombers, which did not however fulfil all the requirements of an offensive aircraft, and the already antiquated fighters of the Fokker type ordered in 1936 from Holland or made under licence in Tampere, the Finnish air force had to fight up to the end of the Winter War.

Among the numerous major military issues which the Defence Council and its chairman had to deal with perhaps the most important were the proposed territorial organisation and mobilisation plans. The Council's first task after its initial meeting on 2 April 1931 'was to express its views on the proposal drawn up by the general staff for a reorganisation of the army on the basis of the territorial system'. The reform marked a break with the cadre system followed previously (by which peace-time units were expanded on mobilisation) and a return to principles which Mannerheim had already asserted in 1918. Formations were to be based on particular localities, using the peace-time units as covering troops on mobilisation. This major reorganisation was planned mainly by Colonel Grandell, aided by Colonel Airo, and became of fundamental importance for the rapid mobilisation of 1939. Mannerheim, as Grandell was to acknowledge, was very active in its realisation.

The tactics used on the Karelian isthmus would play a central part in Finnish defence against a Soviet attack. This, the classic route for an invasion, afforded good defensive terrain, but the proximity of Leningrad enabled the enemy to make concealed deployments on the outskirts of the city. There were spirited discussions on the pattern of the defence, chiefly between the adherents of fortifications on the isthmus and those who favoured a war of movement. Mannerheim went to familiarise himself with conditions on the isthmus shortly after being appointed as chairman of the Defence Council, and soon became convinced that permanent defences ought to be built to provide support for the infantry. Against this Lieutenant-General Harald Öhqvist, who knew the terrain of the isthmus well and had served as a divisional and later corps commander in Viipuri, advocated a war of movement, which however was scarcely compatible with the army's inadequate resources and training. At length a defence line was constructed which at least gave the troops some protection and support. During the critical summer of 1939 it was strengthened by volunteer labour – becoming known as the Mannerheim Line. The Finnish army was thus equipped and trained to fight a defensive war, and within that framework the famous *motti* tactics (breaking-up and encircling enemy formations) could eventually be developed. Here the infantry ski training – partly on the Swedish pattern – was particularly valuable.

Mannerheim's recommendations to the government for improving defence usually encompassed the two factors he regarded as pre-conditions: military equipment and national unity. He therefore continued his efforts at achieving reconciliation and concord, already begun when he was Regent in January 1919. As chairman of the Defence Council and Finland's Field-Marshal, Mannerheim commanded a hearing on the burning issues of the day – not as an eager party politician but as an authority transcending party. Many listened to him and understood his message. As well as sentiments about harmony and the will to defend the country, which people had become used to hearing in his somewhat old-fashioned, stately turns of phrase, the sadness of an old soldier faced by the cruelty and destruction of modern war was also apparent. He made a speech in 1933 demanding not only recognition that the War of Independence had benefited the people as a whole, but also a general solidarity, far above party differences; they had to overcome their own bitter memories. 'Where war is waged, life is trodden down and property devastated. The all-destroying strength of modern weapons confers on war its ghastly grandeur . . . Where chivalry and magnaminity are lacking and hatred commands the sword, there is no room for a lasting peace.' Mannerheim hoped that Finland would be spared the scourge of war. 'But we live at a troubled and threatening time . . . So let us extend on open hand to everyone who wants to work and do his duty in this country. A patriotic spirit, expressed in the will to defend the country and to stand in the ranks like a man if some day it has to be defended, is all we ask. We do not need to ask any longer what position a man took fifteen years ago.'

Similarly Mannerheim strove for a settlement of the Finnish-Swedish language dispute which had become more heated in recent decades, particularly in Helsinki University. In 1935 the press published an appeal for a language peace, signed by him with Walden and Ignatius. The appeal, which was motivated not least by defence considerations, was aimed particularly at veterans of 1918, who were reminded that Finnish- and Swedish-speakers had then shown the same love of country in the common struggle, and warned against being divided when difficult times were again imminent.

The formation and planning of defence policy is closely related to foreign policy. Which way was Finland now to go? Mannerheim was realist enough to look at the different options straight away: should support be sought from the Western powers, from Germany or from Scandinavia? He wanted to avoid dependence on great powers. The Swedish military attaché, Lieutenant-Colonel Curt Kempff, visited the headquarters in Helsinki one day and was given an audience by 'the great man', whom he found eagerly studying maps. 'You see, colonel, my thoughts are constantly occupied with the possibilities of Finland's defence. I was just remembering my last period in the Russian empire on the Rumanian front. The country had simply collapsed before the German armies because it had neglected to take care of defence. A little country must avoid being drawn into great power politics.'

Mannerheim developed his train of thought in several memoranda. In 1935 he wrote: 'The threatening way the European situation is developing, as well as the experiences of the World War and the post-war years, urge us seriously to examine what can be done in Finland to lessen the threat presented by a new world catastrophe or, if war does break out, to limit it if practicable. Unfortunately there is a great danger that an outbreak of war . . . will set ablaze the whole of Europe and even, like last time, most of the world. However, the preservation of peace demands, even in a small country, that one adopts in time all available precautionary measures.' First, a small country had to try to keep out of the war and maintain its neutrality. The support of a great power can indeed 'seem attractive and reassuring . . . but it imposes ties and obligations which, if a war breaks out, may easily draw a small country in on the side of its self-same "protecting" power . . . The right . . . of small nations to exist may indeed be maintained by participation in a war, but only if that participation is on the side of the power or power-group which finally wins. It is safest for a small country to use every means to maintain its neutrality. Mannerheim's aim was ' a powerful Scandinavian neutral alliance', as a member of which Finland would be able to stay outside a European war. The memorandum concludes with the reflection, 'When a system for maintaining peace that embraces all the countries of Europe seems more remote than ever, there is growing interest in a closer association between groups of adjacent small nations. Even an economic and political rapprochement between small nations, which have not lost the will to defend themselves, is calculated to strengthen every one of them.' Before, during and after the Winter War, this was the main thrust of Mannerheim's political activity.

The foremost hopes were thus pinned on cooperation for neutrality within Scandinavia. Ever since 1918 Mannerheim had recommended defence cooperation with Sweden, albeit in vain. Now he wanted to try another way. The orientation towards Scandinavia was demonstrated by an unconditional declaration by Finland of solidarity with the Scandinavian neutral countries, given in parliament on 5 December 1935 by the foreign minister Antti Hackzell and the prime minister Kivimäki. Mannerheim later reported that he had long worked for this solidarity, and had succeeded in convincing the politicians of its advantages. He knew that the threat from Nazi Germany was inducing the left-wing parties in Sweden to interest themselves in Finnish defence, and the Finnish left was interested in his proposal for the same reason. Accordingly the government sent the minister of education Oskari Mantere and Väinö Tanner to Stockholm, and Mannerheim himself arranged a big press conference on 14 January 1935 at which he pointed out the value of neutrality, the risk involved in alliances with great powers, and the need for military cooperation with Sweden. At the same time he warned against dreams of a Greater Finland – of incorporating Soviet-controlled Eastern Karelia in the Finnish republic – which were prevalent especially in right-wing academic circles.

In a statement Mannerheim made shortly afterwards to journalists in Stockholm on his way to London to represent Finland at the funeral of George V, he opened up a further perspective on the significance of Scandinavian cooperation. It was important for Finland to be able to adhere to the settled, traditional policy of Scandinavia; the country needed to gather all its resources in a creative determination to build up the state, safeguard the happiness and welfare of the individual, and bind together more firmly the various interests and strata making up its society. However, Finland's economy did not allow the same level of social welfare that Sweden could provide; 'the ears from the fields yield less grain in Finland than in Sweden', and Finland had to spend more on defence. 'To the extent that Sweden and the rest of Scandinavia respond to the Finnish people's united will for peace and their clearly expressed desire for cooperation within Scandinavia and unity in the North, so will new opportunities be opened up in Finland for a stronger cultural structure, which would also be likely to strengthen Scandinavia as a whole.' This statement was part of a considered propaganda campaign that Mannerheim was directing at Sweden at that time.

The spirit of Scandinavian cooperation also made it possible for the question of the defence of the strategic Åland archipelago to be reopened, with good prospects of a solution. Since 1921 the islands had been unfortified, a result of Swedish efforts dating back to the time of the Crimean War in 1856. When the League of Nations refused to award the Åland islands to Sweden in 1921, the Swedes had ensured that fortifications there would again be prohibited, and the local population was exempted from military service. However, Mannerheim had long been aware that the demilitarised archipelago represented a serious risk, especially as Germany and Russia had made undisguised efforts to control it. As Regent he had tried in vain to reach an understanding with Sweden, based on strategic considerations, and when he became chairman of the Defence Council he immediately took the matter up again, suggesting that the military staffs in Helsinki and Stockholm should open discussions. In 1934 he made a press statement underlining the risks he saw in the present situation of the islands.

Despite the delicate nature of this question, the threat from Germany had increased Stockholm's willingness to cooperate over the defence of Åland. Confidence in the ability of the League of Nations to ensure peace had waned. When Mannerheim discussed the Åland question in London and Stockholm he no longer met any opposition; at first there had been opposition from the government of A.J. Cajander in Finland, but Germany's continuing expansion and the general tension in Europe caused the government to initiate cooperation with Sweden in the spring of 1938. The Swedish foreign minister Richard Sandler had no doubts about the urgency of the Åland question, and negotiations could thus be set in motion. Holsti had wanted to take charge of them, which had several unfortunate consequences – he was known to be an opponent of plans to fortify the islands. 'Regrettably, good sense over the selection of people often has to give way before petty ambitions,' was Mannerheim's comment. His own role was nevertheless important, since on several occasions he was able to intervene to settle differences between Sweden and Finland, and between Finnish aspirations and those of Swedish-speakers in Finland. After a year, agreement was reached on certain defence works in Åland. It included provisions giving Finland the right to station a small number of troops there in peace-time and a larger force if war threatened. If military service were introduced, the islanders would be used first of all for local defence, and Swedish would be the language of command. There was a separate agreement whereby Sweden would be able to share in the defence of Åland by sending in troops and by naval support.

However, this new policy was by no means settled once Sweden and Finland had reached agreement between themselves. There were other interested parties. The plans affected the interests of the Åland population and hence of the signatories of the 1921 Convention and the League of Nations as guarantors of those interests. New difficulties were encountered here which the Swedish and Finnish governments had not managed to overcome before the general political situation became worse. Behind the attitude of the Ålanders themselves lay the additional hope, already aroused in 1918, of reunion with Sweden, for which Julius Sundblom, a local politician, led the agitation. Language and military questions were now the immediate concern; it was Ålanders who successfully demanded that the language of command in Åland should be Swedish and not Finnish as in the rest of the Finnish army, and it was their views on the type of military service to be introduced that prevailed. A powerful campaign against the Åland plans was set in motion in Sweden, supported by many who had completely different reasons for opposition to the plans from the Ålanders themselves. Mannerheim regretted that 'the Ålanders have been brought in, if not indeed as a strictly legal party in the matter, then nevertheless as a particularly vociferous one. And all this to allay a certain opinion which cannot see further than the end of its nose.' The hope remained that with the threat of war, eyes would be opened to the danger of Åland being undefended. But when the relevant parts of the agreement between Sweden and Finland were submitted to the League of Nations in May 1939 they were opposed by the Soviet Union and the plan had to be postponed.

Thus orientation towards Scandinavia formed a considerable part of Mannerheim's work, a fact which Kivimäki was anxious to stress during the ceremonies to mark the Field-Marshal's seventieth birthday. Mannerheim's principal objective in this Scandinavian policy was at once to further Finland's neutrality and strengthen its defence. On the other hand he was not prepared to use this policy merely to further the interests of Swedish-speakers in Finland, as many within the Swedish People's Party would gladly have done. He thought it was imprudent at that time to make Finnish cooperation in the Scandinavian policy depend on Finnish concessions over the Swedish language or university questions. He was prepared to exhort his Finnish-speaking countrymen to show understanding, and did so, but he was sure that if pressure were exerted on them

by Sweden, there would be unfortunate reactions and the political orientation he wanted would become more difficult to achieve. The language
question had to be evolved within Finland, 'despite its crazy and absolutely
unnecessary squandering of the nation's strength' (to Ernst Linder,
27.4.35). If only the Scandinavian orientation could be firmly anchored,
the Swedish-speaking population would certainly obtain juster treatment.
Mannerheim's line was difficult for party politicians to understand.

With the situation so serious and Finland in such a dangerous position,
the leaders of the country had also to try to improve relations with its
neighbours as far as possible. If they had to withstand a severe crisis, they
should at least not do so suffering from unnecessary handicaps. For this
reason Mannerheim energetically advocated amicable relations with the
Soviet Union before the world political situation made Finland's position
even worse. Paasikivi declared in a letter to Tanner that Mannerheim 'has
in many conversations with me always stated what we ought to do to
improve relations with Russia and that we ought always to try to be on
good terms there' (26.7.39). With his military experience, he had a more
realistic grasp of the security requirements of Leningrad than the majority
of his countrymen. He was fully conscious that Russia's traditional policy
was aimed at domination over the shores of the Gulf of Finland, not only
from a defensive but also from an offensive standpoint. He had come face
to face with these political aims during the long negotiations with the
White Russian leaders in 1918–19, and he knew that the Bolshevik leaders
too were afraid of the Soviet Union being attacked through Finland,
initially by the Western powers and later by the Germans.

It was because of this understanding that Mannerheim recommended
certain adjustments to the frontier when the Soviet diplomat Boris Stein
was in Helsinki for discussions in the early spring of 1939. Already the
previous year Stalin had tried to obtain a negotiating contact with the
Finnish government over the possibility of acquiring the so-called outer
islands in the innermost part of the Gulf of Finland. These islands, which
were reckoned of great importance for Russian defence, were close to
Kronstadt and Leningrad; according to the Treaty of Tartu they could not
be fortified. This Soviet initiative – taken by an apparently subordinate
official, Boris Yartsev – came to nothing, since the Finns he approached
did not treat it seriously. It was for this reason that Boris Stein as a more
senior official (he was Soviet minister in Rome) came to Finland for
discussions of a more official character. His proposal included the lease of
the islands to the Soviet Union by Finland for thirty years in return for an
area in Finnish-speaking Karelia north of Lake Ladoga.

The leaders of the Finnish state did not want to consent to the wishes of the Soviet Union, but during discussions about those wishes, Mannerheim vigorously advocated an accommodation; however, the politicians did not at that moment dare to follow his advice – doing so would have made them extremely unpopular, and parliamentary elections were due in the summer. The Swedish government, too, advised against frontier adjustments at that time. In vain Mannerheim offered to accept public responsibility for a settlement himself, explaining to Paasikivi that Eljas Erkko, the liberal politician and newspaper editor who had succeeded Holsti as foreign minister, had handled this delicate matter mistakenly, but on 9 April Stein left Helsinki empty-handed.

Events now moved rapidly towards a great war in Europe. The background to Stalin's attempt to persuade the Helsinki government into an agreement on the islands in the Gulf of Finland was Hitler's occupation of Sudetenland in the autumn of 1938 and the ensuing Prague coup of March 1939. The Western powers certainly attempted to counter German expansion, which was now clearly directed against Poland, chiefly by means of a guarantee of that country's frontiers. But without Soviet assistance such a guarantee could not be of much value, and the next move was therefore for the Western powers to try to win Moscow over to it. In this way the opportunity arose for Stalin to mount his attempt to increase his influence in Eastern Europe and Finland – which the Western powers would find difficult to accept. In Finland, people understood at last the dangers that threatened them.

Mannerheim was certainly well satisfied with the refusal of the Poles to give in to Hitler's demands. 'It really gladdened my old heart that at last someone had the courage to speak out and not, as hitherto, humbly put up with all the Nazis' arrogance and insolence' (to Eva Sparre, 27.2.39). But he also understood that this was an imprudent, perhaps a dangerous game. 'Everything points to the fact that war is inevitable,' he wrote to his daughter Sophy (16.4.39). Mannerheim's insight into Soviet policy and Hitler's tactics enabled him to anticipate a sudden change in the general political situation. Like several other experts on Russia he expected cooperation between the Soviet Union and Germany, which would be aimed in the first place at Poland but would also affect Finland. This particular change in the European political alignment would probably lead to a major European war. In fact it occurred in August 1939 when Germany and the Soviet Union signed their non-aggression pact. War broke out on 3 September 1939, and Mannerheim was not surprised; he had long expected the final conflagration. The question now was: could Finland be kept out of it?

Not long after the German invasion of Poland, Moscow enforced a fateful agreement with the three Baltic states which made them completely dependent upon the Soviet Union, and it was feared that this was only the prelude to their final incorporation in the Soviet Union. On 5 October Finland's turn came: Stalin issued a summons to talks in Moscow. What would the import of this be? Would it 'go badly here', and would 'our eastern neighbour seize us in his claws' (to Eva Sparre, 11.10.39)? He added: 'Events in our country have taken the turn which I had forecasts.' The most immediate measures were an increase in defence preparedness by means of an extensive military call-up and evacuation of the population of Helsinki. Then it was necessary to choose the negotiators to send to Moscow. Mannerheim recommended Hjalmar J. Procopé, formerly foreign minister and now minister in Washington, who was acknowledged as a skilled negotiator; however, the government's choice fell instead on the minister in Stockholm, J.K. Paasikivi, who obtained Colonel A. Paasonen as his military assistant. The first negotiating contact was made in Moscow on 12 October, when it became evident that what Stalin demanded was beyond what Paasikivi had been authorised to accept: a region on the Karelian isthmus, including the fortifications of Koivisto; the town of Hanko with an area of surrounding land; an area of sea and an anchorage at Lappohja; and parts of Petsamo. On 15 October Paasikivi returned to report and obtain fresh instructions.

Intensive deliberations now began within the government and with Mannerheim and the leaders of the defence forces. The majority in the government were against large-scale concessions, while Niukkanen made the important point that if concessions were made now, they would only be followed by new demands in a situation made worse for defence. In spite of this risk, Mannerheim was again anxious to avoid a conflict with the Soviet Union in the greatly worsened political situation which had come about because of its cooperation with Germany. He proposed certain alternatives to Hanko which could be offered during the negotiations, and certain modifications on the Karelian isthmus. On 21 October Paasikivi returned to Moscow with Tanner as his fellow-negotiator. In a letter to H.J. Procopé on 23 October, Mannerheim expressed his regret at how the delegation was made up: 'I only wish – and many share this wish with me – that today when Messrs Paasikivi, Tanner and Yrjö-Koskinen [the Finnish minister in Moscow] reach the end of their journey, you were not away in America but were with them in Moscow.' Later the same day he wrote: 'A special newspaper edition has just now reported that our delegation is returning after a day and a night's negotiations to confer again with the government. This is not a good augury.' The Finnish negotiators had indeed come home for new consultations, and on the evening of 26 October the government discussed the position with Mannerheim. Cajander put to him the question: how long could Finland hold out in a war? The answer was pessimistic; because of the great deficiencies in the defence forces, to risk a war was out of the question. Erkko was displeased and Niukkanen put forward a dissenting opinion. Both ministers were against large-scale concessions. After this meeting the Finns drew up a written reply to the Soviet government. Mannerheim was anxious that it should be drafted flexibly and politely – it was meant for a great power concerned about its prestige – but the tone he desired was missing. He became more and more pessimistic. However, on his last journey Paasikivi did take an alternative offer drawn up by Mannerheim and Niukkanen for a naval base outside Hanko, on Jussarö (or Örö), and a proposal for certain concessions on the isthmus.

Mannerheim had thus tried to facilitate a settlement based on his realistic view of the country's defence. 'The Moscow negotiations and the threat of war come particularly inopportunely for us,' he wrote on 6 November 1939 to Gripenberg. 'We would have needed at least a year's intensive work to be anywhere near ready, but with the exception of Germany hardly any country is ever ready.' They were living in 'very hard times'. 'Woe betide the weak – if he is unable to defend himself, he cannot count on help from others.' Soon all these misgivings were confirmed. The negotiations had been conducted in such a way that his compromise proposal was never even put forward because it seemed to stand no chance. In practical terms contact was broken, something he found inexcusable. The Soviet Union, a great power, could not be treated in this way. But Erkko argued otherwise; he had himself given the negotiators instructions to break off the discussions if the Finnish conditions were not approved. Paasikivi raged in vain over the directions he received: 'In the army there is no one but Mannerheim who understands anything.' The Field-Marshal had told him that 'we must absolutely come to an agreement. The army cannot fight.'

In Helsinki Mannerheim did not hide his bitter criticism of the government's policy, nor did he tire of urging caution on the Cajander government. Contact should be resumed through negotiations. He knew only too well the superiority of the forces the Soviet Union had at its disposal and how defective was the equipment of his own armed forces. 'I regard it

as my duty to point out to the government my deep conviction that everything humanly possible should be done to avoid a war during the present
political alignments.' He believed that the pact between Stalin and Hitler
had brought about a situation in which Finland ran the risk of standing
alone in an armed struggle with the Soviet Union. At last he found the
position untenable. The government were paying no attention to his views,
but trusted instead in the non-aggression pact with the Soviet Union and
above all in its belief that Stalin did not want to start an aggressive war.
The government's optimism found expression also in plans to reduce
military preparedness, but this at least was something which Mannerheim
could prevent. He therefore asked to be relieved of his post. He considered
he was not obliged to act as commander-in-chief in these circumstances,
least of all since the contact represented by the negotiations had been
broken. The intention was for Lieutenant-General Hugo Österman to
take over his responsibilities, and a date was fixed for Mannerheim to hand
over his command to this officer. However, things turned out quite
differently. On 26 November Moscow declared that Finnish artillery had
fired into Soviet territory, the so-called Mainila shots. The statement,
although untrue, provided the Soviet Union with a reason for denouncing
the 1932 non-aggression pact on 28 November. On 29 November it broke
off diplomatic relations.

In this situation Mannerheim withdrew his request to resign. Under the
immediate threat of war, no soldier could leave his post. 'I had not wanted
to undertake the responsibility of commander-in-chief,' he wrote to Sophy
shortly after the outbreak of war, 'as my age and my health entitled
me – but I had to yield to appeals from the President of the republic and
the government, and now for the fourth time I am at war.'

XI
THE WINTER WAR
1939–1940

The attack on Finland began on 30 November at the front and with the bombing of Helsinki and other places. Mannerheim reported in the morning to Niukkanen at the ministry of defence. He said: 'I give notice that I am now assuming the post of commander-in-chief of which so much has been said.' Gone, as Niukkanen later recalled in his memoirs, were depression and the weariness of old age. Indeed this was a moment that demanded vigour and presence of mind. Mannerheim also had to visit the President, who made over to him his military powers.

It was clear that important changes had to be made at government level. Cajander and Erkko, who had failed, were removed and their places taken by Risto Ryti and Väinö Tanner, two men who in the succeeding months had to work with the commander-in-chief and discuss war and peace. J.O. Söderhjelm entered the government as minister of justice and Paasikivi as minister without portfolio, while Urho Kekkonen (prominent in post-war Finland as prime minister and long-serving President) was given other duties.

On the same day Mannerheim addressed his first order of the day to the armed forces as commander-in-chief, which was to become famous. He had written it himself.

The President of the Republic has appointed me on 30.11.1939 as commander-in-chief of the armed forces of the country.

Brave soldiers of Finland!

I enter on this task at a time when our hereditary enemy is once again attacking our country. Confidence in one's commander is the first condition for success.

You know me and I know you and know that everyone in the ranks is ready to do his duty even to death.

This war is nothing other than the continuation and final act of our War of Independence.

We are fighting for our homes, our faith and our country.

This proud call to arms exuded confidence and strength, but its seventy-two-year-old author was pessimistic. The policy of those in office had made him bitter and disappointed, and he felt sad that in his last years he should be compelled to 'preside over a tragedy'. 'I had really hoped to end

111

my days without once more having to go on campaign, but higher powers have decided otherwise and through no fault of our own we have been drawn into a bloody war' (to his nephew Augustin Mannerheim, 16.12.39).

In the fight against an overwhelmingly more powerful enemy, the defence had one enormous advantage: namely, that the nation was almost wholly at one. Thus the situation was plainly different from that in 1918 – a fact which Mannerheim acknowledged with satisfaction. The people of Finland now took a more realistic view of Soviet policy and of conditions inside the Soviet Union than hitherto. On this point Moscow had clearly blundered. Stalin's order to O.W. Kuusinen to proclaim a communist Finnish government in captured Terijoki backfired. On the other hand, the first days of the war brought some acute disappointments. The Swedish government leaders decided not to activate the plan for a joint defence of Åland. The doubts Mannerheim had expressed as to whether a small and inadequately armed country would receive any outside help seemed justified.

Nevertheless the people of Finland turned to their country's defence with such self-assurance and concentrated effort that the gloomy predictions of immediate defeat and collapse did not materialise. The fight they put up has been described by many people and from different points of view, but perhaps best of all by Pekka Peitsi, a pen-name of Urho Kekkonen:

The time of the Winter War was something completely unique in the life of our people, so unique that we can scarcely ever attain its like again. It was a perpetual holy-day, an ecstasy which found no time to die down. It was a compound of faith in a just cause, and in final victory, with a fateful presentiment of the hopelessness of resistance and the ensuing national and individual downfall. The entire nation had, as it were, put on its best clothes.

Unhesitating confidence in the Field-Marshal was an important factor in this state of mind. On 3 December Mannerheim left Helsinki to go to headquarters, which, as had been arranged before hostilities began, were located in Mikkeli. This small town in Savo had fulfilled the same function once before, during the final phase of the War of Independence. 'Here I am sitting in my headquarters in the same building as 21 years ago.' Now for more than five years the town came to be both a military and a political centre. The enormous superiority of the enemy and the ensuing intense pressure, which never relaxed its grip, meant that the commander-in-chief was not able to leave Mikkeli to visit the capital even once throughout the entire Winter War. Thus important political discussions took place there, often with members of the government, led by the prime minister, or with foreign representatives. At his modest headquarters Mannerheim was able to create an environment which was stimulating for his assistants and a suitable setting for work and discussions. Here were gathered the central command of the defence forces: Lennart Oesch, chief of the general staff, and the operations division under the quartermaster-general, Colonel (soon Major-General) Aksel Airo. A peculiar consequence of previous arrangements for the army's organisation was that its commander, Lieutenant-General Hugo Österman, remained under the commander-in-chief with his staff located at Imatra. This proved to some extent a superfluous level of command, and friction resulted.

As had been expected, the main Soviet attack was mounted on the Karelian isthmus. The terrain and such fortification works as had been finished before the war facilitated a tough defence. A great advantage was that the army's deployment had already been completed while the negotiations that preceded the war had been going on. Discussions had already been held about how the fighting in front of the main defence line should be conducted. Should the Finns retire to save the troops, or should they fight to the last? Mannerheim had urged that they should stand their ground for as long as possible; the terrain favoured such tactics, and ground was precious from the point of view of the defence. Österman, however, took the opposite view.

In the first days of the war there was a fairly rapid withdrawal in the forward area. Mannerheim was agitated, and tried while still in Helsinki to put a halt to it. Then, on the way to his own headquarters, he stopped at army headquarters at Imatra for what was a heated discussion. It can be seen with hindsight that his criticism had justification – that the battles of those early days could have been fought to better advantage.

After the preliminary encounters on the isthmus, 'the phase of the covering troops', heavy fighting followed on the Mannerheim Line. The enemy made a violent attempt to break through the main defence positions towards Viipuri, the first major attack being on 10 December, followed by further attacks in the next ten days. The Russians had great superiority in troop numbers and weapons. Against their tanks the Finnish side had to defend themselves mainly with grenades and petrol bombs, which soon came to be known as Molotov cocktails; there was a serious shortage of anti-tank weapons. Enemy superiority was enormous too in the air and put great pressure on the Finns, as did the bombardment by heavy, long-range Soviet artillery, which pounded the fortifications day and night. Nevertheless, the defence held.

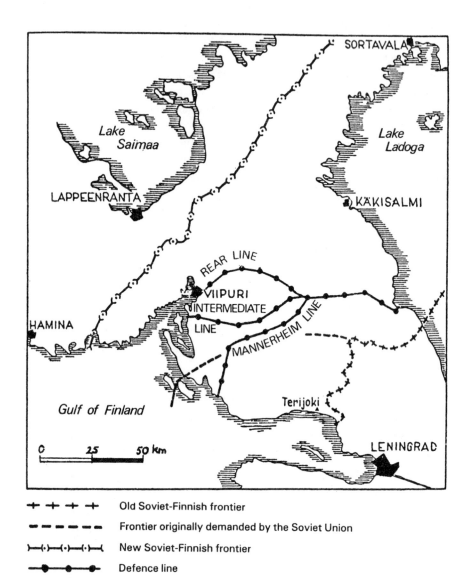

+ + + +	Old Soviet-Finnish frontier
– – – – – –	Frontier originally demanded by the Soviet Union
)—(•)—(•)—(•)—(	New Soviet-Finnish frontier
—•——•——•—	Defence line

The Winter War, 1939–40: frontiers and defence lines on the Karelian isthmus.

The major Russian offensive reached its peak on 17 December, and by 20 December was over for the time being, although local attacks continued till 25 December. The isthmus had not fallen despite the overwhelming odds, and the Finnish army had won a significant defensive victory. The situation was stabilised for a while. The conduct of his troops on the isthmus won Mannerheim's undisguised admiration. 'The capability and tenacious fighting spirit of the Finnish troops' had exceeded all his expectations, and their ability, after Soviet air and tank attacks and a heavy softening-up by artillery, to tackle the enemy infantry with bayonets was something unique. 'You there behind the line cannot even imagine how heroically our troops are fighting,' he said to Ryti during a visit at this time. The fighting was costing the attackers dear, and Mannerheim thought that the Soviet army did not have the expected striking power.

In theory the moment had now come for a powerful counter-attack, and this was urged by Öhqvist, the commander on the western side of the isthmus. Mannerheim, after some hesitation, finally agreed to an attempted pincer operation by II Corps with the 6th Division, but it quickly became evident that his earlier estimations had unfortunately been correct: Finnish firepower was too weak – resources and peace-time training were inadequate – and the operation had to be broken off. Its planning and execution were criticised; Mannerheim expressed this sharply, but considered that despite everything it had been worthwhile for the troops to demonstrate what they were capable of.

The Soviet attack on the long front between Lake Ladoga and the Arctic ocean seemed a more immediate threat in December 1939. Previously it had been thought that the dense forests and wastes of that region would be a sufficient defence against enemy attacks, but the construction of roads and railways in Eastern Karelia had altered assumptions, as had modern technology. The Finnish army could only put two divisions in the field to counter an enemy deployment believed to have amounted to fourteen divisions.

In December strong enemy forces advanced north of Ladoga, partly near the shore and partly somewhat further north in the direction of Ilomantsi. The weak Finnish units withdrew with alarming rapidity. Another force advanced from Russian bases in Eastern Karelia towards the region further north known as the waist of Finland, and further north still, other Red Army units were advancing. It was on these important sectors of the front that the Finnish army won its first successes in actions that were not purely defensive. Successfully applying *motti* tactics, they were able to come into their own. Lightly-equipped Finnish troops on skis could isolate and surround unwieldy enemy units that were tied to the roads in the snowy landscape. Here the great value of winter training was demonstrated; it had been possible to mount exercises of this type in peace time. The enemy's overall superiority could not make itself felt here to the same extent as on the isthmus. In addition to these advantages for the defence, an extremely hard winter set in – which in other ways was a disadvantage for the Finnish army. 'The winter has been extraordinarily cold and hard for my soldiers, but at last snow has fallen, which will cause difficulties for the tanks,' Mannerheim commented in a letter to his daughter Sophy. Could Eva Sparre remember such a temperature from the years of their childhood at Louhisaari? The cold gave the army 'a certain support although we have by no means been equipped for such a severe winter campaign' (21.1.40).

If training and suitable equipment were important preconditions for success, so were the personalities of the senior army commanders, and here Mannerheim's judgement and selection of men were fundamental. The occasion when Colonel Paavo Talvela, later one of the leading fighting generals, received his first command during the war when Mannerheim was still in Helsinki in early December became well-known. Talvela, who had left regular service several years previously and was one of Walden's principal assistants in the Finnish Paper Mills Association, had asked Walden to arrange for him to have an immediate audience with Mannerheim. Talvela at once expressed agitated concern over what was happening north of Ladoga, and said: 'The Finnish army is in flight.' Walden, who was present, felt increasingly apprehensive at Talvela's behaviour but Mannerheim, after asking him a few questions, gave Talvela command of the troops on the most critical sector north of Ladoga. Talvela requested, and obtained, Lieutenant-Colonel Aaro Pajari to accompany him, and by means of vigorous and skilful operations in the lake area around Tolvajärvi they were able to strike and destroy an enemy force which was considerably larger and more heavily equipped than themselves – a success which the commander-in-chief regarded as highly significant. It had given the soldiers back their self-confidence, and Talvela's troops had shown that the army was not only capable of defending itself but also of counter-attacking. It had 'halted significantly superior enemy forces penetrating into the country', Mannerheim summed up in his order of the day.

An equally important success was won during the final days of December by Colonel Hjalmar Siilasvuo's troops at Suomussalmi. Strong Soviet forces – two divisions – were advancing here with the objective of cutting Finland into two in the comparatively narrow area between the frontier and Oulu. In the first of two operations the 163rd Division of the

Red Army was isolated and shattered, and an immense quantity of material was taken. Then Finnish forces succeeded in cutting up the 44th Division, which appeared to be an élite formation from the Moscow Military District. These great successes made a powerful impression both in Finland and abroad. In an order of the day Mannerheim repeated Ryti's judgement on them: they were an historic miracle. Finally, immediately north of Ladoga, two divisions and an armoured brigade of the Red Army were advancing. Major-General Hägglund succeeded in cutting off the enemy forces, which with their heavy equipment were hampered by the deep snow. But the fighting was tough and long-drawn-out – here too the difficulties the Finnish troops faced in going on to the offensive against a well-entrenched enemy were apparent.

Thus at the turn of the year a relative calm prevailed. On the isthmus the Russian offensive had petered out, and on the long northern front immediate danger no longer threatened. The pause in the war gave the opportunity to build up the strength of the defence, and try to obtain help from abroad. But beyond the immediate future, the prospects gave the military command grave concern. On 8 January 1940 Mannerheim was able to inform General Sir Edmund Ironside, chief of the imperial general staff in the United Kingdom, that for the time being the situation in Finland was comparatively good, but the defence suffered from great deficiencies and help was needed, which could not be left to the last minute if it was to be of any use. With help, Finland might perhaps hold .out through the winter. While waiting for the next development, one day was 'just like another at headquarters, so long as no catastrophes occur. Work proceeds so that you scarcely notice how time is passing before it is well into the small hours of the morning' (to Eva Sparre, 21.1.40).

Great sympathy was aroused abroad for the little northern country which was daring to stand up for its freedom – after the initial battles, it had become clear that no new Polish campaign was to be expected in Finland. Clearly, help for Finland would not be wasted. In the neighbouring Scandinavian countries and in Britain and France, there were calls not only for humanitarian aid but also for the despatch of arms and ultimately for active participation with troops. On the other hand, there was no possibility of any military or political aid coming from Germany, since Hitler was bound by the pact with Stalin.

Sweden's policy towards Finland developed in a dramatic way, which disappointed even the realistic and sceptical Field-Marshal. All the work that had been put into achieving a Nordic orientation and cooperation for mutual security at first seemed to have been utterly wasted. E.J. Wigforss (see above, p. 56), who since 1917 had consistently taken a negative stance over Sweden pursuing an active Finnish policy, was now favourably disposed towards the Soviet Union, and a driving force behind Sweden's completely negative policy on Finland. The Swedish foreign minister, Sandler, soon resigned, and in the ensuing political crisis a coalition government was formed which was to last throughout the World War. A career diplomat, Christian Günther, became foreign minister. Friends of Finland had barely succeeded in preventing Sweden from making a declaration of neutrality. However, under strong pressure from an aroused public opinion and with support from the influential defence minister P.E. Sköld, considerable aid for Finland was mobilised – and of this, the rapid deliveries of war material such as ammunition, rifles, gun barrels and aircraft were of vital importance for the Finnish defensive effort. A volunteer corps was organised which finally consisted of three detachments totalling about 10,000 men. There was also substantial humanitarian assistance. However, in the final and most difficult phase of the war all this did not seem to be enough. The main question then was whether Finland might also obtain the help of Swedish troops in its fight.

Indignation over the Soviet attack on Finland flared up too in Western Europe and the United States. The reaction in Britain and France had military significance. The Soviet ambassador in London, Ivan Maisky, wrote in his memoirs that of the many unpleasant displays of anti-Soviet feeling he had experienced, the storm over the Winter War was the worst. There was doubt at first whether the defence would hold in view of the disparity in the relative strengths of the Soviet Union and Finland, but when it did hold, Finland very soon became a political problem of the first rank. Neville Chamberlain, the British prime minister, was at first restrained in his reaction, considering the Finnish front of secondary concern and the outcome there to be clear. However, he quickly changed his opinion, since he had come to believe that the fate of Finland was of decisive psychological importance, even for the Allies. Within the British cabinet Lord Halifax, the foreign secretary – who had known Mannerheim since, as Viceroy of India, he had received him on his journey there in 1928 – was moved by Finland's fate and prepared to send help so far as was possible. The attitude of Winston Churchill, on the other hand (he was then first lord of the admiralty), was determined chiefly by other motives. At first, like Chamberlain, he was negatively inclined, but soon this changed to willingness to send help – to procure for Britain 'a foothold in Scandinavia'. The decisive factor was the hope of stopping Swedish iron ore exports to the German armament industry.

It was decided that Finland was to receive help in the form of weapons. A senior British officer, Brigadier C.G. Ling, was sent to Mikkeli on the proposal of General Sir Walter Kirke (see above, p. 85), to organise this cooperation, his first taste being to obtain information on what equipment the Finnish army needed most urgently. When Ling returned to London with the Finnish list of requirements, this was largely approved, even including anti-aircraft guns. However, there was one important area in which it proved difficult to meet Mannerheim's wishes. The Royal Air Force had still not been built up to the extent that it dared to let aircraft go, especially bombers. However, twelve Blenheim bombers were sent – the determination of the officer commanding Royal Air Force Fighter Command, Air Chief Marshal Sir Hugh Dowding, to retain a concentration of aircraft for Britain's defence meant a lower priority being given to bombers. (The Battle of Britain in the late summer of 1940 proved him right.)

The French provided more important supplies of equipment than the British. Already at the turn of the year, thirty Morane aircraft were sent to Finland, unfortunately by sea. The French also sent a liaison officer, Colonel Jean Ganéval, to Mikkeli. Subsequently they shipped anti-aircraft guns, field artillery, howitzers, lorries, motor-cycles, bicycles, radio transmitters and so on. But there were difficulties over obtaining bombers. When the French high command discussed the aid programme on 4 January, General Gamelin, the commander-in-chief, emphasised that aircraft were extremely important, for with bombers the Finns could attack the Soviet lines of communication, especially on the Karelian isthmus. But the French squadrons were themselves still being built up, and the older aircraft which were being replaced were turned over to training. Thus they had good military reasons for being unwilling to give away anything important.

The war had clearly not been the easy success on which Moscow had counted. Finnish society had shown the unity and strength needed to stand up to this severe test. From the Soviets' point of view the hostile public opinion they had aroused by attacking their small neighbour boded ill, and unforeseeable complications could flow from it. There had been severe Soviet casualties during the heavier battles. The result was that in mid-January Stalin changed his policy: he now wanted to find out what possibilities there were for peace. With this in view Mme Alexandra Kollontai, the Soviet minister in Stockholm, made contact during the latter half of January with various Swedes and Finns, and on 29 January with the Swedish government. However, nothing definite could be learned of what terms the Russians might have in mind – they were possibly more favourable at that point than later.

Ryti visited Mikkeli on 26 January and informed Mannerheim of what had happened. Mannerheim recommended peace; he was now more optimistic than at the beginning of the war, but he pointed out that one never knew how a war would end. Clearly, in spite of foreign help, Finland was still badly equipped. He advised making limited concessions, though more far-reaching ones than those made in the autumn. But when, later, the government had to reply to the Soviet offer, he was not consulted. Annoyance was compounded by his belief that the answer should have been more positive in tone. Ryti took this answer to Stockholm on 31 January. The next step was Tanner's visit to Stockholm on 4 February, when he delivered to Mme Kollontai a peace proposal linked to Mannerheim's conversation with Ryti. Moscow immediately replied that the proposal did not go far enough. It was now clear to the Swedish government that it was possible for Finland to obtain a peace settlement and avoid being crushed, even if more extensive Swedish help were not forthcoming. The Swedish government therefore tried to force the Finns to accept the Soviet peace terms, even if they were harsh ones. This represented the easiest solution from Sweden's point of view, and was undoubtedly what the Russians had intended to be the outcome of their hints of peace. Mme Kollontai explained the actual Soviet terms on 14 February. They were extremely severe.

However, Ryti had heard from Mannerheim that increased foreign, and particularly Swedish, help was absolutely essential if the war was to be continued. Mannerheim had explained his views on this point in a letter to the chief to the Swedish defence staff, General Axel Rappe, a friend of his since 1918. During his visit to Stockholm on 31 January, Ryti requested more weapons, particularly anti-tank guns, and the despatch of Swedish troops. He was promised guns, but on the question of troops Hansson, the prime minister, replied that the matter would be considered by the government. It was indeed discussed shortly afterwards, and the Finns received a dramatic answer. During his conversation with the Swedish prime minister and foreign minister in Stockholm on 5 February, Tanner had expressed the Finnish desire for increased military help, and on that occasion was not given a clear refusal; thus after meeting Mannerheim on 10 February he decided to return to Stockholm for a further attempt. On 13 February he recounted to Hansson, Sköld and Günther the Field-Marshal's wish for assistance, particularly in the form of volunteer units. This time he was given an unambiguous refusal. The Swedish side stressed the risks for them of becoming drawn into the European war. Hansson's negative reply was published in a short communiqué, clearly with the intention of forcing Helsinki into rapidly concluding peace on the basis of the Soviet conditions as then known; indeed for the Finns, who wanted so keep the rebuff secret, this was a major setback. However, there was a storm of indignation from the Swedish public, who regarded the possible collapse of Finland with apprehension. To allay this, King Gustaf explained the government's attitude in a detailed statement.

An important argument made by the Finnish side during the attempts by Ryti and, even more, by Tanner to obtain increased Swedish military help had been the offer of troops by the Western powers. If the situation became desperate, Finland would be compelled to accept the offer by the Allies: would it therefore not be preferable to send Swedish help in time, so that the risks involved in aid being sent by the Allies could be avoided? However, in Stockholm they did not at first want to believe in the possibility of Allied intervention. Tanner had put corresponding arguments to Mme Kollontai: did they not see in Moscow what dangers a continuation of the war might represent for the Soviet Union?

It so happened that official views in London and Paris had moved in exactly that direction. On 5 February the Allied Supreme War Council discussed plans for intervention. It was feared that if Finland succumbed during the harsh campaign, the Western powers would thereby suffer a severe political and psychological reverse. There were other arguments too, notably interest in preventing Swedish iron ore exports to the German war industry. It is difficult to assess the relative significance of the various motives. For Britain's part, Churchill was especially eager to establish the base for intervention on Norwegian and Swedish soil, mainly at Narvik. The result was that a combined Allied operation would be undertaken, but only if there were a Finnish request for help, to be made after Allied preparations were complete. These decisions in Paris changed the political situation in Scandinavia. They might represent the salvation of Finland, but if they were implemented, they would also involve great risks for Scandinavia as a whole. News of a possible intervention by the Allied powers spread rapidly and caused great excitement. Brigadier Ling was to convey the details of the plans, but his authority extended to informing Mannerheim and him alone. The cabinet in London did not trust the ability of the Finns to keep a secret.

From the start, however, Mannerheim was distrustful of intervention by the Western powers. He had not supported the activity of Finnish diplomats in Paris and London, because of his fear that intervention in the north would force Germany on to the Soviet side without, of itself, having any decisive significance for the war being waged by Finland. He did not believe that the Western powers had sufficient resources for such a large undertaking, and he knew the difficult character of the terrain in the far north on the shores of the Arctic ocean. His thoughts turned to the unsuccessful British operations in North Russia during the critical year 1919. He immediately informed Tanner and the government of his scepticism regarding the planned intervention, but they were not of the same opinion. Ryti thought that the Allied plans could at least be used to extract concessions from Moscow and force Stockholm to give increased aid. Paasikivi was enthusiastic at the apparent opportunity to acquire Eastern Karelia. Mannerheim shared the government's hope that the Allied decision might be put to diplomatic use, but otherwise he kept a cool head. On 9 February the government sent Ryti, Tanner and Walden to Mikkeli to discuss the situation with him in greater detail, and in discussions the next day he explained to them how serious the situation was. The Red Army had begun a new and extremely powerful offensive on the isthmus.

The offensive was based on an unprecedentedly heavy concentration of artillery. In addition, the Soviet commander-in-chief had a strong air force and large numbers of tanks at his disposal. The Finnish units, without adequate protection and in comparatively weak positions, were under terrible pressure; Airo's view was that if Finland had possessed a Maginot Line, the Russians would never have got through. The Finnish artillery lacked the range of its Soviet counterpart, and suffered besides from a shortage of ammunition. The number of defenders dwindled every day. Nevertheless at headquarters on 10 February the situation, though critical, was not regarded as catastrophic, and there were still hopes of a new defensive victory. However, on 11 February the Soviet offensive was stepped up, and forward probes were made along the front to find a weak point for a breakthrough. On 12 February the Russians succeeded at last in breaking into the Finnish positions at Lähde (Summa) after a heavy artillery barrage. The Finnish positions were shot to pieces and many of their defenders were killed. In this situation the only possibility was to counter-attack and eject the enemy from the positions, but Mannerheim had no strategic reserves that he could bring into play. On 13 February a counter-attack was attempted, but it was only partly successful. The Finnish units lacked the requisite anti-tank weapons – those requested from Sweden had not arrived. A force of about fifty Russian tanks held back all counter-attacks.

The commander-in-chief at once left with Airo for the threatened point on the front, and on 14 February was in the courtyard of the old castle at

Viipuri during a heavy Soviet air-raid. From there he went on to the
headquarters of II Corps at Saarela manor north of Viipuri. The question
was no longer whether to hold the line of defence in its entirety. It was
clear that the troops in the western part of the isthmus would have to
withdraw from the positions they had held with such tenacity. On the
other hand, the eastern part of the isthmus could be held till the end of the
war. Two possible withdrawal plans were discussed. There was an intermediate position which was in a reasonable state of readiness, although it
was not easy to defend. Then there was a position further from the front,
which offered greater possibilities, but construction work had only started
there in the autumn and was still going on. This position began west of
Viipuri and continued to the Vuoksi. Opinion was divided on which of the
two positions offered better possibilities, and the fact that they would
eventually have to withdraw to it recommended the rear position. However, Mannerheim chose the intermediate position. Partly for political
reasons, he did not want to yield any more ground at this moment, and
furthermore work on the rear position also demanded more time. The final
Soviet successes on 15 February seemed to come as a shock, which was
made all the worse because hopes of increased Swedish help had been
publicly shattered.

On the Karelian isthmus Mannerheim thoroughly reorganised the command structure. Hugo Österman was replaced as commander of the army
on the isthmus by Erik Heinrichs, of whom Mannerheim wrote in his
memoirs that he had strong nerves which he was able to keep in the worst
crises. Talvela succeeded Heinrichs in command of III Corps on the eastern
isthmus, and Öhqvist was to command II Corps and the defence of
Viipuri. The withdrawal to a rear position on the western isthmus was
accomplished successfully, but further withdrawals had to follow. On
21 February Mannerheim ordered the evacuation of the strong coastal
fortress of Koivisto which had been of great value, latterly through the
support its artillery gave to the retreating infantry. The faltering defence
on the Karelian isthmus was eventually decisive for the outcome of the
war, in spite of some notable Finnish successes north of Ladoga where
Major-General Hägglund's troops succeeded at last in annihilating the
Soviet 18th Division and surrounding 168th Division which, however,
was able to hold out till the end of the war in March. Further north,
Siilasvuo isolated the Soviet 14th Division, most of which was cut to pieces
at Kuhmo. Again, the Finnish *motti* tactics were responsible for these
successes.

However, the crisis on the isthmus also prompted increased activity on the diplomatic front, with the government seeking more help from Sweden and the Western powers. In mid-February, when all hope of peace with the Soviet Union on reasonable terms seemed to have vanished, many of Finland's political leaders found the Allied intervention plans more attractive than before. Mannerheim, however, remained sceptical. On 20 February Ling returned to Finland from London; Ganéval, the French liaison officer sent by General Gamelin, arrived at the same time. They now found that the situation on the Finnish front, combined with the actions of the Swedish government, offered the Allies greater opportunities. On 22 February they explained the Western powers' great intervention plan to Mannerheim – who put various questions to them which testified to his level-headed and sceptical outlook. How would the troops be able to pass through the neutral territory of Norway and Sweden, and what would be the reaction of the Scandinavian governments? The officers were unable to enlighten him completely on these points, but in spite of everything the intervention plan gave the Finnish leaders a weapon: the possibility of help from the Western powers ought to be used to soften the Soviet peace terms, and the Swedish government should be persuaded to work in a similar direction. But Moscow was impervious to this approach. Stalin clearly calculated that the Finnish front would not hold out long enough – and perhaps too that Allied troops sent to Finland would never arrive. Throughout these weeks the fighting on the isthmus became even tougher, and despite certain successes the Finnish troops on its western side had to withdraw to the rear line at the end of February.

The final moment of decision was thus approaching, but the government in Helsinki was still not of one mind. Ryti and Tanner agreed that a harsh peace – though without a Soviet occupation – had to be accepted. Paasikivi sided with them, but Niukkanen still refused. On 23 February, after a visit to Mikkeli, Walden was able to inform Ryti and Tanner of Mannerheim's views: they should further examine the significance of the offer by Britain and France, and keep open the negotiating contact with the Soviet Union, but above all try to obtain peace. The government's foreign affairs committee met the same day and heard of the unfavourable turn in the peace negotiations. The Soviet side were demanding the outer islands with Suursaari, a large part of Ladoga-Karelia (the part of Karelia on the north-east shore of the lake), Sortavala, Viipuri and the Hanko peninsula. Paasikivi was appalled by the terms, but wanted to know Mannerheim's opinion, which Ryti and Walden duly reported. Söderhjelm proposed that Ryti and Tanner should travel to headquarters, but not without the whole government being informed. Meanwhile negotiations with the British and French continued, but no promising results were forthcoming. The expeditionary corps, which in any case was only of modest size, could not arrive in Finland before 15 April. Mannerheim's comment was that 'the help will come too late . . . Are there men with the courage to gamble? 15.IV too late.' But discussions must be continued.

On 26 February, more far-reaching demands were put forward by the Soviet side, to which the Finns had to reply within two days. A delegation of members of the government, including Ryti and Walden, was thus sent to Mikkeli on 28 February to learn the the commander-in-chief's opinion and discuss with him the burning question of peace. This dramatic meeting began with Airo presenting a report of the situation in the presence of Oesch. Mannerheim then allowed a number of generals, including Österman, Heinrichs, Martola and Talvela, to speak, and to his surprise the majority opinion appeared to be against the conclusion of peace on the terms offered by the Soviet Union. They said that the army could continue the fight. However, Mannerheim did not abandon his view, and during an interval while the ministers were holding discussions among themselves, he was able to argue further with the generals, as the result of which they took up positions in favour of the peace line. The troops were exhausted, and there was a serious risk of a Soviet breakthrough at Viipuri, with possibly calamitous consequences. However, on the question of the peace terms Mannerheim refused to give an opinion since, he said, it was a political question. But when afterwards he spoke to Heinrichs alone, they agreed that the terms had to be accepted.

During the meeting at headquarters on 29 February, Mannerheim had shown plainly what his view was: namely, that the government should seek peace. However, the time was not yet ripe for this difficult choice. Niukkanen and Uuno Hannula, the minister of education, were still loath to accept Stalin's demands, and Niukkanen could not agree to cede Viipuri. The government bore an agonising responsibility: should they accept a peace if that meant the country losing its independence? Once again the decision was made more difficult by the actions of the Western powers. Ling and Ganéval now returned to their respective capitals for further instructions. The Allied preparations for the expeditionary force to northern Scandinavia still continued; by 5 March at the latest Finland was to issue its request for help, whereupon the transport vessels would sail for northern Norway. Daladier, the French prime minister, appealed to Finland not to give up the fight and to King Gustaf to allow the troops passage across Swedish territory. This made an impression. On 1 March the Finnish government departed from the strict path of peace negotiation, formulating their answer to Moscow's demands in such a way as to gain time. They were taking a risk, but they did not ask the Western powers for help.

On 2 March the Western powers officially asked permission for transit across Norwegian and Swedish territory to enable them to come to the aid of Finland. Both governments refused, but acute concern for the future was felt in the Scandinavian captials, and Christian Günther, the Swedish foreign minister, now pressed Helsinki harder to accept the Russian terms and save Scandinavia. However, the refusal of the Scandinavian governments did not decide the matter. London and Paris could still try to overcome Scandinavian resistance if the Finnish government were to present a request for help in accordance with the plan previously laid down. The decision now lay with Ryti and Mannerheim. To the Field-Marshal, living as he was under the pressure of the heavy battles on the isthmus, it was most important at that moment for help to be increased as soon as possible. In Stockholm the government changed its position to the extent that appreciably more support was made ready as an alternative to the offer from the Western powers; the Swedish volunteer corps would be encouraged, and enlistment increased. Above all Mannerheim wanted help with equipment, notably bombers, as soon as possible. Dramatic meetings took place, especially in London where Churchill and Dowding opposed Finnish demands because of their own state of unpreparedness. The despatch of bombers was eventually made dependent on the anticipated Finnish request for help, and this request never came. When it became clear on 5 March that the negotiating contact with Moscow had not been broken in spite of the non-committal Finnish answer of 1 March, the government finally decided to accept the harsh Soviet terms and ask for an armistice. The peace line seemed to have prevailed at last, but the decision was not unanimous and so, to strengthen its position, the government requested from Mannerheim a written appreciation of the military situation.

On 6 March a delegation was chosen to conduct negotiations, and it arrived in Moscow the following day. The negotiations began on 9 March, but the first meeting between the two sides involved a severe disappointment. The demands put forward by Molotov were harsher than before, thus proving Mme Kollontai's siren calls in Stockholm about modification of the terms and Stalin's magnaminity to have been without foundation. Those in charge of Sweden's foreign affairs had allowed themselves to be duped. As the result, the alternative put forward by the Western powers proved enticing for a last time. Mannerheim had maintained contact with London and Paris, chiefly as a means of obtaining the bombers he sought.

On 7 March he wrote Daladier a letter appealing for help; he recommended, in spite of everything, sending the appeal for Allied intervention in the north which had been expected to arrive by 5 March. If negotiations in Moscow led to peace, the request could be cancelled. When the more rigorous Russian conditions became known in Helsinki on 9 March, voices were raised in the government demanding that the request for Western help should go out immediately. Some members had consistently hoped that this would happen. However, it was during that meeting that the appreciation requested from Mannerheim on 5 March arrived. It was a pessimistic document, and concluded with a recommendation that the harsh terms be accepted. The army lacked reserves, heavy artillery and much else, and the troops were worn out and depleted by heavy losses. To his own appreciation the commander-in-chief had appended one by Heinrichs of a similar tenor. Mannerheim still judged that the promised intervention by the Western Allies would be insufficient. Reliance on it was therefore an absolute danger not only for Sweden but also for Finland. The government's decision – still not unanimous – was to give the delegation in Moscow authority to conclude peace, which came into effect on 13 March. The hard struggle, 'the winter of honour', was over.

The commander-in-chief now addressed a message of thanks to the armed forces, and not only those who had defended the country in the front line, but also those who had worked in the war industries and on the fortifications. It was personal and warm, and expressive of the tragedy that had been enacted. Paasikivi commented in his memoirs that it cannot be read without emotion.

. . . You did not want war. You loved peace, work and progress, but the fight was forced upon you and in it you accomplished great exploits which for centuries to come will shine in the pages of history.

Soldiers! I have fought on many battlefields but I have never yet seen your equals as warriors. I am proud of you as if you were my own children, as proud of the man from the northern tundras as of the sons of the broad plains of Ostrobothnia, the forests of Karelia, the smiling tracts of Savo, the rich farms of Häme and Satakunta, the lands of Uusimaa and South-West Finland with their whispering birches. I am as proud of the factory worker and the son of the poor cottage as I am of the rich man's contribution of life and limb . . .

In spite of all the courage and spirit of self-sacrifice the government has been compelled to make peace on hard terms, which nevertheless can be explained.

Our army was small, and both its reserves and its regulars were insufficient. We were not equipped for a war with a great power. While our brave soldiers were defending our frontiers, it was necessary by superhuman exertions to produce what was wanting, to construct lines of defence which did not exist, to seek help which did not come. It was necessary to obtain arms and equipment, and this at a time when every country was feverishly preparing itself for the storm which is now sweeping over the world. Your deeds have aroused admiration throughout the world, but after three and a half months of war we continue to stand nearly alone . . .

XII

THE PERIOD OF PEACE

1940–1941

The conclusion of peace did not alter Mannerheim's position as commander-in-chief: when legally examined as a result of criticism that the supreme command of the defence forces should have reverted to the President at the end of the war, this was found to be constitutionally proper. However, Mannerheim himself considered that he should retire before the soldiers began to call him 'grandfather' because of his advanced age – as they did Pétain in France. Kallio and Ryti appealed to him to stay on, and thus he had to confront all the difficulties which were now coming to a head.

The new political situation caused important changes to be made within the Ryti government. Two posts were of particular interest to the commander-in-chief, those of defence minister and foreign minister. Niukkanen, one of the few who had voted against the peace right up to the end, was replaced as defence minister by Rudolf Walden, for whom collaboration with Mannerheim presented no difficulties. It was also thought that Tanner should leave the foreign ministry and return to the ministry of finance. The choice of successor proved difficult. Mannerheim wanted G.A. Gripenberg or, as second choice, Carl Enckell, who had held the appointment during the difficult years of the 1920s and was experienced in dealing with the Soviet Union. However, both refused, and eventually the post was accepted by Professor Rolf Witting, a geophysicist who had moved into banking, and had political experience.

The Peace of Moscow created great problems. Historic regions of Finland containing modern industries, ports and the important Saimaa Canal were now lost. Some 400,000 people had to leave their homes and their land and be fitted into Finnish society as quickly as possible. This presupposed an expropriation of land in the remaining parts of Finland – an undertaking which raised difficult questions of fair distribution as well as the nationality problem where the settlement of Finnish-speakers in Swedish-speaking areas was concerned.

The end to the fighting provided no lasting solution to relations between Finland and the Soviet Union. The Finnish government was resolutely determined to try to avoid a new war, and was therefore willing to accept the new frontiers, even if there was a generally cherished hope that somewhat later, after conclusion of a general European peace, Finland would get back a part of what had been lost. It quickly became clear that Moscow did not want to accept the idea of a completely independent Finland with the right to determine its own future within its own borders.

Because of Finland's dangerous situation, the continued expansion of the defence forces became a priority. There were discussions on how to safeguard the south-eastern frontier, which was now more difficult to defend than before; what fortified lines to build, and so on. The task of directing planning in this area fell largely to the commander-in-chief. It was also important to maintain the training of personnel in the defence forces, and the procurement of military equipment was the most pressing need of all. Substantial supplies had arrived during the Winter War but there were still great deficiencies, and a good deal of equipment was worn out. A new system of organisation and other reforms in the army were also tried out.

No less important than strengthening the defence forces was the shaping of relations with the Soviet Union. One Soviet demand followed another in the six months following the peace in March, most of which were acceded to. The first took the form of a strong protest against plans for a Scandinavian defensive alliance. The Swedish government had offered such an alliance to induce Finland to accept a harsh peace, but this plan now had to be abandoned. Germany's occupation of Denmark and Norway, begun on 9 April 1940, worsened Finland's communications with the West still further, and the situation appeared threatening throughout the entire Baltic region. The Swedish government's attitude over the defence of Åland was now different from what it had been at the outbreak of the Winter War: there seemed to be a danger that the Germans would occupy the archipelago as the war in Norway dragged on. The Swedes declared that they would be willing to help defend it in accordance with the Åland plan of 1939, and sought contact with Mannerheim, but the commander-in-chief was instructed by his government to return a negative answer; the Soviet Union made it impossible for Finland to enter into any such arrangement. Finnish forces alone were allocated to the defence of Åland, and would defend the islands even against a German attack.

When Germany rapidly overran France, Finland's position was worsened still further. Stalin hurried to reap the benefits he could expect from the pact with Hitler; on 17 June Moscow ordered the incorporation of the three Baltic states – Estonia, Latvia and Lithuania – into the Soviet Union. The German military attaché in Helsinki, Colonel Horst Rössing, wrote after his last visit to Tallinn, where he had actually witnessed the dissolution of the Estonian republic, that he now regretfully expected the same fate to befall Finland in the course of the following months (to Colonel Matzky of the German intelligence branch, 25.7.40). This opinion was widely shared. Mannerheim's own comment was that 'it has felt ghastly to witness so close at hand the dramatic events which have been staged in the Baltic countries. If the German armed forces win their victories on the battlefield with the speed of lightning, one can say that the tragedies of Stalin's theatrically arranged *coups d'état* are not behind in their tempo. Their direction and effectiveness leave nothing to be desired. Comment is superfluous for anyone able and willing to think' (to Count Erik von Rosen, the Swedish explorer, 27.7.40).

Scarcely anyone doubted that the Soviet Union was preparing a similar development in Finland. Unrest and political demonstrations were organised on an increasing scale with the help of certain groups in Finland and Finno-Soviet friendship societies. The content of Soviet plans was subsequently stated by Molotov during his conversation with Hitler in Berlin in November. Finland was to be incorporated in the Soviet Union by action from within, without a direct war. Parallel with this, Moscow made one political demand after another. The first concerned the important nickel mines at Petsamo in the far north, Finland had been allowed to retain most of this region in the March peace treaty, presumably in deference to Britain, which had major interests in the mines. Now the situation was different, and Molotov asked to have the nickel mining concession transferred from the existing holder, an Anglo-Canadian company, to a Soviet or joint Soviet-Finnish concern. Also, as had become clear during the Winter War, Petsamo had strategic importance. Molotov pointed out to Paasikivi – now the Finnish minister in Moscow – that the question was 'extremely serious'. The government in Helsinki tried to gain a respite, pointing out that not only Britain but Germany also had interests in the nickel production. They would have to open negotiations with the concessionaires, which would take time. Molotov let the matter rest till the end of the summer, when it became the subject of difficult and protracted negotiations.

The next Soviet démarche was made on 8 July, when Molotov unexpectedly put forward extensive demands for the transit of troops and war material to Hanko by Finnish railways. This was a completely fresh demand which had no basis in the peace treaty. The Finns succeeded in limiting the necessary concession so as to reduce the risk that the transit traffic would provide the occasion for a Soviet military takeover. The third difficult question which Moscow brought up concerned the Åland islands.

This too had not arisen during the peace negotiations – Stalin had probably not wanted to annoy Sweden at that point. Now, on 27 June, Molotov demanded that either the islands should be demilitarised or the Soviet Union should participate in the defence works. Mannerheim did not think that in the situation then prevailing, Finland could risk a war for the right to fortify Åland, and therefore recommended giving way. When an answer to this effect was delivered, Moscow increased its demand to include continuous inspection to ensure that Åland had not been fortified.

A demand of a different kind was made on 24 July. It was now stated that the Soviet Union had an interest in the internal development of Finland, and it was therefore now demanded that Väinö Tanner, the foremost and most trusted leader of the Social Democrats, should be removed from the government. The authority he carried within the working-class movement – he had always, even in 1918, followed a democratic line and was well known as an anti-communist – had become an embarrassment. Even this demand was gratified. In the first week of August the Swedish military attaché Curt Kempff reported: 'The foreign and domestic political barometers showed such a low pressure that it approached an earthquake' (26.8.40).

In this tense situation the government decided to investigate the possibilities of obtaining foreign support in a crisis. Mannerheim still persisted in the orientation towards Scandinavia which he had been partly responsible for creating. They should first ask Sweden whether Finland could count on such support, but the answer came back that it could not. Only Günther, the Swedish foreign minister, recommended a more positive reply. Nor could the Finns count on German assistance; the Germans made it clear in different ways that their treaty relations with the Soviet Union put any such support out of the question. Mannerheim was informed of this both by Hermann Göring (through the latter's former brother-in-law, Count Erik von Rosen) and by the German military attaché, Colonel Rössing. However, from mid-July intimations began to come from Germany that the leadership no longer rejected support for Finland so clearly. At the end of July, both Ryti and Mannerheim were visited by a notable German diplomatic agent, Dr Ludwig Weissauer, who was to play a considerable role in Finnish politics during the years ahead; he was frequently used as an unofficial envoy for Ribbentrop and possibly for Hitler also. His message was that Finland could count on receiving weapons to defend its independence, although Germany had to observe discretion in relation to the Soviet Union. In Berlin at the beginning of August, representations in Moscow in support of Finland were being considered. Above all it was German involvement in northern Norway that came to increase the interest of the German military command in Finland.

In Sweden too there was a changed attitude to Finland, where developments were being closely watched. The Swedes feared that if they showed a complete lack of interest in its future, Finland would eventually be forced into a policy oriented towards Germany, which many regarded as dangerous; Swedish observers there reported clear signs of this. In Sweden a group of people interested in Finland, centred around the industrialist Major Svante Påhlson, had the aim of preserving the independence of both countries by means of far-reaching cooperation, and ultimately through a union between them with a common foreign and defence policy. As an industrialist Påhlson had long-standing links with Rudolf Walden through the Paper Mills Association; and as a Swedish army officer he had good military contacts, notably with General Axel Rappe. A friend, Major Sven Wijkman, had drawn up a memorandum containing this programme which was set out many months later, in June 1941, in a pamphlet entitled *Decemviri*. Påhlson brought this memorandum to the attention of a number of Swedish politicians and sent it to Mannerheim, Walden and Ryti. It aroused interest. On the same day – 18 August 1940 – that Påhlson's memorandum reached him, Mannerheim also received an important message from Berlin. This was from Kivimäki, now the official Finnish representative there. A German officer was to come at the behest of Göring for discussions with Mannerheim and him alone. Both communications – Påhlson's and Kivimäki's – were brought by a Finnish businessman, Baron Ernst Fabian Wrede, who was flying home from Berlin to Helsinki via Stockholm. Wrede met Mannerheim at Malmi airfield, where the Field-Marshal was about to fly with Walden to be present at the formation of the Veterans' Association at Jyväskylä. Witting and Erik Heinrichs were there too.

Göring's emissary was Lieutenant-Colonel Josef Veltjens, one of his former air force comrades and now an arms dealer. His mission was to offer Finland the opportunity to purchase weapons in return for permitting transit across Finnish territory for military personnel travelling from northern Norway to Germany and back. The men would be mainly those who were sick or going on leave. Mannerheim received him on 19 August, and immediately explained that he could not take a such a decision alone but would at once contact his government. The German proposal seemed attractive in Finland's current situation, and provided evidence that the limitations imposed on Hitler by his cooperation with Moscow were not excessive. Still, Mannerheim hesitated. He immediately informed Ryti of

Veltjens's proposal – President Kallio was ill and staying at Kultaranta, his official summer residence near Turku – and Ryti gave his approval. (This sequence of events, once obscure, has now been made clear.)

Further discussions with the Germans were to be the concern of the defence minister, Walden, who entrusted them to Talvela, now no longer serving with the forces. An agreement was concluded on 22 September setting out in detail the routes and forms of transport. The latter could involve only limited use of the railway since the line ended at Rovaniemi, and it was therefore necessary to arrange staging points and set up supplies throughout the long road up to northern Norway. A great deal of attention has been given retrospectively to the agreement on transit facilities for the German army. At the war responsibility trial in 1945 it was interpreted as a preliminary to the Continuation War waged against the Soviet Union from 1941 to 1944, so that the question of how the agreement had originated was regarded as fundamental in establishing responsibility for the war. However, this is a wrong approach because at the time when the Finns decided to comply with the German request, the possibility of a war between Germany and the Soviet Union was still regarded as remote. Hitler had not yet taken a clear decision to attack the Soviet Union, even if his thoughts were already occupied with it. The political gains Finland could achieve through compliance with the German request were a supply of arms when these were badly needed and an indication of Germany's interest in Finland's independence. This certainly made an impact in Moscow, which nevertheless still hoped to be able to carry out its plans in Finland without opposition from Hitler. From the Finns' point of view, the transit agreement with Germany could be regarded as parallel to the agreement forced on them a few months earlier by the Soviet Union over the transport of troops to Hanko. The agreement also had a parallel, as far as neutrality was concerned, with the one Sweden had been obliged to conclude in June 1940 for the transport of soldiers on leave to and from Norway. However, in other respects the Swedish-German agreement clearly had foreign policy implications different from those of the agreement between Germany and Finland, while a larger number of German troops had to be transported across Swedish territory than through Finland.

During the autumn the Finnish political leaders had continued contacts with Stockholm over a common approach to neutrality to safeguard both countries, and after familiarising themselves with the Påhlson memorandum through Walden and Mannerheim, they wanted further discussions with the Swedes. These led quickly to a decision to work out the possibilities of forming of a union. What was then believed and hoped both in

Stockholm and Helsinki was that a Swedish-Finnish neutrality alliance, and hence a pacification of the Baltic region, could be brought about which would be in the interests of Germany and the Soviet Union, and welcomed by both. The union plan fulfilled for Mannerheim a desire he had cherished for decades. Talvela was sent back to Berlin on 5 December with the task of clarifying German political reactions to the plan. Talvela put the question to Göring, who promised to obtain Hitler's view; however, Hitler gave a point-blank refusal. The Soviet reaction was the same when reports of the union plan penetrated to Moscow. What the Swedes and Finns could not understand was that both Berlin and Moscow harboured entirely different plans – in which both wanted to dominate Finland.

Parallel with Finnish efforts to form a union with Sweden went a debate on the forthcoming presidential election. Kallio had been ill, having suffered several strokes, since the late summer of 1940, and thus a new head of state had to be chosen. It was considered that the choice should be made by the same electoral college as had elected Kallio; it would scarcely have been possible to arrange new elections because of the great movement of population after the peace in March. Various candidates had been discussed during the run-up to the election, Mannerheim among them. However, on 6 December Paasikivi was summoned by Molotov and told that the Soviet Union could not give its approval to four possible candidates: Mannerheim, Svinhufvud, Tanner and Kivimäki. This was yet a further scandalous interference in Finland's internal affairs.

During President Kallio's illness the prime minister, Ryti, had stood in for him. On 17 December Mannerheim called on Kallio, who had always loyally supported him and whom he had grown to appreciate as a fine and good man. That evening he recounted the visit in a letter to his sister Eva Sparre. 'I am pleased I managed to present the first commemorative medal to our outgoing President, who invited me to the palace to say farewell. The President was greatly moved and this did not fail to affect me to some extent. His strokes have left only light traces. Both his legs are working, as is his left arm, and he talked for quite a while without noticeable difficulty. He puts his right arm inside his jacket and was amused when I told him that in this respect he resembled Napoleon. Towards the end of my visit he was a little upset and then he had difficulty in speaking.'

The final farewell to Kallio was dramatic. Mannerheim and many senior officers accompanied him to the train north. As he stood 'in front of the centre of a guard of honour to the sound of the Pori March, the poor, sick President's strength deserted him, and he staggered and collapsed and quite simply disappeared within his overcoat. With a great effort we succeeded, with the chief of the general staff, the President's aide-de-camp and a couple of other people in getting hold of him and carrying him to the carriage a few paces further on. A couple of doctors who had rushed up found him unconscious, and the end came a few moments later. Yet another victim of war had done his duty and departed into the unknown. It was an impressive death, if such is wanted, but one would so gladly have let this dutiful man spend the evening of his life far from the bustle of the world among his own people in his beloved Nivala. . . . Mrs Kallio, who is a wonderfully courageous and warm-hearted woman, invited us into the carriage where with the words ''Now the journey is accomplished'' she came out and thanked everyone. It was all deeply touching.'

Risto Ryti was elected as the country's new President on 19 December. 'I am pleased about Ryti's election,' Mannerheim wrote in a letter, 'but I almost believe that he would have done a greater service to the country [by continuing] as prime minister than in his new appointment. However, we must hope that, where our strength proves slight, higher powers will direct the destiny of the country.'

As to war in the east, Hitler's decision to attack the Soviet Union in the spring of 1941 became firmer during the previous autumn. Molotov's visit to Berlin in November led to no new agreement; Hitler rejected outright his attempt to get a free hand to incorporate Finland into the Soviet Union in the same way as the Baltic states – Mannerheim was immediately informed of this Russian proposal through Göring's Swedish relative, Erik von Rosen. German plans for the campaign were worked out and confirmed on 18 December. The code name, as later became well-known, was 'Barbarossa'. An important element in German planning was surprise, and it is clear that Hitler succeeded in keeping the plans secret. This was of great military and political significance – not least for Finland, which therefore could not be a party to the invasion plans.

During the autumn of 1940 Talvela was sent to Berlin three times on different missions besides the agreement on the transit of troops. He was to work for better contacts with the German military authorities than had existed after the Winter War. Relations with the Soviet Union were already at such a low level that Mannerheim as well as the government thought they should examine the possibilities of obtaining German support of some kind if the Soviet Union launched a new attack. Mannerheim wanted to point out to the German command that two regions, Åland and Lapland, were especially difficult to defend. He hoped also to obtain Germany's consent, and perhaps its support, for persuading Sweden to help defend Finland against a fresh Soviet attack. It cannot be claimed that

Talvela's Berlin missions achieved any great success. He had to wait a considerable time before he could even gain access to the men in key positions. He was able to state the wishes of his government to the chief of the German naval staff, Vice-Admiral Otto Schniewind, but he found no interest in an active Germany policy on Finland's behalf. Eventually, however, he succeeded in obtaining an audience with Göring and Halder, the chief of the general staff. Halder asked him various questions which may well have been connected with the planning of grand strategy that was then in progress. However, Talvela was unable to answer them, and he in turn was given no definite information about Hitler's war plans. Still, his final report to Mannerheim makes it clear that he had heard rumours which he dared not commit to paper – probably the same as later reached the Finnish legation in Moscow concerning German invasion plans, to which Paasikivi at any rate was unwilling to give credence. Erik Heinrichs, when sent to Berlin in January 1941 to give a lecture about the Winter War, also received no definite information about Hitler's aggressive plans. He too had the opportunity to meet Halder, who repeated the questions already put to Talvela about how long it would take Finland to mobilise and what were its strategic plans if a war with the Soviet Union were to break out.

The Finnish leaders thus lived for a long time in a state of uncertainty about the future. The opposite has often been claimed, but what undoubtedly had been understood in Helsinki was that Finland could count on German military support if the Soviet Union should threaten its existence. Plans were also made for Finnish operations if that situation arose and resulted in military cooperation with German forces. Several senior German officers visited Helsinki in February, but this failed to clarify Hitler's political aims; however, the Germans occupying Oslo had by then prepared a plan for operations in the Petsamo region, code-named 'Silver Fox'. The German General Hans von Seidel made contact with Mannerheim on a visit, and out of courtesy was invited to tea at his home, but the conversation did not touch on politics or even on current military problems. More important was the rather longer visit to Helsinki of the German Colonel, subsequently Major-General, Erich Buschenhagen. This was to play a big part during the war responsibility trial, because the Russians extracted a deposition from Buschenhagen in 1945 on supposedly close collaboration with Mannerheim and his staff. However, sources from the late winter of 1941 made it clear that while Buschenhagen certainly informed himself on conditions in Finland that had relevance for the conduct of a war in Lapland, his information-seeking was mainly concentrated on preparing for possible future cooperation if Finland should be attacked by the Soviet Union, and not linked to the Barbarossa plan.

For Finland the winter of 1940–1 was overshadowed rather by Soviet demands and threats. Throughout the winter the Soviet leadership kept up its demand for influence over the Petsamo nickel mines, which it had already put forward in the autumn. Nickel, which was essential for steel manufacture and thus for arms production, was then a rare commodity. The Finnish side was unwilling to accept these demands in their entirety; above all, the Finns wanted the management of the mining company to continue to be Finnish. They had tried to reach a compromise in negotiations during the autumn, but in vain. On 14 January 1941 Moscow sharpened its tone; other methods would be found of attaining their objective if the Finnish government continued to be awkward. A week later Paasikivi was summoned to a new conversation where the Soviet side were even more threatening. At the same time Moscow halted exports to Finland and recalled its minister from Helsinki – the connection with the nickel question was obvious. Russian troops were thought to be concentrating along the Finnish frontier. Because of this Mannerheim wanted to mobilise two divisions, but Ryti did not think there was any reason to do so. The Finnish government still wanted to try for a compromise solution over the management of the planned firm, and discussions continued till 12 February when Molotov, unwilling to abandon the Soviet demand for complete authority over the mining concern, broke them off.

Two contrary schools of thought on the future development of Soviet-Finnish relations were now revealed within the Finnish leadership. Paasikivi insisted on yielding to Soviet demands, and prepared a proposal for an agreement on those lines. The basis for this was his absolute conviction that German-Russian cooperation would continue. The inner circle in Helsinki saw the matter differently; they did not know if Germany would go to war with the Soviet Union, but they had become aware since the autumn of German interest in Finland's continued existence, and were therefore anxious not to take any steps which might lose them German support. They believed that complete acquiescence in Soviet demands regarding Petsamo must imply that risk. Mannerheim and Walden submitted their resignations on 10 February 1941, because they did not want to be parties to a policy which resulted in one concession after another. The resignations were not accepted, and Paasikivi's approach was thus prevented from succeeding.

When Paasikivi returned to Helsinki in March, his view of the Petsamo question and that of the inner circle were at odds with each other. They did not differ over the significance of German support, but over whether such support would actually be provided. Paasikivi attached the greatest value to information he had received from German diplomats in Moscow, especially from Count von der Schulenburg, the ambassador, who had gained the impression from Hitler that a war with the Soviet Union was out of the question; he would not be so imprudent as to go to war with Stalin. Both Paasikivi and Schulenburg were admirers of Bismarck's policy of attempting to maintain good relations between Germany and Russia, and believed that Hitler was ready to continue it. Thus Paasikivi considered it essential to make concessions to Soviet wishes he feared a repetition of the catastrophic policy pursued by the Finnish government in the autumn of 1939, and wanted no part in it. He was, as he wrote to Ryti, a pro-German of long standing, but his standpoint was now determined by his view that German-Soviet friendship was assured.

In 1939 Mannerheim and Walden had shared Paasikivi's opinion of Soviet policy, but they could not do so now. On the contrary, they saw a great danger in a concession to the Soviet Union because Hitler would scarcely approve of access to the Petsamo nickel mines being lost to Germany, since the mines were vital for its arms production. The discussions which the temperamental Paasikivi had with Mannerheim and Walden were once again heated, as was often the case.

Certain signs began to be apparent in 1941 that a great war in the east was being prepared. German troop concentrations along the eastern frontier naturally did not escape notice. However, it did not seem likely that Hitler intended actually to attack the Soviet Union so much as to build up a strong position in advance of new discussions with Moscow after the meeting with Molotov in Berlin had led to no results. In Helsinki, as in other capitals, no one was prepared to believe that Hitler would embark on a gigantic struggle with the Soviet Union as long as the war with Britain continued.

But other ideas too were current in Finland at that time. These were partly inspired by wishful thinking about a war in the east which would restore to Finland what it had lost and more besides, and partly by German propaganda regarding a future war which had been quietly spread about. There were also those who, out of opportunism or genuine admiration for the Germans, were prepared to express solidarity with the National Socialist state. Under the direction of some convinced pro-Germans, enlistment was started in the spring of 1941 for a Finnish SS battalion. Neither Finland nor the Soviet Union was a belligerent at that time, and Mannerheim strongly disapproved of the enterprise. He considered that Finland needed its own men for its own defence. But there was nothing he could do to prevent the recruiting, and three more years passed before he could take action.

In April Mannerheim found the situation in Scandinavia sufficiently quiet for him to go to the Swedish spa, Ulricehamn, to recover his health; on 8 May he was back in Finland. Meanwhile, on 22 and 24 April the Swedish military attaché in Helsinki, Gösta von Stedingk, had sent rather detailed reports to his government of the German concentrations in the east which came very close to the great secret, mentioning that he had received this information from his German colleague Colonel Rössing. Finland was supposedly committed to take part in a war of aggression due to begin at the end of May, and considerable cooperation was said to have taken place. Stedingk's reports were largely based on a combination of the rumours then current in Finland; still, they caused a stir in Stockholm where those in charge of foreign policy had hitherto refused to believe reports that Germany was planning a major attack in the east. Günther, the foreign minister, committed a grave indiscretion by asking the German minister, the Prince of Wied, a question about whether or not Hitler intended to go to war in the east. Stedingk himself has recorded that Günther even mentioned who had been Stedingk's informant. In his anxiety, Günther decided to go across to Helsinki to obtain clarification of the matter, since Wied had categorically denied what Stedingk had reported.

At the same time as Günther's visit, Ryti received Dr Ludwig Weissauer, the secret emissary for Ribbentrop and Hitler (see above, page 132), who told him what was being spread throughout Europe, namely that Hitler had no intention of going to war with the Soviet Union but wanted negotiations with Stalin. The German minister in Helsinki, Wipert von Blücher, simultaneously denied all reports of German aggressive intentions; he and his staff had been instructed not to discuss preparations for war in the east or Finland's possible role in such a war with the Finnish authorities. As in Finland, so in Moscow the Germans denied that Hitler was considering an invasion; Ambassador von der Schulenburg was recalled to Berlin to be assured of this by Hitler himself, and he believed it. Stalin did not want to look reality in the face, and allowed himself to be caught off-guard. Thus when Ryti told Günther that he did not expect war to break out in the east, he clearly did so in good faith, and Günther returned to Stockholm reassured. However, after what happened subsequently, he believed that Ryti had deliberately misled him, a misjudgement which undoubtedly aggravated his relations with Finland.

However, a real stormy petrel now appeared in Helsinki in the person of Karl Schnurre. On 20 May 1940 this German diplomat and Scandinavian specialist, of ministerial rank, visited first Ryti and then Mannerheim. He had been sent at the behest of the officers at OKW (*Oberkommando der Wehrmacht* – supreme army headquarters) to prepare the cooperation which would become essential when the Barbarossa plan was put into operation. But he was not to mention anything about this, and was only to discuss a hypothetical Soviet attack on Finland and its consequences. Schnurre hinted at the possibility of a German-Soviet war, as a last resort, but he emphasised that Hitler wanted to negotiate and not to wage war. Finland ought to determine what frontier alterations it desired, and then Germany would help to attain them. At the same time Schnurre delivered an invitation for some senior Finnish officers to be sent to Germany for discussions. According to what he shortly afterwards told Mannerheim, Ryti replied that Finland did not want to be drawn into the European war, and that the Finns did not intend to attack the Soviet Union but would fight in self-defence if attacked themselves. In such an event they would be grateful for assistance. As to the invitation to send a military delegation, the Finns did not want to reject it in the present situation. However, Mannerheim wanted to send officers who were below the most senior level of command; he wanted to emphasise, through their lower rank, that the journey was concerned with information only. Schnurre was dissatisfied with this because a number of senior officers would be receiving the visitors on the German side. To oblige the Germans Mannerheim therefore chose Erik Heinrichs, in whom he had complete confidence, as leader of the delegation, but in his instructions Heinrichs was forbidden to conclude any binding agreements. The delegation left on 24 May for Salzburg, where they were received by Field-Marshal Keitel and General Alfred Jodl from supreme headquarters. Jodl gave the customary appreciation of the situation: negotiations with the Soviet Union were in progress, and a preventive war might become necessary. Not a word was said about the Barbarossa plan. However, as distinct from earlier occasions, war was now said to be not just conceivable but probable.

Jodl wanted answers to three questions, all of them assuming an outbreak of war, notably a Soviet attack on Finland: could the Finnish army offer any help to the Germans in northern Finland if they should need it? Was there a possibility of concentrating German troops there? And in what way could the Finnish army go over to the offensive in the southeast? Heinrichs said that he had no authority to adopt any position with regard to the German proposals, but he answered the three definite questions on the assumption that a war had broken out in which the Finnish government had decided to undertake military operations. As to operations in the south-east, he offered no enlightenment at all. They also discussed the position of Hanko and the Åland archipelago. From Salzburg the Finnish officers travelled to Berlin, where General Halder, the chief of the general staff, presented a different picture of the situation. He said that war in the east was very probable, and he stated Germany's wishes more precisely. These were concerned with, among other things, Finnish cooperation in an attack on Leningrad – against which Heinrichs immediately reacted. He later asked Commodore Bürkner, the head of the foreign intelligence section (*Amtsgruppe Ausland*) at supreme headquarters, which statement was to be taken as authoritative: Jodl's in Salzburg or Halder's in Berlin. Bürkner replied that Jodl's was the conclusive one.

These conversations had been unsatisfactory from the Germans' point of view, and Jodl therefore sent Buschenhagen again to Helsinki, accompanied by Colonel Kinzel, to continue them. On 3 June discussions began with the Finnish command, and developed in a way that surprised the Finns. Hitherto Mannerheim and those responsible for Finnish foreign policy-making had been able to avoid binding Finland to any particular German political programme, but this was now much more difficult. They had to admit that current developments made the outbreak of war increasingly probable, that to continue keeping a distance from Germany represented too great a risk. Finland would be dependent on German support either if Hitler attacked or if he succeeded in reaching a new agreement with Stalin by negotiation. What had occurred from August 1939 onwards told its own story. When Buschenhagen now demanded whether Finland was willing to join in an aggressive war, and what it would require if it were to do so, Mannerheim tried at first to lead the discussions towards the question of what Finland would do if attacked again by the Soviet Union. In this eventuality, he said, it would defend itself, but if it became drawn into a German-Russian war as a result of such an attack, Finland would not require anything, but would be grateful for help.

Buschenhagen wanted a clearer reply, and therefore Mannerheim referred the question of Finnish policy to the government. He was able to recommend that certain Finnish formations in the far north should be placed under German command, which would bring about practical advantages. He could also permit a concentration of German troops in Lapland: the relatively small Finnish force there could be increased by two German divisions, one technically on its homeward journey from Norway and the other on the way out. Thus two German divisions could be concentrated in Lapland for a while within the formal framework of the transit agreement covering men on leave. The original German proposal was designated Operation Blue Fox. This measure could form a link in the German attempt both to exert pressure on the Soviet Union and to safeguard Finland while negotiations with the Soviet Union were going on. At the same time it could form part of the deployment for a German aggressive war. The government approved this 'transit of men on leave'.

The reply to the principal German question on Finland's willingness to take part in an aggressive war was formulated with great care so that the Finnish government would retain its freedom of action. Finnish cooperation was assumed to depend on a later decision by the government, but the aim, as Ryti and later Heinrichs believed, was to reject the German demands. The minutes composed by the two sides reflect their respective wishes. The Finnish version emphasises the country's wish to remain neutral. During the following weeks a certain degree of collaboration developed between the Finns and the Germans. There was no agreement on waging war in common, or on military operations of any kind, but it is clear the leaders in Helsinki believed that, in the situation as it was, they had to take account of German wishes. They were equally afraid of a new German-Soviet understanding and of a Soviet attack. They collaborated with German naval units and German forces in general to an extraordinary extent. General Waldemar Erfurth arrived from Berlin as representative of supreme headquarters, and Mannerheim sent Lieutenant-General Öhqvist on a reciprocal mission to Berlin. Altogether the situation was judged to be so serious that the army was mobilised on 14 and 17 June. A Soviet attack was expected – with good reason, because Soviet diplomats had said on several occasions that in the event of a war with Germany the Soviet Union would immediately launch an offensive against Finland.

On 22 June the code word 'Altona' – which meant the implementation of Barbarossa – was sent out to the German forces. The great war between Hitler's Germany and Stalin's Soviet Union was beginning. The Finnish authorities had been uncertain up to the last moment of what would happen. The German attempts to conceal and deceive had been remarkably successful. When Erfurth came to the general staff building in Korkeavuorenkatu in Helsinki at lunch-time on 22 June, Mannerheim had already gone out and Erfurth had to tell the great news to Erik Heinrichs. The principal reaction of Heinrichs was surprise, since the sheer scale of an attack on the Soviet Union had made such an undertaking seem to him improbable. This outbreak of war, however, did not have any immediate consequences for Finland; no agreement had been concluded with Germany which bound the Finns to take part.

Tense days followed. The Soviet air force delivered heavy air raids on Finland on 22 and 25 June, and this eventually proved decisive. The raids were subsequently justified by the fact that German troops were present in the country, but the bombardment was not directed solely against those troops. We can never know how events might have developed if the Soviet Union had not attacked Finland; in a letter to Eva Sparre on 17 July, Mannerheim said that Finland would probably have kept outside the conflict. In fact the government prepared a declaration of neutrality.

To Mannerheim it was a fundamental and self-evident fact that the war, involving Finland, which had now begun had been caused by Soviet aggressive actions, and was not an element in Germany's Barbarossa plan. To make this unambiguously clear, it was represented as 'the Continuation War', in other words a consequence of the Winter War which had started with the Soviet attack on 30 November 1939. However, Mannerheim also understood that his country would probably not be able to maintain its neutrality once both great powers were at war and fighting had spread northwards. One or the other would find reasons to make moves against Finland.

Formally, Finland's political and military leaders were free in their relations with Germany in 1941, and during the years that followed they succeeded in maintaining that position. Time after time they gave indications that they were at liberty, whatever Hitler might say, to conclude a separate peace with Moscow. Only in the desperate situation of June 1944 did Ryti promise not to enter separate peace negotiations, but Finland was able to cut loose from this commitment quickly enough when Ryti resigned the Presidency and Mannerheim succeeded him.

XIII

THE CONTINUATION WAR

1941–1944

Thus Finland found itself at war again with its great eastern neighbour, yet this time it was not alone as in the Winter War. It could count on Germany to help with arms, food and fuel. The German command had been anxious to transfer a division from Norway to the new theatre of operations even before Finland had entered the war, but it was necessary for the Swedish government to give its permission before this could be done. The transit proposal was made on 22 June and acceded to the next day after a severe crisis over it in the Swedish government. Mannerheim was nevertheless rather embarrassed to have this formation – the German 163rd infantry division, commanded by Lieutenant-General Engelbrecht – at his disposal. He did not consider that he needed it, and indeed its combat value soon proved rather limited.

When the war went on for longer than had been expected, Finland became increasingly dependent on Germany, and thus withdrawal from the war became ever more difficult. But for Mannerheim, as for many other Finns in leading positions, the close relationship with Hitler's Reich was and remained a severe problem. He had become known ever since the First World War as a critic of German aggressive policies and the arrogant German mentality, and what he had seen of National Socialism had disgusted him and aroused his apprehension.

Despite Finland's difficult situation, Mannerheim's aim was to preserve the country's independence. The Finnish army's military successes in reconquering lost territories and advancing into Eastern Karelia made this easier, but the commander-in-chief's own personality and bearing had a significant influence. He managed to avoid military operations which might have jeopardised relations with the Soviet Union, and he successfully opposed all German attempts to carry out Hitler's racial policy with its persecution of the Jews. He was able to help in individual cases of suffering, and he criticised Nazi oppression in the Baltic countries, Poland and the Soviet Union. However, he also regarded it as his duty not to aggravate the essential cooperation with the Germans. He had done the same in 1918 when he had treated von der Goltz and his staff correctly and civilly although in many ways he disapproved of the German general and his involvement in politics. When Gripenberg remarked to him in 1942 that Germany was sure to lose the war, Mannerheim warned him against saying so if, as he hoped, Gripenberg became foreign minister. 'Think of me,' he urged his colleague, 'I am loyal!'

Cooperation and coexistence with the German military and politicians put a considerable strain on the commander-in-chief's tact and self-control, but he was helped by the reserved attitude to people which over the years had become an element in his personality. With several of the German representatives with whom he came in contact Mannerheim was able to achieve good personal relations. Some, especially of the older generation and in particular General Waldemar Erfurth, he liked and repected; and for his part this cultivated, gifted and correct officer, with his traditional concepts of honour, came to feel a devotion bred of respect towards Mannerheim, whose background was so different from his own. On the other hand Mannerheim felt antipathy towards the German commander-in-chief in Norway, Colonel-General R.N. von Falkenhorst, and got on better with his successor as commander of the Mountain Army in the north, the lively and dashing Bavarian, Eduard Dietl.

However, current developments not only brought Finland closer to Germany as a great power but led it into a conflict with Britain. Mannerheim was of course compelled by the circumstances of the time to see the Soviet Union as the country's principal enemy and Germany as a helper, but the British government, and Churchill in particular, saw the situation from precisely the opposite point of view: Hitler's Reich was a deadly threat not only to Britain but also to the whole of human civilisation, and all cooperation in Germany's war was therefore inexcusable. Finland thus merited a hard fate. However, Churchill's categorical condemnation of Finnish policy was not endorsed by the entire British leadership, and in the Foreign Office it was commented that now – as distinct from during the Winter War – the interests of Britain and Finland unfortunately collided, and those threatened by a monster do not choose their means of defence after carefully considering the balance of world politics.

Mannerheim himself attempted, as far as was in his power, to reconcile the growing conflict of views. He was anxious to release from internment the British volunteers who had remained in Finland, and he ensured that they were able to enter Sweden. For this he was warmly thanked by Britain. When the foreign minister Rolf Witting, under German pressure, broke off diplomatic relations with London in July 1941, it was against Mannerheim's wishes, and he protested when Witting tried to blame this step on the army and on Mannerheim in particular. The responsibility certainly did not lie in that quarter.

Supreme Headquarters was again located in Mikkeli, and as before the commander-in-chief and his closest colleagues took offices in the large senior school building in the centre of the town. For the greater part of the Continuation War Erik Heinrichs served as chief of the general staff; however, during the major offensive operations of 1941 Mannerheim appointed him to the important post of commander of the independent Karelian Army formed at that time. In his absence Major-General Tuompo, head of the adjutant-general's staff, and then Major-General Hanell took Heinrichs' place, but when operations in Karelia were halted at the end of the year, Heinrichs returned to headquarters. Aksel Airo, as in the Winter War, was quartermaster-general and headed the operations division; he was generally regarded as the brains of the headquarters staff. In Vilho Petter Nenonen the staff had an extremely capable artilleryman. For most of the war Colonel Aladár Paasonen was head of the intelligence service. Lieutenant-Colonel Ragnar Grönvall served as before as aide-de-camp; he remained with Mannerheim in this capacity during his Presidency and also served the two succeeding Presidents, Paasikivi and Kekkonen. At headquarters also was General Erfurth – mentioned above – who served as liaison with the military command in Germany.

As in the Winter War, Mannerheim was able to carry out his duties with surprising and impressive energy and purposefulness. He could be criticised for retaining the power of decision himself to an excessive extent and for intervening too readily in matters of all kinds without regard to the established chain of command. But his motive was efficiency and the need to get things done properly. 'In his great eagerness for work he wants to do everything himself,' Erfurth noted in his diary. 'He also wants to know everything that is going on . . . During my long service I have experienced many commanders-in-chief but none where headquarters receded into the background to quite the same extent. Mannerheim's authority can perhaps be compared with that possessed by Seeckt [the general who led and preserved the German army in the 1920s].' The intensive work at Mikkeli meant that existence in that relatively isolated place was less monotonous than might otherwise have been feared. As Mannerheim wrote to his sister-in-law Palaemona, 'I am so strenuously occupied from morning till late at night that one does not notice how the weeks hasten by. Yes, the recent years have also been so full of work and above all full of threatening excitement that they have changed at almost the speed of pictures at a cinema.'

Many have praised the Field-Marshal's invariable courtesy and the attentiveness which he showed to his guests down to the minutest detail. His politeness and general manner of conducting himself inevitably had an effect on his surroundings, though he also possessed a marked aloofness and by means of this and, when needed, a sharply ironical turn of speech, he was more than able to maintain his integrity. Erfurth wrote in his memoirs from Finland that Mannerheim's headquarters was at that time the one where good form was most conspicuous. At headquarters, as throughout the armed forces, Mannerheim not only enjoyed a unique authority but also received the devotion and loyalty that are bred of esteem. The qualities he required of his colleagues were above all sincerity and truthfulness; he had no use or sympathy for yes-men. As long ago as the Russo-Japanese War he had criticised in his diary officers who submitted fallacious reports in order to ingratiate themselves, and thus became unreliable. Every officer was to express his true opinion, even if it was a dissenting one, because the nature of the commander-in-chief's work required that he should always know the truth. The only proviso was that the correct forms of conduct should be observed. His close collaboration over many years with such independent men – each in his own way – as Airo and Talvela proves his ability to accept advice and respect the opinions of others.

As commander-in-chief Mannerheim had the sometimes difficult task of choosing those who would command army operations at a high level. 'Among my duties is the appointment of the army's generals in the way that I believe can best serve the defence forces,' he wrote to a deserving officer (Öhqvist) who was disappointed at not being given a task for which he considered himself particularly suitable and for which he had long prepared himself. Decisions of this kind could be very sensitive; a mistake could not only have a bad effect on the man passed over but could also cause harm throughout the entire army. Mannerheim was never sentimental over such matters, nor did he take account of irrelevant considerations; and indeed he has never been criticised on these grounds. On the other hand he could be indulgent towards military leaders of genuine merit who had overstepped the limits of what was proper. In such cases he tried to find solutions which would remove difficulties and restore cooperation. But in the last resort he would unhesitatingly use his full authority to reestablish order when it had been disturbed.

Mannerheim had a great interest in people and in detail, and wanted appreciation and gratitude to be shown when these were appropriate. The system of orders and medals was a practical way of doing thus, and to this end a new order was introduced into the Cross of Freedom, which had been founded in 1918; it was called the Mannerheim Cross and had two classes. Modelled on the corresponding decorations of the great powers – the Cross of St George in imperial Russia which Mannerheim had received in 1914, the Victoria Cross in Britain, and the *Pour le mérite* in Germany – it was to be awarded to both officers and other ranks in the armed services for exceptional achievement. The first recipient was Lieutenant-General Ruben Lagus, the tank commander, and the second was Talvela.

Mannerheim was undoubtedly a humane leader; with his long experience he could easily understand the soldiers and their problems. According to Heinrichs, he could be a hard commander when necessary, but, as another general (Adolf Ehrnrooth) testified, 'his concern for his soldiers knew no bounds . . . With a few simple words he could show the human qualities within him. Over important disciplinary matters, he could be sympathetic towards those who had strayed. When soldiers refused to fight or deserted, he recommended reprieves if they returned to the front and their subsequent conduct was good. Talvela and others, on the other hand, considered a reprieve to be the root of all evil, and that death sentences were beneficial for the fighting morale of the troops. Mannerheim was of the contrary opinion.

Already during the hard days of the First World War Mannerheim had come to realise – after several tragic episodes – the need to avoid operations which would lead to excessive loss of life, but in the Finnish army, with its limited reserves, such caution was imperative. The commander-in-chief's consideration extended also to the families of those who had died in battle. The Finnish army was unique in attempting to return the dead to their home districts and to provide them with fitting graves and memorial stones. In the same spirit he took up a suggestion sent to him by a soldier to show gratitude and sympathy to the mothers of the dead. On 10 May 1942 he issued his notable order of the day 'To the Mothers of Finland' as a gesture of thanks to those who had brought up the young men of the country and especially to those who had lost one or more sons. The order of the day concluded by announcing his award to the mothers of Finland collectively of the Cross of Freedom as an expression of the country's gratitude and esteem. This order of the day hangs in all Finnish churches.

At the beginning of the war three Soviet armies were concentrated on the frontiers of Finland under the command of Marshal Voroshilov. One was

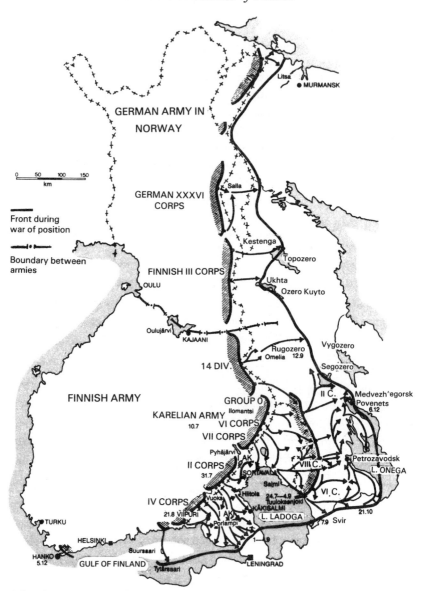

The Continuation War

Main offensives, summer 1941

From the south: IV Corps (Oesch) attacked towards Viipuri on 22 Aug.;
II Corps (Laatikainen) towards the Vuoksi-Suvanto line on 21 July; VII Corps
(Hägglund) towards Hämekoski and the shore of Lake Ladoga on 10 July;
VI Corps (Talvela) towards Värtsilä and Korpiselkä on 6 July. III Corps
(Siilasvuo) began its offensive towards Ukhta and Kestenga on 1 July after the
German XXXVI Corps (Feige) and the Mountain Corps Norway (Dietl) had
begun their attack on 29 June.

The President gives a reception for Paasikivi's government, November 1944. J. K. Paasikivi is to the left of Mannerheim

The Marshal as President with Prime Minister Edwin Linkomies

The outgoing President leaving the Palace after visiting his successor, J. K.
Paasikivi

Mannerheim convalescing in Switzerland in 1947

Mannerheim's villa in Kaivopuisto

Mannnerheim's study at his villa in Kaivopuisto

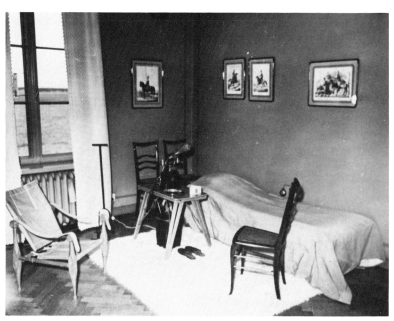

Mannerheim's bedroom at his villa in Kaivopuisto

The funeral cortège on its way to the military cemetery at Hietaniemi, 4 February 1951

Guard of honour at Mannerheim's grave, 4 February 1951

on the Karelian isthmus, a second north of Lake Ladoga and a third further north. The Finnish military command had to choose between a passive defence and offensive operations, and it quickly chose to attack. From a military viewpoint they wanted to push back the Russian forces and control the air bases near the Finnish frontier. The population from the ceded territories would be able to return home, with considerable advantage to the country. A further consideration in planning operations was how far to cooperate with the German armies.

It became necessary rather quickly to decide on the direction the offensive would take. The alternatives were to advance first via Viipuri on the Karelian isthmus, with Leningrad as the ultimate objective, or to move north of Ladoga and follow its shore as far as the mouth of the river Svir. It had been assumed by the Germans in preliminary discussions that in the event of war the Finnish army would attack across the isthmus, but Mannerheim dissented: he was absolutely opposed to an operation directed towards Leningrad. When he agreed to continue as commander-in-chief, he made it a condition that this was something the army would never do. With the new outbreak of war, when future operations had to be decided, it quickly became clear that they ought in the first place to be directed towards the regions north of Ladoga (a variation recommended by Talvela involved the incursion of troops into the valley of the Vuoksi to save the important and valuable industrial installations there). On 10 July the offensive could begin. The concentration of troops had been completed, and the German invading armies in the Soviet Union·had attained the objectives which had been considered essential for these Finnish operations: Dvinsk (Dünaburg, Daugavpils) had fallen and the offensive had turned northwards.

Before the Finnish advance Mannerheim issued the 'Karelia' order of the day. This has been severely criticised, being expressly cited as proof that Finland was not only trying to get back what had been taken from it by the peace treaty of March 1940, but was also harbouring imperialistic designs, specifically the incorporation of Eastern Karelia into Finland. Plans on these lines had existed ever since 1918; Eastern Karelia was an area inhabited by Finnish-speaking people and of cultural importance as the homeland of the singers of the Kalevala, the Finnish national epic. During the insurrection of 1918 Lenin had held out the prospect of this part of Karelia being handed over to a Finnish Soviet Republic, and Mannerheim had answered this propaganda with a declaration that he would liberate the Finns' kinsfolk there and not sheathe his sword until that task had been accomplished. Now he made a reference to that order of the day – somebody on the staff had chanced to see the order and had reminded him of it. One can scan the carefully composed text of 1941 in vain for any clear expression of annexation plans; what, however, is clearly expressed is the hope of freedom for the population of Eastern Karelia.

For operations towards Ladoga-Karelia, Mannerheim had selected VI Corps commanded by Talvela and VII Corps under Hägglund, and because it appeared too difficult to direct formations from Mikkeli, especially as they would be operating in distant and difficult terrain, he combined the two corps into a separate Karelian Army commanded by Erik Heinrichs. This decision disappointed Talvela, who had hoped for an independent command directly under the commander-in-chief. VI Corps formed the centre and VII Corps the right flank of the Karelian Army. In a vigorous and skilfully planned attack, Talvela succeeded in breaking Soviet resistance, and at the end of a week the north shore of Ladoga was in his hands. Talvela was now eager for a rapid offensive down to the mouth of the river Svir – a bold operation which matched the wishes of the Germans, who regarded a linking-up on the Svir as the goal of German-Finnish cooperation. However, Finnish operations did not proceed at this pace. Mannerheim and Heinrichs, who feared a reverse, were wary of advancing so rapidly, and Talvela's troops were obliged to halt on the old frontier. It was to be a long delay, and meanwhile VII Corps managed in the course of heavy fighting to drive the Soviet troops out of Sortavala and the north-west coastal region of Ladoga which they were holding. The left flank of the Karelian Army met with even greater difficulties in advancing in the area of Suojärvi. The help which should have been given by Engelbrecht's 163rd German division proved of little value in the unfavourable terrain. Only at the end of August did Finnish troops succeed in driving the enemy out of this district near the old frontier.

Towards the end of July the time had come for an operation towards the Vuoksi, Viipuri and the Karelian isthmus, a vital area from the Finnish point of view. The Germans no longer objected to this since they had not advanced towards Leningrad and the Svir as rapidly as they had anticipated. Operations began on the left flank of the front with an attack towards Hiitola, with the aim of cutting the enemy's communications between the Karelian isthmus and the troops north of Ladoga. The fighting was hard and long. Already before it was over, General Pajari's division swung down towards the Vuoksi; on 21 August it reached the great waterway, and the attack on Viipuri could be started. This involved a deep enveloping movement against the enemy forces. The Soviet command could not fail to be aware of the danger of being encircled, and evacuated the town, so that on 29 August the Finnish flag could once again be raised over Torkel Knutsson's ancient castle in Viipuri. Mannerheim thanked General Oesch, the commander of IV Corps, 'for these very capably led and brilliantly executed actions'. To the President of the republic he sent the statement that 'the blue and white flag is again flying on the tower of the old castle as a proof of the heroic deeds of our soldiers and as a symbol of the inner strength of our people and their readiness to make sacrifices'. On 16–18 September he visited the isthmus and Viipuri. He was able to see how Leningrad lay open to German artillery fire, and his thoughts turned to the imperial city where he had lived and worked for so many years.

In the far north German troops under Falkenhorst had attempted an offensive in the direction of Murmansk and Kandalaksha on the White Sea and towards Loukhi. After initial successes these various operations had come to a halt; the resistance of the Soviet troops was tough and the terrain along the Arctic coast was difficult for troops unfamiliar with it. Towards Murmansk the Germans did not succeed in crossing the river Litsa, and in the direction of Kandalaksha General Feige's troops got into increasing difficulties. By early September it could be said that the areas of Karelia ceded in the March peace had been recovered, and the old national frontiers restored – although Hanko still held out in the west. Now the momentous question had to be decided whether the army was to remain on the frontiers or whether operations should be continued into Soviet territory – and, if so, how far.

After these great operations had been completed, Mannerheim summed up his thoughts in a sad letter to Eva Sparre: 'We have occupied a great part of the territory taken from us when peace was last concluded and also a bit of Far Karelia. However, the fighting is incredibly hard, even harder than last winter, perhaps because this time we do not have the cold and snow as allies. The Bolsheviks are fighting with a tenacity and bitterness which borders on the incredible, especially because it is occurring everywhere. . . . However, pleasure over the successes that have been won is overshadowed by daily reports of the numbers of killed and wounded, which show how many brave Finnish boys will never again see the homes for the defence of which they took the field.'

On one sector of the front the Finnish army reached the old frontier much earlier. But Talvela's corps had been ordered to halt on the line Tuulos-Vieljärvi, on the north shore of Ladoga. Talvela was eager to continue towards the Svir, and considered that the commander-in-chief was mistaken in not utilising the favourable situation he was in. He expressed regret at the delay in a letter to Walden, and Erfurth too became uneasy. Mannerheim was clearly only half-hearted about resuming the offensive: what did he have in mind? He obviously considered that to continue the advance was still too dangerous. The attack demanded thorough preparations, and Finnish casualty figures were worrying him increasingly. German operations had by no means achieved the success that an optimistic command had predicted, and were meeting resistance that became tougher all the time. The German political and military leaders had committed some fateful mistakes, and Mannerheim became increasingly cautious. Finally events moved towards a crisis. German supreme headquarters wanted a speedy advance to the river Svir, and Finnish cooperation with German troops south of it. Keitel openly requested on 2 August that the Finnish army should take part in a planned attack on Leningrad, with the city being surrounded and bombarded from the air and with artillery. The Germans asked for Hanko to be captured as soon as possible.

Mannerheim gave a very negative reply. He did not intend to cross the old frontier on the Karelian isthmus, and Finland wanted nothing to do with an operation against Leningrad, since the necessary equipment simply was not available. East of Ladoga the Finns had planned an advance only as far as the Svir and no further. If new military objectives were being proposed, he would have to consult the government. Thus when he replied to Keitel on 24 and 26 August, he rejected most of the German requests. He strongly emphasised that too much was being demanded of the Finnish people; the casualty figures were alarming, and the government would make difficulties if he asked for its agreement to a crossing of the old frontier. Mannerheim's only concession was to agree so re-start the advance towards the Svir. An attack on Hanko was out of the question. Thus in one respect Mannerheim's reply to the Germans was perfectly clear: he refused to attack Leningrad – a decision to which he held fast throughout the following years. As he observed in his memoirs, it represented a carefully considered political position. The Soviet state must not see an independent Finland as a threat to its second city.

The German army command were disappointed by Mannerheim's rejection of their wishes, and were unwilling to accept it. His decision has sometimes been criticised even by Finns, and Talvela thought it a mistake of world-shaking significance. Mannerheim's letter of 26 August was cautiously worded, but Erfurth suspected that the Field-Marshal was inclined to break off the advance to the Svir. Opinions in the government were divided as to whether the army should continue into Eastern Karelia or not. Ryti, like Mannerheim and Walden, seems to have had doubts, especially because industry and the economy generally felt the drain of manpower into the armed forces. At that time the more pro-German ministers were still in a minority, albeit a strong one.

In the end Ryti changed his mind, and on 31 August gave Mannerheim authority to go on to the Svir and Petrozavodsk. The reasons behind this fundamental expansion of the scope of military operations were primarily strategic. As long as Soviet forces controlled the broad area adjoining the frontier, their air force threatened the Finnish population. Whether or not it was intended in the future to incorporate the occupied Soviet territory into Finland can only be conjectured, although it is clear that Mannerheim was not eager for a solution of that kind. In any case he was careful after the Eastern Karelian districts had been occupied not to show any such intention but to observe scrupulously the rules of international law relating to occupation. On the other hand it is plain that he and many others in the political leadership hoped for a revision of the frontiers in accordance with old plans, both Finnish and Russian, which would make possible the transfer to Finland of areas where Finnish was still spoken. That other groups, particularly in Finnish-speaking Finland, hoped for bigger territorial gains is also clear.

On 4 September the operations began which were to lead to the occupation of Eastern Karelia. At first the offensive was directed towards the Svir. The right flank of the Karelian Army, commanded by Talvela, rapidly broke through the Soviet defence (Heinrichs was in overall command of the Army) and the armoured units commanded by Major-General Ruben Lagus advanced through the gap. On 5 September the town of Olonets (Aunus) was captured, and two days later the Svir was reached. Already on 8 September Mannerheim, accompanied by Walden, went to visit this sector of the front and was able to look out across the mighty river. At the same time the left flank of the Karelian Army had taken up its starting positions for operations against Petrozavodsk, the capital of Eastern Karelia on the shore of Lake Onega. The attack, carried out by Hägglund's VII Corps, began on 15 September parallel with the advance of units of Talvela's VI Corps towards the town. Soviet troops abandoned the defence of Petrozavodsk on 10 October and it was occupied by the Finnish army. The next objective was the isthmus between Onega and the big lake of Segozero (Seesjärvi), and the town of Medvezh'egorsk (Karhumäki) at the north-western corner of Lake Onega. The attack was begun immediately. Mannerheim wanted no delay, as it was necessary to take advantage of a favourable situation. However, the army met with stiffening resistance in difficult terrain, and it was some time before it had

the great Masel'ga (Maaselkä) isthmus in its hands from the Stalin Canal
in the south to Segozero in the northwest.

The Finnish successes in Eastern Karelia alarmed the Soviet leaders. In
London the Soviet ambassador, Maisky, put pressure on Churchill to try
to halt the advance, which might be aiming at the White Sea and the
important Murmansk railway. Stalin demanded a declaration of war by
Britain, and Churchill judged a concession to his wishes on this point to be
necessary. The German armies were making considerable advances on the
central front at that time. Britain therefore sent Helsinki an ultimatum,
which was reported at a government meeting on 28 November attended
by Mannerheim. Moreover, on 29 November Churchill (remembering
their earlier conversations and correspondence) addressed a personal and
private message to Mannerheim which was transmitted by the American
minister in Helsinki, Arthur Schoenfeld. In it he asked for the Finnish
offensive to be broken off, failing which he would be compelled to take the
regrettable step of declaring war. He wrote that he was convinced of a final
Allied victory, even more so than he had been during the critical years 1917
and 1918. Churchill emphasised that the need was not to make a public
declaration, but only to stop the fighting – for which the severe winter
would be sufficient reason. It would be painful to Finland's many friends
in Britain if the country had to sit in the dock with the guilty and defeated
Nazis.

Churchill's letter reached Mannerheim on 1 December after he had
returned to Mikkeli, and he hastened to write his reply – which, he
thought, had to be brief and phrased in general terms. He referred to the
impossibility of halting military operations before the army had reached
the positions which, he believed, would afford the necessary security. It
would be regrettable 'if these operations undertaken for the safety of
Finland should bring my country into conflict with England, and it would
deeply grieve me if England felt itself compelled to declare war on
Finland.' The reply concluded with thanks for Churchill's kindness in
sending a personal message 'in these critical days'. It can be seen, if the letter
is read carefully, that Mannerheim had gone as far as he could possibly go at
that time; He pointed out that the the war was being fought with the
object of safeguarding the security of Finland, and was thus not bound up
with Germany's aggressive war. He mentioned that operations would be
concluded when the intended positions had been reached; what these were
he could hardly specify. Those who have criticised Mannerheim for not
giving Churchill more detailed information have not taken into account
that at Mikkeli they had to assume that Churchill was acting on the

instigation of the Russians, that he had informed Maisky both of his ultimatum to the Finnish government and of his personal letter to Mannerheim, and that he would therefore also inform him of Mannerheim's
reply – all of which did indeed happen. The British declared war against
Finland on 6 December. On the 5th, Finnish troops had taken
Medvezh'egorsk, and on 7 December they occupied Povenets (Poventsa).
With that the operations ceased.

The decision to occupy Eastern Karelia as far as the western shore of
Lake Onega had thus been carried out. The occupation did indeed give
Finland the desired protection against Soviet attack by air and land
throughout the war, but it had led to an unwanted conflict with Britain.
It also became a handicap later in the war when the military situation in
Eastern Europe underwent a radical change; this clearly complicated the
possibilities of reaching a peace agreement in that public opinion in Finland
found a retreat from these successfully conquered positions difficult to
countenance. Furthermore, there was division within the country over the
wisdom of the Eastern Karelia operations; in a letter to Ryti on 25
November 1941 Tanner criticised them strongly and dissociated himself
from all annexation plans.

The advance of the army to Medvezh'egorsk opened the possibility of
an attack on the Murmansk railway. Such an operation would finally cut
the railways, and Allied consignments of arms to the Soviet Union through
Murmansk would become impossible, with significant consequences for
the Soviet capacity to wage war. As long as the Russians controlled the
railway from the Arctic ocean down to Belomorsk (Sorokka) on the
White Sea, transportation could continue unimpeded because a railway ran
from Belomorsk via Archangel into the interior of the Soviet Union. The
other branch of the railway, running from Belomorsk to Leningrad, had
been cut by the Finnish army during the occupation of Eastern Karelia.
Earlier, on 25 September, Mannerheim had intimated to Keitel that he
was willing during the winter to mount an attack on the Murmansk
railway and particularly Belomorsk from the positions which he would
have attained in Eastern Karelia. However, this plan lost its interest when
Hitler announced on 10 October that the bulk of the Soviet armed forces
had been broken and destroyed; there remained no reason to use an attack
to tie Soviet forces down in Finland. The German army command in the
north soon took up the question again, since the victorious communiqués proved not to correspond with the true situation, but a Finnish
attack towards the White Sea coast had now become politically more
sensitive. Ryti, disquieted by reports that Siilasvuo had attempted to

advance on Loukhi, approached Mannerheim – who shared his apprehension but indicated to Erfurth that he would attack Murmansk, Kandalaksha and Belomorsk later in the winter. Erfurth proposed that operations should be coordinated under Mannerheim's command, an idea Mannerheim did not reject. During November and December various operations of this nature were proposed and discussed – none of which, however, was to be put into effect before the military situation had radically altered.

At this point the German supreme headquarters decided to reorganise its forces in the north. Falkenhorst was to return to Oslo and the command in Lapland was to be assumed by General Eduard Dietl (see above, page 146), who had distinguished himself in the capture of Narvik the year before and who enjoyed Hitler's confidence; his first task, Keitel announced, would be to prepare an attack on Kandalaksha in March 1942. However, in his reply of 4 December Mannerheim was already guarded. He pointed out the difficulties for the Finnish army in joining in such operations so long as the Germans had not captured Leningrad. But he suggested the possibility of Finnish troops being used against Belomorsk.

On 14 December Mannerheim was at last able to leave for the German headquarters at Rovaniemi to discuss on the spot the cooperation between them in the fight against the Soviet Union – Falkenhorst had not yet left for Norway – but no decision was taken. After returning to Mikkeli Mannerheim set out in a letter to Keitel his reasons for aiming a decisive blow at Belomorsk, but in the letter he made it clear how well he understood the great difficulties the Germans were encountering on the Eastern Front and the problems faced by both the Finnish army and the civilian population at home. The German supreme headquarters was immediately prepared to abandon plans for an attack on Kandalaksha and was willing to approve the proposal for an attack on Belomorsk in March. Mannerheim had thus gained the right to decide this sensitive question: he now had the option of carrying out the operation or not, depending on future developments in the Soviet Union. However, the situation became easier for Finland when the Red Army evacuated Hanko on 3 December. 'Hanko was a relief,' Mannerheim acknowledged in a letter, 'yes, a great relief, for the narrow headland with numerous defence lines would have been a hard nut to crack and would surely have cost much blood.' In his order of the day of 7 December he thanked the troops at Hanko and, at the same time, the Swedish volunteers who had taken part in its encirclement.

As 1941 ended it was clear to Mannerheim that Finland was facing a dangerous crisis. The German army had not been able to attain its objectives. Leningrad was indeed beset on many sides, but its communications with the east were maintained by land and water across Lake Ladoga. The Germans had succeeded for a short time in occupying the important railway station at Tikhvin on the line to the east, but the Red Army had recaptured it. In any case the war would not be over before winter as Hitler had promised. Mannerheim's misgivings increased all the time. To an old riding companion in Sweden he wrote that it remained to be seen when Hitler's victorious communiqués would be fulfilled. 'The world situation is now so complicated that it is most discreet not to play the prophet, and in war this is even a golden rule' (to Clarence von Rosen, 9.3.42).

An important factor in the conduct of the war proved once more to be the severe and early winter. In Finland they knew from their experience of the Winter War what this could mean. Sometimes, Mannerheim wrote on 20 November 1941 to Eva Sparre, the seasons are as confusing as what we see in the world we live in. 'A professor had promised a long Indian summer and there are still to be found those who believe in the professor's infallibility and . . . are unshakably convinced that ice and snow will soon give way to sun and warm winds. Those who think otherwise are our brave soldiers in their cold and damp trenches and dugouts.' Some weeks later he noted a temperature of $-25°$C. ($-13°$F.) on the Svir. 'I am afraid we have a winter ahead of us like that of 1939–40.' He was shocked when he heard that the German troops were without winter equipment. Casualties through frostbite, he told Erfurth, weigh more heavily on a commander's conscience than battle losses.

The German armies had one reverse after another. On 20 December Erfurth was summoned to the commander-in-chief, who was unable to hide his concern and who, as Erfurth realised, had finally lost his confidence in the German command. From that day Mannerheim's policy and strategy changed. When Erfurth referred to some soothing words by Witting about the military situation, Mannerheim rejoined that the foreign minister understood as much about war as Alexander the Great's horse. When Ryti visited headquarters on 21 January 1942, Mannerheim told him: 'The catastrophe is already upon us.' Mannerheim made the logical deductions from this judgement. Finland had to avoid steps which could worsen relations with the Western powers; it also had to prepare an exit from the great war, which was altering its character exactly at this point. On 7 December 1941 Japanese aircraft bombed Pearl Harbor, and the United States thus became a belligerent. Hitler further hastened the course of events by his own declaration of war on the United States, which meant that the greatest armed conflict in world history had now begun.

Mannerheim clearly saw the importance of this for Finland: it was essential at all costs to avoid a conflict with the United States, even if Germany and the United States were now at war.

Heinrichs was sent to Germany in January 1942 to see Hitler and thus – so it was hoped – to obtain some enlightenment on the military and political situation. The meeting proved interesting, but far from encouraging for the future. Talvela was later sent to Berlin as a military observer, to provide continuous reporting on the war situation. However, it soon became clear that under the influence of his surroundings Talvela was tending to be over-optimistic. The headquarters at Mikkeli had other, more sceptical informants.

To begin with, Mannerheim broke off all offensive operations, although it was often difficult to combine this passivity with the degree of cooperation which Finland's relationship with Germany made necessary, and so avoid Hitler's reprisals. He openly announced that he would make no more attacks. From the start of 1942 the Finnish army remained stationary, thus tying down the important German forces in the north, and from this time the front remained unchanged right up to the dramatic days of June 1944 when the Soviet offensive began. However, there were a number of fresh German proposals for attacks at different points on the long front between the Arctic coast and Ladoga, which were always to be aimed at a final breach of the Murmansk railway. Keitel tried in a letter of 28 January 1942 to bind Mannerheim to his own outline of a winter operation against Belomorsk, and soon afterwards Dietl, the new German commander-in-chief, appeared at Mikkeli to try cajoling Mannerheim into greater activity. He now met with a definite refusal: there was no possibility of attacking Belomorsk in March or in the summer. A short time later, he explained to Gripenberg, who had come to Finland from London, that he should naturally take Belomorsk, but it was now impossible because of the United States (25 May). Strategic objectives had to yield to political ones.

For the time being it was too dangerous to take direct peace initiatives, since counter-measures by Hitler were always possible. However, Mannerheim was fully conscious that because of the way events were shaping, an attempt to end the war would soon follow. The war had followed diplomacy, he said in May 1942, but 'when war ends, diplomacy begins again.' It was necessary to be prepared in advance for negotiations. He was anxious to 'emphasise the importance of having as our diplomatic representatives men who have a good capacity for work, are well trained, disciplined, educated and with good judgement. It probably will not be long before the country's defence will be completely taken over by our representatives abroad, and then it will be a little late to seek out suitable ones who will represent this skill alongside other emissaries' (to Rudolf Walden, 19.4.43).

Mannerheim did not allow himself to become disheartened and pessimistic in the light of the threatening prospect now opening up. Nor did German victories cause him to lapse into wishful thinking. The one threat he perceived with complete certainty was Bolshevism, and he did not see Finland's salvation as being solely through Germany, as Paasikivi still did. They should seek support for Finland's peace endeavours first of all in Sweden. Ever since the beginning of the Continuation War in June 1941, Mannerheim had tried to prevent anti-Scandinavian statements from appearing in the press and elsewhere, and had to fight numerous battles with political romantics or opportunists. Swedish help might mean anything from deliveries of food supplies and arms during a delicate transitional phase, to efforts to get the Germans out of northern Finland or promising a future defensive alliance. Similar plans were also developed in various quarters in Sweden, but German pressure was still so strong that the Swedish government did not dare to take them up. It was still necessary to wait. The Germans had sufficient forces in 1942 for a major offensive in the Soviet Union. If such an offensive were successful, Finland might be able to find some way of withdrawing from the war.

In the midst of these preparations, on 4 June, came Mannerheim's seventy-fifth birthday. Initially he did not want the occasion marked in any way, thinking it would be in poor taste to have a celebration at headquarters while officers and men were roughing it and seeing their comrades being killed. But the President and the government wanted to call on him, and this he could not prevent. Finally, he made a counter-move by insisting that if his birthday had to be celebrated, then the whole army should be given a treat of some sort. However, during the evening of 3 June Mannerheim received a message which totally altered the programme: Hitler, chancellor of the German Reich and commander-in-chief, was flying in from his headquarters the following day. He arrived with Keitel, his ADC General Schmundt, and the Reich press director Otto Dietrich. The visit might be politically difficult, but it had no immediate political content and was rather an expression of Germany's admiration and regard for Mannerheim and Finland. Mannerheim interpreted the German dictator's courtesy visit as an apology for having left Finland to its fate during the Winter War. Throughout the visit Hitler appeared reasonable and restrained – a role he was able to play when necessary. 'The Reich chan-

cellor won much sympathy through his simplicity and natural behaviour,'
Mannerheim commented. He had feared – groundlessly, as it turned out –
that Hitler would press demands for cooperation in offensives against
Belomorsk or Leningrad. In fact Finland had for the time being ceased to
be a focus of attention. German offensives were now planned in the south,
against the Ukraine and the Caucasus.

Mannerheim's own demeanour during the visit was watched with close
attention. His critical attitude towards Hitler's activities was scarcely a
secret, but it was understood that there would hardly be any possibility of
expressing personal feelings. Observers quickly recognised that his long
experience of appearing in public on ceremonial occasions, stood him in
good stead, and they could not help admiring the assurance and faultless
politeness with which he was able to deal with his scarcely welcome guest
without binding either Finland or himself in any way. The German military
attaché Colonel Kitschmann noted the bizarre contrast between the
Finnish marshal, 'a man of the world, a tall and slender apparition, with
the unaffected movements of a *grand seigneur*', and 'Hitler, thick-set, with
lively, definite movements and an imperious expression'. Thus a small
nation, due to the personality of its representative, was able to hold its own
against the leader of a great power. In Paris it was said with satisfaction
that he had shown great dignity. Hitler for his part was highly satisfied and
dreamed of providing Finland with a prominent place in the future world
order he was planning.

Thus 4 June 1942 assumed a pattern entirely different from what
Mannerheim had wanted. The government expressed its appreciation by
conferring on him the new rank of 'Marshal of Finland'. He valued highly
the address by organised labour paying homage to his work for national
unity, and emphasising the importance of his great efforts to remove the
traces of the events of 1918. Mannerheim replied that he saw in that a proof
'that my dreams and efforts over decades have now been fulfilled'.
Mannerheim tried to sum up his impression of the great day in a letter to
his sister Eva Sparre' 'It was all . . . moving. A people who are fighting
for the right to live in the land which their forefathers made with great
toil, and where the church bells daily toll their sons into their eternal rest,
and who show me in such an overwhelming way their trust and recognition, a trust which you understand is difficult to bear . . . It was something
very different from the seventieth birthday which you attended. Nothing
of the glamour of pageantry which you remember, but now instead a
gathering in the midst of a world war of men in positions of responsibility,
of whom even the youngest had shown what they were capable of . . .

The government's address and the President's speech were very fine, and moving in their recognition of work and intentions which unfortunately have not been even remotely realised. I do not need to tell you how overcome I was . . . by all the kindness, esteem and gratitude of which I was the object, but the celebration of an anniversary is one time when people are always apt to go to extremes, perhaps even more so than usual when it is likely that this will be the last.'

Hitler's visit demanded a return in kind, and thus on 27 June Mannerheim set out, taking with him Tuompo, Paasonen, Grönvall and others. He regarded the journey with alarm and anxiety, fearing once again that there would be increased German demands. But even now Finland's war was evidently not reckoned as of any great importance. Instead the Finns were to hear a lecture from General Alfred Jodl on the planned great offensive against Southern Russia, a region which Mannerheim had known well in the First World War. Göring interposed with the remark that the war would soon be decided, and Mannerheim was duly sceptical. Even now Mannerheim's character made an impression, as Talvela, who had come from his observation post in Berlin, noted. Several times Mannerheim could not avoid showing by his reserved manner his deprecation of strikingly arrogant and extravagant behaviour, especially that of Göring.

Before the tide of war finally turned, the Germans again raised the question of Finland's position. At the height of the summer, when Hitler assumed that Soviet communications in the south could be broken and that he could seize the Baku oil wells, the Germans began drawing up plans for the northern front. Leningrad was to be taken and the Murmansk railway cut. Finnish troops should take part in the realisation of these plans, now called Operations *Nordlicht* ('northern lights') and *Lachsfang* ('salmon catch'). The Finnish army ought to seize Belomorsk and Dietl's troops Kandalaksha, and the Germans and Finns in conjunction would take Leningrad, by September at the latest. To Mannerheim this prospect was displeasing, since he assumed that an attack on Belomorsk would bring down an American declaration of war on Finland, which ought to be avoided if possible. On the other hand great caution was necessary with the Germans. He decided to lay down various conditions for possible cooperation, for example over Belomorsk; raising objections, he thought, was their only way of gaining time. He was suspicious of the wide-ranging German plans, while Talvela was enthusiastic and Ryti considered that Finland should give in and cooperate with the Germans. In this situation Mannerheim decided to send Erik Heinrichs to Hitler for one more conversation in the hope of acquiring information. Mannerheim now heard that the attack on Leningrad, commanded by Field-Marshal Manstein, was to begin on 14 September and that Finnish cooperation was required in certain respects. Erfurth's comment was that over this the Finns would, as before, show themselves to be extremely reluctant.

The written reply to the various requests of the Germans was composed with great care, but it was soon to lose its significance, since the military situation in the east put paid to all the German plans. The great offensive planned for the summer of 1942 was to have shattered Soviet resistance, but it led instead to German reverses which altered the whole strategic situation. Hitler's attempt to cut the traffic on the Volga became a large-scale catastrophe, and ended in the capitulation at Stalingrad. The Finnish army was directly affected when the German encirclement of Leningrad – never complete – was broken by the recapture of Petrokrepost' (Schlüsselburg) by the Red Army. From Leningrad a Soviet offensive could be aimed at the Karelian isthmus, with the effect of surprise because the troops could be concentrated in the metropolis and its outskirts unobserved.

Naturally, such important events influenced the political situation in Finland. It was difficult to make people aware of the world situation as it really was – many were unwilling to recognise the dangers threatening their own country – but caution was necessary in informing the public. Mannerheim was anxious that in any case members of parliament and other people in public life should be correctly informed and not fall a prey to wishful thinking. On 11 February 1943 headquarters arranged for the head of the intelligence division, Colonel Aladár Paasonen, to brief a selected group on the real situation. Paasonen had been able to form a realistic view of the situation through his connections, among whom was Admiral Canaris, head of the German intelligence service and one of the leaders of the resistance against Hitler. What Paasonen revealed came as a shock; some refused to believe his statements, and strong indignation was felt. Mannerheim was compelled to let Heinrichs present a more guarded briefing some days later.

Increasingly the old Marshal appeared to represent the country's last asset. His name was now being mentioned in connection with the approaching presidential election in March 1943. The Agrarians and the Swedish People's Party in particular put forward his candidature. But he refused to be a candidate if he could not count on a unanimous election. Eventually the Conservative Party and the Social Democrats proposed the reelection of Ryti. This election was followed, in accordance with custom, by the formation of a new government – which, in this case, marked the beginning of a change in the direction of policy. As prime minister Ryti appointed Professor Edwin Linkomies, a representative of the Conservative Party. The choice of foreign minister was important. Mannerheim's candidate was still G.A. Gripenberg, with Carl Enckell in second place, but he could not get his way with Ryti – although he did later succeed in having Gripenberg appointed minister in Stockholm, perhaps the most important diplomatic post in the current situation. Eventually Henrik Ramsay, who was prominent in shipping circles, and an experienced negotiator with good British connections, became foreign minister. Mannerheim, to whom he was a close friend, valued his prudent and amiable nature.

In any case it was clear that Finland would now attempt to extricate itself from the war and from dependence on Germany – a task as difficult as it was important. Mannerheim, with the approval of the political leadership, had sought contact with the government in London through his British connections, but for this work Ramsay was the primary instrument. However, the strongest pressure on the Finnish government now came from Washington. Ramsay received various proposals from the Americans for mediation, but when he tried to obtain precise information from them about Soviet peace conditions he was not successful. The US leaders plainly did not want the trouble this would involve, nor were they interested in trying to induce Stalin to moderate them. The Finnish government, in their view, ought to initiate peace negotiations itself.

Ramsay's first initiative was far from being a success. He wanted first to discuss the situation and Finland's scope for action with Ribbentrop, the German foreign minister, and therefore travelled to Berlin on 25 March 1943. Mannerheim was informed of Ramsay's journey and doubted its wisdom. During his conversation with Ribbentrop, Ramsay mentioned the attempt of the United States to mediate. The result was only an outburst of rage on the German side, a categorical rejection of the Finnish proposal, threats and, above all, a demand for a political agreement which would pledge Finland to fight alongside Germany. Hitler had previously shown no interest in such a demand, but now that Germany's situation had deteriorated he saw it in a different light. It would have signified the end of Finland's peace endeavours. Ramsay's trip to Berlin also threatened to lead to a breach of the fragile connection which Helsinki had hitherto succeeded in preserving with the United States. Washington had already delivered a memorandum to that effect to their chargé d'affaires, Robert McClintock, when at the last moment he received a counter-order to exercise greater consideration towards Finland; this was prompted by the

Germans discovering the Russian mass graves of Polish prisoners-of-war at Katyn.

Mannerheim had been ill during this eventful period; his doctor had found it necessary for him to spend some time in a mild climate, and so he had gone to stay in Lugano in southern Switzerland. When he returned on 10 May 1943 the political leadership had to decide their attitude to Hitler's demand that Finland should commit itself to his war policy by treaty. Mannerheim used all his authority – successfully – to prevent concessions, and Hitler was induced to abandon his demand. Mannerheim wanted at the same time to use the situation to continue the process of extricating Finland from dependence on Germany. Early in 1941, between Finland's wars, a volunteer Finnish SS battalion had been set up by private initiative. This had been against his will, but in June 1943 the soldiers' contract with the Germans expired, and Mannerheim was finally able to arrange for the SS command to relinquish the Finnish auxiliary force. The negotiations leading to this conclusion were difficult and sensitive, and undoubtedly left the German side with a feeling of mistrust and let-down. The outcome showed that the balance of power in Europe was continuing to change.

The main line of Mannerheim's peace efforts was still to seek Swedish support. While Ryti still believed that it was possible for Finland to quit the war by agreement with Germany and hoped for a separate German-British peace, Mannerheim saw clearly the necessity of freeing Finland completely from the Reich. The summer of 1943 threw up an interesting parallel in Italy, where a similar approach was attempted and on 25 July Mussolini was overthrown. At Mikkeli they waited in suspense to see how Hitler would react.

At meetings on 1 and 2 July in Helsinki with the inner cabinet and Gripenberg, Mannerheim put forward a plan for withdrawal from the war. In order to obtain security, they should try to obtain a guarantee of Finland's continued independence, preferably a defensive alliance, from Sweden; otherwise its future alongside an aggressive great power would always be precarious. Walden emphasised that to gain confidence in Sweden they would have to break down anti-Swedish sentiment in Finland. They also discussed the possibility of getting support for the removal of the German troops in Lapland. Gripenberg stressed that Finland had to make clear that it had never had any intention whatsoever of annexing the region of Eastern Karelia. But when he tried in Stockholm to gain a sympathetic understanding for Mannerheim's schemes, he encountered a negative attitude from Hansson and Günther, who did not now want Sweden to become involved in peace efforts but preferred to remain passive.

However, in the late summer of 1943 a new Soviet peace initiative began which led finally to real peace negotiations in the spring of 1944. Certain conversations which the Soviet minister in Stockholm, Mme Kollontai, and the counsellor of her legation, V.S. Semenov, had with the Belgian minister, the Prince de Croy, were noteworthy. The Soviet side suggested the possibility of negotiations, and in Stockholm the invitation was judged to be honestly intended; Stalin would surely give Finland back its 1939 frontiers. Ryti and Mannerheim were both prepared to accept a peace on terms such as these (there would be bitterness in the army if all the gains in Eastern Karelia had to be given up, but it was agreed that this had to be done). They worked out a reply emphasising Finland's readiness for peace if the country received its 1939 frontiers with certain adjustments in favour of the Soviet Union. When Semenov received this answer, the tenuous negotiating contact broke. Stalin's conditions were clearly more severe, but at that point they had not yet been made known.

The way events were now moving in Europe required the Finns to act with extreme caution. In reaction to the Italian government's attempt at the beginning of September to go over to the Allied camp, German troops on 8 September occupied the greater part of Italy. This was a terrifying warning. Finland was dependent upon German supplies and weapons, and therefore could not risk a breach. Without having changed his mind on the peace question, Mannerheim on 21 October urged restraint on the government. This advice was justified, because Hitler had in fact already cut off part of the supplies to Finland. At the same time he sent General Jodl to give Mannerheim a description of Germany's strength, albeit in guarded terms, and simultaneously to make soundings and veiled threats. He observed that it was open to Germany too to make a separate peace with the Soviet Union.

However, it was not long before various signs of Soviet interest in peace were discerned once again. A background to these signs was the Allied foreign ministers' meeting in Moscow in October and the conference of the war leaders in Teheran on 28 November-1 December 1943. There they had decided to demand unconditional surrender by the Axis powers; this was an initiative of the United States, which however made an exception of Finland. In Stockholm Mme Kollontai made numerous attempts to spur the Finns into peace negotiations and held out a false prospect of favourable conditions – they would be allowed to keep Viipuri and Hanko, she said, using the same tactics which had been successful in March 1940. It was necessary to get the Finns to Moscow because after that they would find it difficult to return to cooperation with the Germans.

The consequence was that the Swedish government again pressed the Finnish government towards peace overtures, as it had done during the Winter War: Mannerheim was of course quite clear that the Swedes were looking after their own interests, but he was disposed to follow their exhortations. He judged the situation mainly from the military stand-point. But when the question arose of formulating a reply to Moscow, he wanted instead to send somebody there for actual negotiations, rather than letting the exchange of views proceed through the Swedish foreign minis-try and its permanent secretary Erik Boheman. But the government con-sidered this too risky. When the written reply that had been drafted was submitted to him for comments, Mannerheim thought it too abrupt, and succeeded in giving it a more positive content and a more courteous formulation. His position was stronger now than in the autumn of 1939 when he had been unable to gain a hearing for similar views. However, some weeks later the government in Helsinki was prepared to send a representative to Stockholm or, in an emergency, to Moscow to obtain clarification of the Soviet conditions. But who was to be sent? Paasikivi wanted this mission and was eventually given it. Before taking its decision, the government had been subjected to both political and military pressure, since the Soviet Union was now beginning air raids on Helsinki and other places.

As a first step Paasikivi went to Stockholm on 11 February to meet Mme Kollontai. He returned on 24 February, bringing with him certain Soviet conditions. These were very severe: Finland's frontiers were to be those agreed in the March peace, and all German forces in the country were to be interned. The inner circle of the government were shaken by these conditions, and Linkomies proposed that Mannerheim should take over the post of President immediately, reckoning that only he would be able to conclude a peace on such terms. This was opposed by Tanner. The imme-diate question now was whether negotiations should be continued at all, and if so in what form. A debate in parliament showed that there was a majority in favour of continued negotiations, but the vote had been won by an alarmingly narrow margin. Could they really proceed with opinion so divided?

In this situation Paasikivi appealed to Mannerheim on 4 March. Only the soldiers could inform the people accurately about the war in the east:

'You are the only man the Finnish people trust.' Could the Marshal not see some members of parliament to give them the necessary briefing? Finland no longer had any real choice but to accept hard conditions, and they would get harder still as time went on. Negotiating at least offered the possibility of some improvement. This was the way they had to go. Paasikivi recalled the decisions that had been made in the autumn of 1939, with such unfortunate consequences. Appeals to try to influence the course of events came from another direction too. The King of Sweden in a confidential statement expressed the hope that the Marshal would be able to unite the Finnish people in support of a decision to begin peace negotiations. Unfortunately King Gustaf's statement became known to the press and thus news of it travelled abroad.

However, Mannerheim was not prepared to act on these lines. As commander-in-chief he was entitled to express his opinion on military questions, if called on to do so, but not on political ones; these were for the government. He did not believe that the army could withstand an attack by the Red Army, using its full strength. Therefore, when an answer had to be sent to Moscow on the peace terms offered to Paasikivi in Stockholm, Mannerheim was anxious that its preparation should be gone into in detail and with great care – advice that was not followed completely, with the result that the Swedish foreign ministry, which was to transmit the reply, advised a different form of words. A new reply was therefore drafted, in which the government emphasised its desire for peace and recalled its obligation under international law to expel the German troops if the country again became neutral. Negotiations were requested.

Moscow was not satisfied with this reply, and on 12 March demanded in the form of an ultimatum that the Helsinki government should accept the proposed peace terms before 18 March and pledge itself to intern all German forces in the country. The government was united in rejecting this demand, and at this point it also asked Mannerheim's advice. Talking with Ramsay by telephone on 13 March, he emphasised that they ought to take account of the great military resources of the Soviet Union and the fact that Finland would be standing alone, unable to count on help from anywhere. Mannerheim thought that nobody could fail to understand his meaning, but the government's reply to Moscow, although conciliatory in tone, signified nonetheless that it did not want to continue negotiating on the basis of the latest preconditions. This seemed to break the negotiating contact, but Moscow quickly played a new card by inviting Finland to send delegates to obtain more precise information concerning the Soviet peace terms. Again Mme Kollontai held out the prospect to both Sweden and the Finns that these terms would be surprisingly mild. Despite its mistrust of such a promise, the Helsinki government decided to accept Stalin's invitation, and Paasikivi and Carl Enckell (who spoke Russian perfectly) were chosen as delegates. A proposal, mooted by some Soviet diplomats, to send Mannerheim to Moscow came to nothing. The delegation left on 25 March.

What had happened during the peace negotiations four years earlier was now repeated. Once the Finnish delegates had arrived, the terms were made significantly harder: they included even the cession of the Petsamo region and an indemnity of an amount unheard of at that time, 600 million US dollars. The German troops were to be interned within a period eventually prescribed as two months. As soon as the delegation returned to Helsinki on 30 March there were intensive discussions, first within the narrow circle and then in the entire government with Mannerheim present. Ryti had also summoned him, together with Heinrichs, on 1 April to discuss the situation with Linkomies, Walden, Tanner and Reinikka, the minister of agriculture. During this meeting Mannerheim was almost inclined to recommend an agreement on the Soviet terms, although he was dissatisfied with Paasikivi's way of conducting the negotiations, which had come to his knowledge through the minutes drawn up by Georg Enckell as secretary of the delegation. An agreement in any case would not be upset by the tough conditions concerning the German troops, although as commander-in-chief he would have great difficulty in carrying them out. He was more hesitant over the huge war indemnity, the significance of which he did not believe himself competent to judge. The decision was slightly delayed because Easter week now intervened. Various proposals were made for obtaining Mannerheim's opinion in writing, but eventually they were abandoned; the decision had of course to be a political one, and on that he was not prepared to give an opinion. Dietl, who visited headquarters at this time, found him deeply pessimistic.

The government and parliament finally decided on 12 April not to accept the Soviet peace proposal. There were many reasons behind this. Besides misgivings over the indemnity and the necessity to intern the German troops within so short a time, there had to be anxiety regarding the reaction of the Germans. For as long as Hitler's army controlled the Baltic states and the coast of the Gulf of Finland, there was every reason to expect heavy German reprisals, including the bombing of Helsinki, which was unprotected; Hitler's actions against the attempt by Hungary to break itself free was yet one more cautionary example. However, in the last resort it was the government's inability to reach unanimity on the peace terms that proved decisive. The Agrarians – including Reinikka – threatened to resign, and Ramsay therefore considered it preferable to wait for a more favourable opportunity. In London Churchill explained that he well understood Finland's plight; the demand for the internment of the large German forces in the north, like the indemnity, was too severe. However, his appeal to Stalin to modify his attitude regarding the nine German divisions was in vain. In Stockholm too Moscow's diplomacy caused shock and disappointment; it was embarrassing to have been hood-winked once again. Mannerheim was dissatisfied with the outcome, and was anxious that the government's reply should be drafted in such a way that the negotiating contact should not be broken. Memories of the autumn of 1939 crowded in upon him, but his views were not given a hearing. The weeks that followed were difficult. Mannerheim hoped to the very last that the government would find a new negotiating contact, but it never came. His position was the result not only of a realistic perception of Finland's military capacity, but also of his knowledge of the Russians' sensibilities over their prestige as a great power. There was also a hope that the Russians would not want to divide their forces before the great final battle which was now approaching on the continent, where the Allied invasion from the west across the English Channel was expected.

A major Soviet offensive on the Karelian isthmus would represent an enormous trial and danger. There had been major technical developments in weaponry since 1939, and a country as small as Finland had little opportunity to keep up with the larger powers in this respect. In addition Hitler, out of mistrust for the Finnish peace policy, had stopped the more important arms supplies. It was also clear that the long period of quiet along the fronts since 1942 must have dulled the preparedness of the Finnish forces. Mannerheim had tried to counteract this with inspections and warnings, but this was a factor that could not be ignored. His fears were undoubtedly justified. Accustomed to thinking far ahead, he recommended that they should prepare in time to form an alternative government which could emerge if a catastrophe occurred.

The Soviet offensive on the Karelian isthmus began on 9 June and, as Mannerheim had feared, achieved surprise. It struck once more, and in devastating strength, along the classic military route into the centre of Finland. They had discussed at headquarters whether the defence of the isthmus could be strengthened by the transfer of troops from Eastern Karelia, but Mannerheim did not want to do this to any great extent because of the big Soviet offensive he anticipated on the Svir.

The enemy were now equipped with modern weapons against which the Finns had no defence. The fire from an unprecedented concentration of artillery completely swept away the Finnish front line on the western side of the isthmus. From the air, over 1,000 planes carpet-bombed the defensive positions on the isthmus; then the Soviet infantry went into the attack, supported by numerous heavy tanks. The main defensive position was broken through in many places. Counter-attacking was hopeless, and the situation had all the marks of a total disaster. The defence had a bad day on 10 June; then the third day of fighting brought a glimmer of hope, but on 14 June the enemy succeeded at Kuuterselkä in breaking through the line, previously the second defensive position and now the main one. The Finnish army did better in the central sector of the isthmus, and at Siiranmäki Major-General Martola's division conducted a distinguished and courageous defence which boosted morale along the whole front.

From Mikkeli it was dificult to survey the situation, so complex had it now become. Mannerheim therefore created a level of command between himself and the corps commanders on the isthmus, which he entrusted to Oesch, who had last commanded the troops in Olonets. Oesch considered it necessary to withdraw still further to the last defensive positions on the isthmus – an opinion Mannerheim shared. The fighting was approaching Viipuri, and some days later, on 21 June, the troops were compelled to evacuate the town – a tragedy for the people of Finland.

Also on 21 June, the Red Army's big offensive began on the Svir front, and on the previous day Soviet forces had also advanced on the Masel'ga isthmus further north. An overwhelmingly powerful attack also began across the Svir under General Krutikov, whose forces comprised more than eight divisions, with tanks and modern artillery, and a breakthrough followed. The opposing force of three Finnish divisions, commanded by Talvela, was compelled to retire to the old frontier. Olonets was lost, but it was possible to save the defending troops, who now had hard battles on their hands in the rear lines. Further north the troops were also in retreat, halting at Tolvajärvi and Ilomantsi.

Marshal L.A. Govorov, commander of the Soviet armies on the Leningrad front, and his generals had won considerable victories, and because it was clear that Moscow was now seeking a military decision, Mannerheim asked Germany for help. There was nothing else to be done. At first he proposed the resumption of deliveries of German supplies, which had been interrupted – to some extent secretly – when Hitler learned of Finnish peace moves. Above all there was a need for air support on the western Karelian isthmus and for anti-tank weapons. Firm support was given by Dietl, who travelled down to Helsinki from his headquarters at Rovaniemi. He immediately sent anti-tank weapons from his own stores and called on German supreme headquarters to send assistance quickly to prevent a Finnish collapse. Some days later the German air force provided welcome fighter and bomber support, and more anti-tank weapons were supplied. With this help the Finns were able to meet the Soviet forces on the river Vuoksi. Mannerheim also wanted troops – preferably six divisions. To expedite German assistance, Dietl flew to Berchtesgaden to see Hitler. He proposed that the forces in the north should be withdrawn and committed on fronts where they could be used to better advantage. Above all he requested help for the Finnish army. Hitler rejected the first proposal but approved the second: Finland would receive help, but only on condition that it finally deferred to Germany's wishes. Dietl was to meet Ribbentrop in Helsinki to conclude the negotiations, but on the way there his plane crashed and he was killed.

Meanwhile the government in Helsinki discussed the possibilities of attaining an immediate peace. As a first step the question was again raised of a change of President, whereby Mannerheim would assume political as well as military responsibility. Ryti, Ramsay and Walden went to Mikkeli on 17 June to attempt to persuade Mannerheim, but he rejected the proposal although he urged the formation of a new government. On 18 June there was agreement that the government should be reconstructed in order to be able to get peace negotiations going again. Various proposals were discussed. The post of prime minister was finally offered to Ramsay on 19 June, and he had his list of ministers drawn up that day. However, there was to be no Ramsay government. This was because Mannerheim wanted to wait and see how the situation developed. He was now more optimistic about the military position; the troops were fighting well and it ought to be possible to attain a stable situation before negotiations were started. 'Because the Marshal wants a postponement, it is impossible to achieve unanimity over a new government,' Ramsay observed. The same day, the President had asked the commander-in-chief for a military appreciation of the situation, which he provided in a tone of restrained optimism. 'The enemy's capable leadership and their superiority . . . led to initial successes during which we were compelled step by step to draw back to the general line Viipuri-Vuoksi . . . Gradually during this time we became accustomed to the effectiveness of the enemy's new weapons . . . The spirit of the Winter War [has] awakened in the army.' However, the situation was 'extremely serious'. Mannerheim had reached a more favourable view of the ability of the Finnish army to resist and of how strong the Russian offensive actually was.

On 22 June – an important day – Ramsay put to Mme Kollontai the question whether her government was willing to negotiate, and the answer was a demand for unconditional surrender. There were even some members of the government in favour of surrender, but this was opposed by the prime minister, Ramsay and Walden, and by Mannerheim, whose attitude was certainly influenced by the recently improved prospect of German help. On the same day, 22 June, Ramsay received the surprising news that Ribbentrop was coming to Helsinki. During discussions that followed, Ribbentrop offered arms, aircraft and men for the defence of the Karelian isthmus – with the condition that Finland should sign a treaty undertaking not to enter into peace negotiations with the Soviet Union without Germany's consent. Hitler was thus repeating the demand for Finnish subjection which he had already made in the winter of 1943 after Ramsay had visited Ribbentrop, but which it was then possible to reject. Now the situation was different.

Hitler's conditions for help in the fight against the Soviet Union presented the Finnish leaders with a difficult decision. There were military reasons for accepting them, because without help in the form of weapons they would be in an extremely critical situation. Their need for aircraft and anti-tank weapons was especially desperate. However, they would face political destruction if they entered such an agreement with Hitler. An internationally binding treaty would require approval by parliament, which could not be guaranteed. Eventually a solution was found which avoided a treaty. In a letter to Hitler on 26 June, President Ryti declared that Finland would not begin peace negotiations with Moscow on its own initiative, or come to any peace agreement without Germany's consent, and Ribbentrop was eventually persuaded to accept this precarious undertaking. Mannerheim had recommended this kind of agreement, and considered it unavoidable in military terms. However, when Ribbentrop wanted to meet him at headquarters he refused, pleading the tense situation at the front. 'It was the military command which insisted that war material should be procured at once,' Ramsay informed Gripenberg. 'Ideologies and preferences carry little weight when a nation's life is at stake.' 'A meritorious civic deed' was how Mannerheim described Ryti's action.

The fighting began to die down along the fronts from the middle of July. The opportunity had arrived to try to take the country out of the war, but the situation remained complex. The President was bound by his undertaking to Hitler that neither he nor his subordinates would begin negotiations for a separate peace.

XIV
PRESIDENT
1944–1946

There was only one way forward: a change in the presidency. If Ryti resigned, his successor – according to the Finnish interpretation – would not be bound by the Ribbentrop agreement. In this situation Ryti decided that his authority should be handed over to Mannerheim, and those members of the government who still did not want a peace treaty on Soviet terms could not dissuade him. But was Mannerheim prepared to take up the heavy burden? And was Stalin prepared to enter new negotiations? Was peace attainable without surrender?

On 26 July Rudolf Walden received from Stockholm the important news that Mme Kollontai was interested in peace negotiations. The inner circle round Ryti immediately agreed to offer Mannerheim the presidency, which would mark a significant step in the direction of peace. The decision was made on 28 July at Mikkeli, to which Ryti and Tanner had gone – Walden was already there. Mannerheim made it a condition of his acceptance that Ryti should declare himself willing to resign – there could be no question of his taking any disloyal action towards the head of state. Ryti confirmed that the great political question had been decided, so it now remained for the full government to be informed and to decide what formalities were necessary for the transfer of power. A presidential election as required by the constitution could not be arranged at this time, and thus they had to proceed instead by means of a special law. This was passed by parliament on 4 August 1944.

Mannerheim was inaugurated the same day in the parliament building in Helsinki. Wearing his Marshal's uniform he mounted the podium, and the speaker, Väinö Hakkila, read out the decision of his appointment as head of state; then he took the oath in the country's two languages and, conducted by Hakkila, went to greet the members of parliament. After the brief ceremony he emerged on the steps of the parliament building, and there was a burst of cheering from the crowd which had gathered below. The new President enjoyed the confidence of the public and his presence in the highest office of state aroused hopes for a brighter future. However, it was an old man who came out of the parliament building that day. In his memoirs Mannerheim wrote that it was a heavy sacrifice for him, feeling ill and tired, to take on the task of head of state at the most difficult moment in Finland's history. With the presidential election of 1919 in mind, he recalled that he had never been successful in political activity. 'Now I began to trudge my thorny path,' was how, looking back later, he characterised this moment, as he stood on the threshold of a period of many anxieties and reverses.

Mannerheim's first duty as President was the formation of a new government, which proved more complicated than he had expected. He would have liked his well-tried colleague and friend Rudolf Walden as prime minister, and there was political support for this, but Walden was in poor health and the doctors were absolutely against his appointment, which Mannerheim had to respect. Many other names were mentioned but some were ruled out because of their previous political leanings, while others were opposed by influential groups within the parties. Mannerheim had to threaten resignation if he was not given the support he needed among the politicians. Walden's confidant and one of the most prominent figures in the so-called 'peace opposition' (i.e. those opposed to the continuation of the war), Holger Nystén, compared his friends in that grouping to a flock of hens. Antti Hackzell, the head of the employers' organisation, at last undertook to form a government, and its membership was finally settled – it had a conservative tinge, probably for the sake of a smooth transition. Carl Enckell, an old friend of the Mannerheim and well acquainted with Soviet affairs, became foreign minister. Walden remained as minister of defence. Ernst von Born became minister of justice; out of regard for Mannerheim, the Swedish People's Party, to which he belonged, had been satisfied with only one ministerial appointment, which was necessary to make the formation of the government possible. Of the Social Democrats Tanner remained, but the leading Agrarian, Kaarlo Hillilä, the governor of Lapland province, became minister of the interior.

The immediate task facing the new President and the government was to open up a proper contact with Moscow. Throughout this time the military situation demanded constant attention, with battles continuing on all fronts, though now with an important Finnish victory at Ilomantsi. However, the long-term outlook could only be viewed with pessimism. On 12 August Mannerheim summoned the new prime minister and foreign minister, together with Gripenberg, to Mikkeli. He was fully aware of Germany's deteriorating situation. The Finnish forces could perhaps hold out for a few months if there were a new Soviet offensive, but their power of resistance could also be broken in a few days if the Red Army launched a full-scale attack. Mannerheim did not reveal his plans. On several occasions he let it be known that he regarded his principal task as being the conclusion of peace, but relations with Germany were far too sensitive for him to say more. A premature break would leave Finland completely dependent on Moscow and therefore had to be avoided. Stalin's actual terms were still unknown, and it was essential to find out what they were as soon as possible. It was also necessary to know what degree of support – economic, political and in terms of relief – could be counted on from Stockholm. Relations with Hitler were quickly clarified when two German military leaders, Colonel-General Schörner and Field-Marshal Keitel, visited Finland on 3 and 17 August respectively. Keitel received a clear statement of the Finnish position on the pact: namely that when Ryti relinquished the presidency the Ribbentrop agreement had ceased to be valid. Keitel appeared extremely agitated. However, Mannerheim did not want, at this difficult moment, to omit a gesture of courtesy on the departure of his German guest, who found a large basket of Finnish crayfish awaiting him in the aircraft. Sweden meanwhile clarified its position: it could not enter into any precise obligations in relation to Finland.

On the main European fronts the Allies continued to make headway. Paris fell on 24 August. At the same time, Rumania collapsed. On 24 August Mannerheim took the crucial decision; he had summoned Hackzell, Walden, Tanner and Gripenberg to meet him in the presidential train at Herttoniemi on the eastern side of Helsinki, and they agreed to enter into negotiations with Stalin. Once again, a turning-point had been passed.

It fell to Gripenberg to seek a new contact with Mme Kollontai in Stockholm, armed with a letter of recommendation from Enckell. She received him the same evening following the mediation of the Swedish foreign ministry. However, some anxious and tense days had to pass till 29 August when Moscow's reply was received. This was favourable to the extent that the Soviet Union did not demand unconditional surrender, but there was now a different problem – relations with Germany and the German troops in the north. Before negotiations could begin in Moscow, the Finnish government had to accept two conditions: to break off relations with Germany and to request the Germans in Finland to leave the country within fourteen days. It was now facing precisely the situation that had been feared ever since 1943. If it accepted the Russian preconditions, this would mean an irrevocable break with Berlin, and nothing was yet known of what the Russian peace terms really were, if these proved unreasonable, no return to cooperation with the Germans would be possible. If they rejected Moscow's conditions, the war could start up again and Finland would have to fight without the backing of any other power.

Faced with this decision, Mannerheim arranged a conference to which he summoned not only Hackzell and members of the new government but also Ryti, Linkomies and Heinrichs. He emphasised that if he accepted the Soviet preconditions, they would all be taking a step into the unknown. Ought he to do so? He was more uncertain than before. It was agreed not to break the negotiating contact but to try to persuade the Soviet side to allow a rather longer time for the removal of the German troops. However, this proved impossible. Mme Kollontai expressed annoyance at the delay in the Finnish reply, and some of her remarks were interpreted in Helsinki as an ultimatum. The result was that she received a statement from Gripenberg accepting the preliminary conditions; he did not risk making any reservations over the timetable for the withdrawal of the German troops. Mannerheim had in fact directed him to avoid anything which might give the impression that they were using delaying tactics.

There thus remained the open and immediate break with Hitler's Germany. Mannerheim was anxious to behave correctly up to the last moment, and it was essential too to keep their plans secret for as long as possible – otherwise there was the risk of dangerous countermeasures. The German army leaders and diplomats had long realised that Finland would try to leave the war, and on the very day – 2 September – when the Finns accepted the Soviet preconditions, Dietl's successor, Colonel-General Lothar Rendulic, an Austrian, asked for an audience with Mannerheim to try and clarify the situation. However, no clarification was forthcoming; Mannerheim only chatted. In the end Rendulic decided to remind him that they had long ago fought each other in the Carpathians during the First World War. At the same time Carl Enckell informed von Blücher, the German minister in Helsinki, that his government had decided to break off relations with Germany. Their meeting was stormy. At this point it was essential to Mannerheim that he should justify Finland's policy and his own conduct in a letter to Hitler as Germany's head of state and commander-in-chief. He stated that his duty was now to lead his people out of the war, and he expressed his hope of being able to do so without 'any avoidable aggravation'. He never received a reply.

Wanting to demonstrate in a special way his liking for Erfurth and gratitude for his loyal cooperation, Mannerheim invited him to lunch at Tamminiemi, the presidential residence on the north side of Helsinki. The German general requested and obtained from his supreme headquarters permission to accept the invitation. It proved a sad farewell – but they were to meet once again after the war, when Mannerheim visited Erfurth at his home in Tübingen.

After the breach with Germany, the preconditions for continued negotiations with Stalin had been satisfied. Mannerheim now proposed an armistice; this was agreed, and it came into force on 4 September. Negotiators had to be appointed as soon as possible. Mannerheim did not now want to choose Paasikivi, in whom he did not feel sufficient confidence after the spring of 1944, choosing instead Hackzell, Walden, Erik Heinrichs and General Oskar Enckell. The delegation left on 6 September but was only able to begin negotiations on 14 September. On that day Hackzell visited Molotov, and learned that Moscow also wanted to take possession for an indefinite time of the Porkkala area only a few miles west of Helsinki, and of the MacElliot coastal fortification (built before 1914). The detachment of a fairly large area inland from the coast would cut the coastal railway from Helsinki to the west, enforce an evacuation of the population and, in military terms, put extremely strong pressure on Finland. For Hackzell the shock was too great: when he returned to his hotel room he suffered a severe stroke and was paralysed. Carl Enckell had to come from Helsinki to take his place and continue the negotiations.

It now seemed that what was on offer was not a peace but rather an armistice to be followed by a final treaty at some uncertain date in the future. This, however, was not a Soviet demand but a British one, an element in the plans covering agreements with the states allied with Germany. Stalin would have preferred a definitive peace, enabling him to know precisely what the Soviet Union had won so that he would not need to fear later disadvantageous revisions under pressure from the Allies. In other ways the terms corresponded broadly with the Soviet demands put forward in March. The indemnity had been reduced to 300 million dollars, but the significance of this was quickly diminished when the Control Commission tightened the rules for fixing the prices of the products which Finland had to supply.

The Soviet demand for the Porkkala area was very difficult for the government in Helsinki to accept, and various alternative proposals, such as a new lease of Hanko, were discussed in the days that followed. Above all, many members of the government recommended offering the Soviet Union territory in the Åland archipelago instead of Porkkala. Mannerheim, supported by the justice minister von Born, opposed this on account of relations with Sweden, but they were eventually compelled to accept the will of the majority in the government, and instructions to offer territory in Åland were sent to the Finnish negotiators. However, the proposal was never put forward since Enckell considered it pointless. On 18 September Molotov presented the Finnish delegation with an ultimatum to sign the Soviet proposal for an armistice agreement on 19 September, or else go home. This proved decisive, and the government in Helsinki submitted.

The attempt to avoid having Soviet troops in the Porkkala area by offering the Soviet Union territory in the Åland islands appeared to the Swedish military attaché as fairly natural in the circumstances. Although never put forward, news of it became known in Stockholm as the result of an indiscretion and caused indignation even among politicians who had previously shown little interest in Åland. As Mannerheim had feared, it temporarily strained Swedish-Finnish relations.

Hackzell's stroke in Moscow not only complicated negotiations with the Soviet Union. It also had consequences for Finnish internal politics, the most immediate of which was the need to appoint a new prime minister. The choice fell on U.J. Castrén, a respected lawyer who was president of the supreme administrative court. At the same time the Social Democrats K.A. Fagerholm (speaker of parliament after 1945) and Wuori (from the 'peace opposition') entered the government. However, it was not long before the Castrén government collapsed, and Fagerholm and Wuori resigned. The result was a new crisis. It was proposed from several quarters that Paasikivi should form a government. Mannerheim, who thought his old colleague garrulous and ineffective, opposed this choice for as long as possible, but in the end some politicians from the old pro-German circles put the President in a difficult situation by proposing directly to Paasikivi, on their own initiative, that he should create a new administration. Mannerheim felt himself so strongly committed that he yielded. However, he was unwilling to accept participation by the Communists in Paasikivi's government, especially when this meant giving them power over the police. Paasikivi hoped to win the Communists over to a 'patriotic' (national) Finnish policy if they were allowed to participate in government. Mannerheim considered this idea naive, but had no choice but to yield. His view finally proved to be correct.

At first Paasikivi's position was weak. He belonged to the Conservative Party which he had once led, and which, after the end of the war, found itself exposed to sharp criticism from the left, and soon isolated. Paasikivi's first post-war government represented an abrupt radicalisation. It was based on a coalition between the Agrarians, the Social Democrats and the Communists (Urho Kekkonen played a significant role in its formation), a consequence of which was that a Communist, Yrjö Leino, received a ministerial appointment, much against the President's will. The Swedish People's Party was also given a place in the government.

The Progressive Party (Liberals) did not at first want to participate because of the presence of a Communist minister. Carl Enckell and Rudolf Walden still remained, but shortly afterwards Walden suffered a stroke, which Mannerheim felt as a severe loss both personally and in political terms. He was succeeded by General Valve.

The time that followed was hard, not least for the President. Nevertheless, he continued to fulfil his obligations as head of state and commander-in-chief. Throughout this time he played an indispensable role, since his authority within the army and in the country generally served to legitimise the change of policy that was taking place – from a war in cooperation with Germany to an agreement with the Soviet Union, which presupposed a complete break with Hitler's Reich and eventually military operations against the German forces in Lapland.

In the autumn of 1944 Mannerheim was suffering from tension and nervous strain, the outward signs being constant severe eczema and other allergic symptoms. When the situation began to stabilise in the spring of 1945 his health and strength recovered for a while, but a physical breakdown occured later, caused by a stomach ulcer. This was the final consequence of his exertions over the years, and proved difficult to cure. Sometimes he threatened to resign but, as Tanner predicted, his sense of duty always prevented him from drawing back from the task he had taken on. Even early in 1945, when the worst months were over and the situation had stabilised somewhat, he was still under strong psychological pressure. 'My wings are clipped,' he wrote to his sister Eva Sparre just before her seventy-fifth birthday on 30 June 1945. He could not travel to Stockholm 'in view of the suspicion which surrounds us'. 'This terrible war has left no room for anything humane, still less for the least sentimentality. Indeed, one can almost believe that it will be a very long time before considerate human feelings again recover their rightful place – if it ever happens at all.' At the end of his time as President, Mannerheim confessed that he 'had a very taxing time with constant worries, cares and disappointments . . . When the entire burden of responsibility lies upon yourself, and you have to take decisions in spite of uncertainty and hesitation – then you become nervous.'

One of the consequences of the armistice agreement was the Allied Control Commission. This was principally a Soviet authority, with the task of ensuring that Finland carried out the armistice terms. The Commission had considerable powers – ultimately its leaders could always threaten a Soviet military intervention and the occupation of Finland. It was headed by Colonel-General A.A. Zhdanov, with General Savonenkov as his second-in-command. The most important decisions were usually referred to the Kremlin; other matters were decided by Zhdanov. In the course of time Soviet personnel on the Commission became very numerous. There were also a number of British officers and officials: the diplomat firancis Shepherd was Britain's political representative and it was with him that Mannerheim mainly had to deal. Among the military representatives was a former agent of the timber trade in Finland, Shamus Magill, who had been in the country with Brigadier Ling during the Winter War. However, Finland had little satisfaction from the British members of the Commission; their instructions and conduct were affected by the appeasement policy towards the Soviet Union that prevailed at the time, and which prevented independent British action. According to article 22 of the armistice agreement, the Control Commission's task was limited to the execution of the agreement, but quite frequently it went beyond that limitation. In the last resort (as we shall see strikingly illustrated below) there was little the Finnish authorities could do other than accede to the demands of the all-powerful Soviet representatives.

The agreement in Moscow immediately posed many serious problems for the Finnish leadership. The first of these concerned the German forces in Finland. The time-limit for their evacuation which the Soviet Union had set on 2 September was clearly too short. There was no way that such a large force as the German Mountain Army, nine divisions strong, with its enormous stores, could be transported from the fronts in Eastern Karelia and Petsamo to Norwegian territory within two weeks. Stalin certainly must have understood this, and have fixed the short period of time with the intention of embarrassing Finland. When the period ran out on 15 September even before the armistice agreement had been signed, the Finnish army had to go ahead with measures to force the German formations to complete their evacuation of northern Finland. Already in the course of the negotiations Moscow had shown the deepest suspicion of Finnish intentions, and this was a view the Control Commission was to express repeatedly after its arrival in Helsinki.

In the interval Finnish headquarters tried to make plans for what had to follow. Airo hoped to be able to carry out 'autumn manoeuvres'; the Germans would withdraw towards Norway, and Finnish troops would advance to occupy the area they had evacuated. There was some contact with the German army command in the north – Lieutenant-Colonel Haahti had been sent to Rovaniemi from Mikkeli for discussions. On the Finnish side they were anxious to avoid any unnecessary sacrifice of lives at this point; the local population and property in the north had to be considered. Haahti and the Germans tried to find solutions in accordance with Airo's plan, but things turned out otherwise. Stalin's intentions were entirely different; he wanted to force the Finnish army at any price to mount a heavy attack on the German forces. On 27 September several Soviet officers came to Mikkeli on behalf of the Control Commission and asked to see the plan of attack for the internment of the Germans in the north. No such plan existed and one had to be prepared in the greatest haste. This completely failed to satisfy the Soviet officers, and indeed Mannerheim was not satisfied either. He had realised even before this that Finnish forces would have to attack in the north to avoid risking a breach with Moscow. To this end he appointed Siilasvuo on 22 September as commander in northern Finland, with the overall task of interning the German troops remaining there.

Siilasvuo, an energetic and active general who had won the victory at Suomussalmi during the Winter War, immediately planned a surprise attack on the coastal towns of Kemi and Tornio, but at the last moment news of the plan reached Colonel Nihtilä at headquarters. Nihtilä was alarmed and immediately informed Mannerheim in the hope that such a reckless operation could be stopped. Mannerheim certainly shared Nihtilä's fears, but considered that he was prevented from taking any overt action to forestall Siilasvuo's plans. Because of his political commitment to the Soviet Union he could not halt the enterprise: 'If I forbid it, there will be a catastrophe for the whole country.' However there was agreement between Siilasvuo and headquarters that the assault landing should be directed only against Tornio, thus involving less risk. The operation succeeded, and on 1–2 October Tornio was taken. This occurred only in the nick of time, because on 30 September Savonenkov had sent a letter to Castrén, the prime minister, calling in agitated terms for active military measures, which had not hitherto been in evidence. He also accused the Finnish army command of doing all in its power to prevent the implementation of the second article of the armistice (concerning the German forces in Finland). This was an extremely serious accusation, directed against Mannerheim. The Russians demanded that by 08.00 hours on 1 October at the latest, the Finnish army should launch an attack to disarm the Germans in the north. Airo had now to draw up a more active plan of attack than the earlier scheme, but by the time this was delivered to Savonenkov, the news from Tornio already afforded concrete proof of the army's offensive spirit. From their bridgehead the assault troops there tried partly to advance further along the river Tornio, and partly to follow the coast down towards Kemi, which was simultaneously attacked from the south. Some days earlier, fighting had begun to the north-east of Oulu towards Pudasjärvi on the way to Rovaniemi. The Germans, who had to safeguard their retreat northwards, offered stubborn resistance; and indeed during the first week of October the toughest and most fluctuating battles of this war were fought in southern Lapland.

The Finnish army's attack had plainly come as a surprise to the Germans. Rendulic had believed that he would receive some warning if the Finnish headquarters intended to abandon the tactics they had hitherto applied in concert; he said he had obtained a promise from Haahti which he considered binding on the Finnish supreme command. He reacted strongly, writing letters on 30 September and 1 October demanding the cessation of the Finnish actions in accordance with what he considered had been agreed; otherwise the area in which the Mountain Army was operating would be treated as enemy territory. Hostages had already been taken – Rendulic had previously held a command in the Balkans, and intended to wage war in the same way as he had done there. Mannerheim received a telegram to that effect from Rendulic on 2 October and immediately asked Haahti whether he had had any authority in Rovaniemi to conclude an agreement; he himself had conferred no such authority on Haahti – who duly confirmed that he did not have the authority in question. Mannerheim at once pointed out that the understanding between the countries, to which Rendulic referred, did not exist. Rendulic, however, persisted in his interpretation of the conduct of the Finnish army. He now pleaded a confidential agreement between soldiers, independent of all political considerations, and accused his former brothers-in-arms of making a cowardly and treacherous attack; the Finnish armed forces had lost everything, he asserted – not only their freedom but also their honour. Although the allegation was unfounded, since it did not take account of the country's parlous situation, it influenced German opinion for a long time to come.

The war continued. The Germans put up a strong resistance, and their troops fought well. The Finnish formations, for their part, were handicapped in their fight by the destruction of the roads, which were also soaked by the autumn rains. In addition the Control Commission persisted in its demand that the Finnish army should be demobilised in accordance with the armistice agreement – which, however, also provided for the Red Army to assist it if required. But when Airo on 5 October and Mannerheim on 7 October made a request for Soviet intervention in northern Lapland to cut off the German line of retreat, Zhdanov did not want to agree; the request, he said, had been made too late. Soon the true objective of Soviet strategy became clear: control of the Arctic coast. On 7 October the Red Army began a powerful offensive against the German troops who still held Soviet territory east of the frontier and were occupying Petsamo, pushing them back to Kirkenes in Norway.

For the Germans, who now feared an imminent Allied attack on

Norway, a rapid withdrawal of the whole 20th Mountain Army was the most important task, and on the whole Rendulic succeeded in accomplishing it in accordance with orders given by Hitler. Siilasvuo attempted on several occasions to surround the German troops and intern them in accordance with the provisions of the armistice, first at Rovaniemi, and then in the great wildernesses of western Lapland, but the Finnish army was thwarted each time by the physical conditions and the skilfully-led German withdrawal. The mood in the Control Commission once again turned to irritation: on 16 October Mannerheim received a letter from Zhdanov full of criticism and mistrust, concluding with threats that the Soviet military command might be compelled to take 'such measures as it considers essential', clearly implying in the last resort a possible military occupation. Mannerheim's first reaction was to send an extremely peremptory demand to Siilasvuo to advance with greater vigour and purpose – this has to be regarded as part of the preparation for the reply to Zhdanov delivered on 17 October. In this letter the various difficulties which the Finnish army was encountering and which prevented greater successes were stated: the terrain, destroyed roads and bridges, the capability of the Germans, the autumn weather, and so on. Even now the Finnish army did not succeed in carrying out the strategically impossible task of surrounding the Germans, who managed to reach safety across the Norwegian frontier. Only in January 1945 had they almost completely left Finnish territory.

Many points in the armistice agreement affected Mannerheim closely, even personally. The Control Commission interpreted some of the points in ways which the actual text did not justify, but he did not consider it politically possible, or at any rate prudent, to raise objections. Article 21 obliged Finland to dissolve immediately all pro-Hitler organisations 'whether political, military or para-military' and other organisations conducting propaganda hostile to the Allied nations, in particular the Soviet Union. That the Commission should require the dissolution of nationalistic Finnish organisations such as the IKL (the fascist party) and the AKS (the expansionist Academic Karelia Society) was scarcely surprising, but when it was demanded that the Civil Guard, the Lotta organisation and the Veterans' Association should also be disbanded, it was clear that the Commission was exceeding the terms of article 21. The Civil Guard was an auxiliary defence organisation dating back to the War of Independence, with a membership open to all citizens, and Mannerheim had been its honorary commander since 1919. The Lotta organisation was a women's auxiliary defence force. The Veterans' Association was a body Mannerheim had formed in 1940, principally for social work. He now led an intensive effort to transfer the Civil Guard's significant and geographically scattered assets, mainly to the Finnish Red Cross, but he only succeeded in part.

The end of cooperation with the Germans and the removal of their forces thus constituted a difficult task, demanding time and sacrifices. The resumption of relations with the Soviet Union was an even greater problem in which the future seemed much more problemetical. Mannerheim's policy was now above all to build up reasonable relations with Moscow, settle existing differences and win confidence in Finland's leadership. As for Mannerheim, this programme corresponded with views he had held earlier; indeed he was one of the originators of the policy Finland was now to adopt in a changed world. After a conversation with Mannerheim on 14 October 1944, K.A. Fagerholm declared: 'Finland can no longer undertake the role of a bastion for the west against the east. We must stop this kind of talk. We shall no longer lend ourselves to any such policy. Our army shall never again wage war against Russia.' Mannerheim realised the seriousness of Finland's situation; in fact, on the whole he regarded the country's future too pessimistically. When, in a conversation with Gripenberg at the beginning of January 1945, he said with a some satisfaction that 'we have for the time being avoided a severe conflict with the Russians', he added: 'Our situation is still very worrying: of the future one can say nothing at all' (G.A. Gripenberg, 6.1.45).

Up to this point Mannerheim's views were at one with Paasikivi's, but they differed fundamentally from each other. This was due not so much to different opinions on the aims of Finnish policy – this is clear from Mannerheim's statements on the subject – but rather to a difference in temperament, experience and political methods. Mannerheim thought now, as on other occasions, that the country's leaders would not achieve their ends by submitting or trying to ingratiate themselves with the Russians. On the contrary, they would get further if they kept their dignity, stuck to their principles and were logically consistent without displaying arrogance or unfriendliness while so doing. In justification of his views he could point to his extremely long experience of Russia; and he could recall his dealings with the Germans, particularly during the Continuation War when, by resolutely but courteously rejecting unreasonable demands, he had been able to defend Finland's independence and interests. The same would surely be possible – despite all the differences – in relation to the Soviet Union.

Mannerheim therefore thought that the Finnish government should not make unlimited concessions to Soviet demands and wishes. There were limits which, except in the most extreme necessity, ought not to be exceeded. Thus in connection with the actions of the Control Commission, he pointed out emphatically to Gripenberg 'that we nevertheless could not comply with the Commission in all respects, but must sometimes have sufficient determination to say no' (6.1.45). After his resignation he explained to Gripenberg that 'he had told Enckell and also Paasikivi that the Finnish government, while naturally observing all courteous formalities, ought to have protested against all those Russian demands which were not in strict accordance with the armistice agreement but which we could not avoid fulfilling. It was necessary only to say that we did not consider ourselves bound to do what we were compelled to. But our present leaders did not have the courage for anything like that.' Mannerheim warned against further grovelling and fawning. It was important, especially in Finland's position, to act with dignity; one could not risk being regarded with contempt.

Paasikivi, on the other hand, was prepared to go much further in making concessions. In support of his policy he adduced a historical philosophy linked to the tactics of the Old Finnish Party during the oppressive regimes of Bobrikov and Seyn, governors-general during the final decades of Russian rule in Finland. His authority was Yrjö-Koskinen, the historian and politician who had tried to comply with Russian demands in the interests of the Finns. It did not worry Paasikivi that his present views were at odds with those he had espoused on the same subject at other times in his career. Even in his way of looking at the world, there were definite limits to what Finland could tolerate, and he emphasised to Gripenberg 'that Russia and things Russian are in every respect so foreign to Finland and its people that we could never feel any intellectual affinity with our eastern neighbours. We belong once and for all to the Scandinavian north.' The differences in opinion between the President and the prime minister emerged clearly many times, as over the war responsibility trial and the Soviet deportation of Finnish citizens of Russian origin or Russian refugees who had lived in the country for many years. However, the political situation often prevented Mannerheim from asserting his opinion against that of the government.

The most notable demonstration of Mannerheim's endeavour to normalise relations with Moscow was in his discussions with Zhdanov over defence cooperation, an important initiative in relation to the treaty of friendship, cooperation and mutual assistance signed in 1948. The question was brought up by Mannerheim when he raised particular objections to Zhdanov's demand that Finland should dismantle all heavier artillery even west of the Porkkala peninsula. In a letter of 20 December 1944 he pointed out that it might also be in the Soviet interest if the western coasts of Finland were to have a strong defensive system. At first Zhdanov made only a limited concession: the number of 120mm. guns could be doubled, although heavier guns were not to be put in position but kept in store. However, Mannerheim reminded Zhdanov in a new letter that this demand had no proper basis in the armistice agreement, and here he developed in more detail his thoughts on the need for, and possibility of, defence cooperation. He assumed that the Soviet Union now understood that the people of Finland would not only fulfil all their obligations in the agreement but would also endeavour to live as good neighbours. They were willing to cooperate in the common defence by both countries of the northern Baltic. These were positive ideas which Moscow could appreciate, and from this it was a short step to discussions. On 18 January 1945 Zhdanov visited Mannerheim, and sent him a letter the following day which clearly shows that what they had discussed was a friendship and defence pact, or at least some form of cooperation in treaty form. Mannerheim replied that he would unfortunately be away for the days immediately ahead, but that he would be available the following Monday to discuss the question Zhdanov had raised on 18 January. The journey that Mannerheim had alluded to was to the old headquarters at Mikkeli, and during that visit he talked with his most trusted colleagues, among them Generals Erik Heinrichs and Oscar Enckell, about the possibility of an agreement with Moscow.

On 22 January at 3 p.m. Zhdanov and Admiral A.P. Aleksandrov with other Soviet officers arrived at Tamminiemi, where some of the Finnish army's most senior officers had been summoned to meet them. While talks went on in the study, Mannerheim entertained his principal guest in the drawing-room, and an agreeable and sometimes positively cordial conversation took place between the two of them. Heinrichs, at Mannerheim's request, produced an aide-memoire for these discussions on the question of an agreement; the first of several, it was dated 20 January 1945 – in other words during the visit to Mikkeli. Mannerheim himself composed, in Russian, several proposals for a treaty of cooperation based on model texts which he had earlier received from Zhdanov: these were the Soviet treaties with Czechoslovakia, France, Poland and Jugoslavia. Mannerheim modified and limited Finnish obligations and opportunities for the Soviet Union to intervene in Finnish affairs. Later he passed information on his discussions with the Soviet authorities to Paasikivi and Carl Enckell, who themselves had talks with Zhdanov in the spring of 1945. Hopes now rose of increased Soviet concessions, perhaps even extending to the giving up of Porkkala and a part of Karelia. But the Finns soon had to acknowledge that plans for a pact could not yet be realised. A peace treaty had to come into effect before there could be a treaty of that nature.

Peace came into force in the autumn of 1947, and not long afterwards Stalin again took up the idea of a treaty of friendship and cooperation. However, the situation in February 1948, when he approached Paasikivi directly by means of a personal letter, was very different from that of the winter of 1944–5. In the immediately preceding period the Soviet Union had conducted a frighteningly active policy: Poland, Rumania, Hungary and Czechoslovakia had all been taken over by the Communists, and the Allied powers were under extreme pressure in Berlin. So attitudes towards a treaty with Moscow could not reasonably be the same as they had been earlier. In Stalin's proposal to Paasikivi for treaty negotiations there was a reminder of the earlier discussions with Mannerheim. Carl Enckell gave an account of these discussions when he attempted to describe the origin of the treaty to a number of Finnish politicians.

The parliamentary elections of 17–18 March 1945 marked a turning-point in Finland's policy after the end of the war and in the position of the President. They were awaited with great suspense. The war and the migration of the population from Karelia had hitherto made elections impossible, and the previous ones had been held in 1939. Mannerheim observed of the 1945 elections that they went better than he had feared. The majority in parliament remained non-Socialist, but only by a narrow margin. But the government that now took office was in many ways a disappointment to him. Paasikivi succeeded in remaining as prime minister, but he was forced to allow the Communists and People's Democrats (left-wing Socialists, allied with the Communists) increased influence. The Communist Leino now became minister of the interior in succession to Hillilä, thus acquiring control of the police. Mannerheim did his utmost to ensure that the defence ministry would go to a professional soldier, but he was compelled to accept instead Mauno Pekkala, a People's Democrat. This meant an appreciable radicalisation and a lessening of the President's scope for action.

The consequences were soon apparent. Shortly after the formation of the new government, Zhdanov pressed home his demand that a score of people should be arrested and extradited to the Soviet Union. Some of these were Finnish citizens and some were Russian refugees who had lived for a long time in Finland. Two of them had belonged to the Finnish SS battalion, but had not been accused of any war crime. This was not treated as a matter for government but was dealt with administratively below ministerial level. German demands for the hand over of Jewish refugees during the Continuation War had been handled in similar fashion. Mannerheim, who had made a strenuous intervention on behalf of the Jewish refugees, was extremely angry when he heard of this Soviet demand, and considered immediate resignation. However, he decided to stay in office to try to save what still could be saved.

The change of government and the presence of Leino in the powerful post of interior minister had an important effect on the armed forces. The role of the Communists was particularly notable in the embarrassing arms concealment affair. The background to this was the fear of a Soviet occupation of Finland felt in many quarters in the autumn of 1944, and the desire, if this happened, to have access to weapons for a last defence. An organisation was formed within headquarters under the leadership of Nihtilä and Haahti, who concealed their activity from the higher authorities so that the latter would be shielded in the event of investigation. Local representatives were appointed in country districts to set up arms dumps in their localities consisting of rifles, machine-guns and other weapons that could be used if the large ordnance depots were seized by the enemy. The organisation was already being dissolved in the spring of 1945 when the police and the Control Commission got wind of it as the result of informers. At first the Soviet reaction to the news was relatively mild, but it is clear that the Communist leaders tried to provoke a strong reaction in order to compromise the defence forces and the officer corps, whose offer of a voluntary investigation was rejected.

There has been harsh criticism, mostly exaggerated, of those who were engaged in the concealment of arms. In fact no criminal acts – according to the code then existing – had taken place, and the government was therefore compelled to pass a retroactive law so that those responsible could be indicted. The police, now under Communist control, handled the matter roughly, and the Control Commission also took on a threatening posture. At this point Mannerheim intervened by appealing to the officers most directly responsible, through an intermediary, to state openly what had happened. Complete openness and veracity were essential if the Finnish government was to be able to command confidence. However, those who had taken part in the affair had expressly agreed to disclose nothing about their activities and thus an investigation into them was virtually impossible, but faced with Mannerheim's appeal Haahti decided to change his tactics, and in a detailed letter to the President on 29 June 1945 he assumed responsibility for what had happened. For the sake of public good he was ready to disclose what he knew, but he wanted the decision as to how he should act to rest with Mannerheim, relying on his 'faultless character, magnaminity and far-sightedness'; only he was master of the situation as a whole and could perceive what really was the public good in both good times and bad.

Mannerheim soon decided what he had to do. By word of mouth he divulged the content of Haahti's letter to Leino, the interior minister, who was not backward in abusing the information. In parliament he called the arms concealment affair an 'armed, reactionary act of violence, in the preparation of which extremely important and influential circles took part, particularly within our army'. Then, in an extensive police operation, 564 people were arrested and an excessively large investigatory system was set up. Of the senior officers Airo and five distinguished generals were arrested. However, the operation was intended ultimately to compromise those even more highly placed, namely Heinrichs and Mannerheim himself. In this it failed, but Heinrichs was nevertheless forced to resign as commander-in-chief. Legal proceedings followed, which lasted two years and in which Airo and many of the generals were acquitted.

Another difficult question during Mannerheim's presidency was the obligation to try war criminals. This concept, when interpreted straightforwardly, was aimed at soldiers who had transgressed laws on the conduct of war. Immediately after the armistice Mannerheim made arrangements for investigations to establish if there were any war criminals who ought to be indicted. What these enquiries mainly revealed was that a limited number of offenders could be accused over the treatment of prisoners-of-war, and these subsequently received sentences. At first the Control Commission directed its attention to war crimes of this kind; it delivered a note demanding that measures be taken against a number of individuals – sixty-two in all – on grounds of war crimes they had committed. The list bore the number one, which was thought to mean that further lists would follow. Of the sixty-two, thirty-two were arrested and held in the prison at Riihimäki; they were then tried, some being found guilty and others acquitted. However, Mannerheim was angered by many of the names on the Soviet list (number one), especially those of Major-General Pajari, a soldier known for his bravery, and Major-General Palojärvi, who had lost his wife and son in the war. Both generals, Zhdanov maintained, were war criminals of the worst type, although this description was never explained. Possibly a Finnish informer had been responsible for the Soviet action. Mannerheim called both generals to see him, and let them choose between letting themselves be arrested, going underground or fleeing the country. They chose to go to prison, and before their arrest he invited them to dinner. He was deeply disturbed by this turn of events; he saw a risk, with disastrous implications, that the Soviet Union would demand their extradition to stand trial there – how could he allow that? He wanted at that moment to resign – connivance in any such proceeding was impossible. He could plead his illness, and indeed he had done enough. In fact, the case of the two generals had a remarkable conclusion. After a while it became clear that Zhdanov had lost all interest in them, and he remarked in a conversation with Paasikivi that if the Finnish government had no charges against them they could be released.

However, Moscow on the one hand and Finnish radical politicians on the other were soon showing keen interest in the question of responsibility for war crimes from an entirely different viewpoint. They now wanted to fasten responsibility on the men who had begun the war or delayed its conclusion. Neither Finnish law nor international law recognised any such crime, and thus the problem was discussed at different political levels for almost a year. The government pointed out to Zhdanov that no legal proceedings on this basis were possible in Finland – a view for which Paasikivi made himself spokesman on several occasions. Eventually, however, government and parliament were compelled to accept the enactment of a criminal law which would enable a war responsibility trial to take place. Mannerheim fought against this to the last and attempted during the drafting of the law to introduce qualifications, in some cases successfully.

The most interesting question was ultimately who was to be prosecuted and what was to be the basis of the indictment, and political decisions, or at any rate attempts at political decisions, can be discerned in the way it was resolved. That Ryti should be prosecuted was inevitable from the assumptions behind the law. Witting and Walden were dead. Tanner, who had not then been a member of the government, and had later sought peace, was prosecuted out of political motives. The Agrarian ministers Reinikka and Kukkonen were eventually indicted, and Mannerheim was annoyed when great efforts were made by political friends to release them – although they had clearly been pro-German. Kivimäki, on the other hand, was to be prosecuted at all costs although, as minister in Berlin, he had only been carrying out official policy. All attempts to save him from prosecution were in vain. Henrik Ramsay, who had become foreign minister only in 1943 to initiate a peace policy and had done his best to pursue it, was indicted, mainly because he had been involved in the Ribbentrop agreement – an agreement concluded when the country had faced a desperate emergency.

And what of Mannerheim himself? It was in any case clear that Moscow had made no demands concerning him; his attitude before the Winter War and his policy of caution during the Continuation War were well known in the Kremlin. The Soviet leaders must have realised that in him they now had a firm and dependable opposite number enjoying an unprecedented authority in his own country, as had already been demonstrated by the army's disciplined conduct during and after the armistice negotiations. On at least one occasion Mannerheim received a clear statement from Moscow that nobody there had any intention of adding him to the band of war criminals. After his retirement he told Gripenberg that there had been an occasion when he was a patient in the Red Cross Hospital in Helsinki and there were demands in the Finnish government, and especially on the left, that he should resign from the presidency. The acting head of the Control Commission, Lieutenant-General Savonenkov, presented himself at the hospital and announced that Moscow was making no demand at all for his indictment. The Soviet attitude to Mannerheim also prompted the Finnish Communists not to demand his prosecution, and there was also no more in that direction during the preliminary investigation by the supreme court judge Onni Petäys. Reports to the contrary are incorrect. What actually occurred was that Mannerheim himself invited Petäys to come for a talk if he wanted any information on the events of 1941–4. Before their meeting Petäys prepared various questions which the President answered. The aide-de-camp, Grönvall, took minutes of the conversation. No one other than Grönvall, Mannerheim and Petäys was present, and the occasion completely lacked the character of judicial proceedings.

Mannerheim's health collapsed in the early autumn of 1945. He suffered from severe stomach pains and feared at first that, like three of his brothers and sisters, he had fallen victim to cancer. However, he was soon able to inform Eva Sparre that X-rays had shown that the cause of his pain was a gastric ulcer of which the ultimate cause must have been the exertions and nervous pressure of the war years. At first the doctors hoped that if he spent more time in a milder climate he would throw off his symptoms permanently. Mannerheim reluctantly accepted their advice, and went to a seaside resort south of Lisbon, leaving by boat for Stockholm on 4 November, flying from there to Paris, and continuing by train, which required caution because of the blockade of Franco's Spain then in force. He was received with great courtesy in Portugal, the prime minister Salazar placing a car at his disposal, but his stay there did not bring about any lasting improvement, and the ulcer erupted again when he was travelling home by train through Spain and France. Meanwhile his absence from the country had caused problems. In accordance with the constitution, the office of a President unable to carry out his duties – as during Kallio's severe illness in the autumn of 1940 – had to be exercised by the prime minister, in the present case the almost equally old Paasikivi, and it was soon being discussed within the government whether Mannerheim ought to place his office at the disposal of parliament. Some of those who made this suggestion had political motives, while others were mainly concerned for Paasikivi, who was keen to exchange his heavy task as prime minister for the less taxing presidency. So long as there remained a hope that Mannerheim's health would recover, the question of a change of President could not be urged strongly, but it was a different matter when Mannerheim returned at the beginning of 1946 still in extremely poor health. He himself was now prepared to hand over power, preferably to Paasikivi. On the other hand, with his strong sense of propriety and of what the country's good repute demanded, he was not willing to resign under pressure, or to discuss the timing of his resignation with the government. The only person with whom he thought it appropriate to discuss the question was the speaker of parliament, K.A. Fagerholm.

Mannerheim wanted to put off his resignation until the verdicts had been given in the war responsibility trial. Then he would have fulfilled the important tasks for which he had been appointed head of state. The Germans had been compelled to leave Finnish soil, and the war had ended, although only an armistice and not a peace was so far in force. The obligations of the armistice agreement had been fulfilled in so far as they lay within his power. He would now, therefore, be able to relinquish his office for reasons which were not dishonourable to the country's reputation or his own. Sadly, and perhaps with some bitterness, he acknowledged that it was generally known that Finland's elderly Marshal 'could no longer cope with his duties' (to Eva Sparre, 12.2.46). He added political reasons to the medical ones: the solid majority bloc in parliament led by the Communists made 'my exercise of the powers of the head of state illusory'. Nobody could ask that he should remain as a mere figurehead when he had already accomplished more than had been asked of him at the time of his appointment in August 1944.

However, it was to be longer than he had thought before Mannerheim could resign. The reason was the long time taken by the war responsibility trial. The Control Commission was extremely dissatisfied when it came to know of the planned verdicts (through Hertta Kuusinen, a Communist member of the court and daughter of O.W. Kuusinen, head of Stalin's Terijoki government), and considered that the sentences had to be increased. However, from the point of view of the administration of Finnish justice, this was an objectionable demand, and time was needed before the court could be induced to yield to the Soviet demands. The trial was further complicated when the Control Commission received from the Soviet Union a deposition made in captivity by the German General Erich Buschenhagen, according to which Finland had taken part in the aggressive war against the Soviet Union and been involved in the preparations that preceded it. He had been told by Hitler of the Barbarossa Plan and believed that Heinrichs had been told of it too. In February 1941 he had visited Helsinki and discussed operations on the White Sea with Heinrichs, Airo and Tapola, and there was no time when the Finns had not been ready to participate in them. Mannerheim and Walden had been told of the plans. The Field-Marshal had received Buschenhagen and Kinzel at his home and had been pleased to renew their brotherhood-in-arms dating from 1918.

This testimony naturally caused a sensation in Finland. It provided a new version of the origin of the Continuation War differing from that which the Finns had previously accepted. Not only many of the accused but Mannerheim also appeared to be compromised. The attorney-general immediately arranged an investigation into the German general's information, and it now transpired that there was no factual basis for his narrative. Mannerheim, who had returned to Helsinki on 3 January 1946, at once gave evidence in which he absolutely denied the statements about his meeting and discussion with Buschenhagen. At his one meeting with Buschenhagen in Helsinki in February 1941, they had talked about hunting in India, not about politics. We know now – and he admitted as much after being allowed to return to West Germany – that Buschenhagen, under duress in captivity, gave an untruthful account of his visit to Finland in the spring of 1941.

The sentences were passed on 21 February 1946, and now the time had come for Mannerheim to leave the presidency. He therefore informed the government in writing on 4 March 1946 that because of his worsening health he was no longer able to carry out the duties that fell to the President of the republic. He had – as he further explained – fulfilled the tasks which had been entrusted to him 'at a fateful moment for our country'. He had indeed only resumed his duties the previous day, 3 March, and he used that day to send a sharp rebuke to the commander of the defence forces, Lieutenant-General Lundqvist, over the measures he had taken to reduce the number of officers – this had also represented a political purge.

Mannerheim's successor as President was, not unexpectedly, Paasikivi. Their relations had sometimes been tense during the most recent years, but Mannerheim acknowledged that his successor was a courageous man who was now shouldering a heavy responsibility. For himself, as he wrote to his sister-in-law Palaemona, he was free 'from many heavy responsibilities, indeed it is delightful to be free at last.' He was able to start his life as a private citizen at his villa in Helsinki and on his estate at Kirkniemi in Western Uusimaa. This estate had been bought with capital belonging to the endowment which had been given to him on different occasions, beginning with the national collection of 1920, and on which he had the right to use the interest.

XV
LAST YEARS
1946–1951

During his last years, Mannerheim had to struggle continuously against illness. He was supported by his doctors, notably Professor Lauri Kalaja in Helsinki and Professor Nanna Svartz in Stockholm. The gastric ulcer diagnosed in 1945 was not operated on, and he suffered fresh attacks. In 1946 he had an operation on a perforated ulcer in Pietarsaari, and the doctors soon considered a bigger operation essential. This was carried out in Stockholm and gave him a respite for several years. For convalescence after his various attacks and operations, Mannerheim usually stayed in Switzerland, amid the Alpine scenery of which he was so fond. 'It is true', he wrote to one of his correspondents, 'that one carries with oneself the consuming burden of cares and sorrows, but if there is a place on this earth to forget, to have tranquillity and rest, it is Switzerland.'

After Mannerheim's major operation in 1947 his strength gradually returned, and he now contemplated undertaking a large task. Several times previously he had formed plans to write his memoirs, but had always been prevented from translating them into action. He considered it was his duty to give an account to the Finnish people of his life's work. He wanted to describe the reasons behind Finnish policy and its development. His memoirs were to be a work about the history of Finland, especially since 1917, with the emphasis not on his own life but on the fortunes of the country. He did not want to concentrate on criticism or blame for other people's actions, or to cast ridicule on old friends and colleagues. The proposed work was thus to have a distinctive tone.

The great memoirs were to be compiled in Switzerland – Mannerheim considered that only there could he and his closest collaborators find peace and quiet and political security. He chose to live in a convalescent home near Montreux recommended by Professor Nanna Svartz, and there he stayed for most of the time, only returning to Finland on a few occasions when he felt himself obliged to do so, such as to exercise his right to vote. He also decided that at his age he would not be able to draft the entire text himself but had to call on collaborators. His own authorship was limited to certain sections; for the rest he dictated recollections and gave descriptions which were subsequently written out for him to correct. He received assistance from many people, who prepared drafts and provided source material. His chief collaborator was Colonel A. Paasonen, who for many years had directed the Finnish intelligence division at headquarters, and who now lived in Montreux and remained with the Marshal till the end. But Mannerheim called upon many others to assist with different sections, among them Generals Heinrichs, Grandell, Olenius and Martola and the military historian Colonel Viljanen. With his customary care he scrutinised the outlines he received in this way, and eventually the memoirs approached completion. But they were not in their final state when in January 1951 he suffered a severe gastric attack, which probably had its ultimate cause in the operation on his ulcer a few years earlier. On 23 January he was taken to hospital in Lausanne and operated on; on 28 January he died. He had realised that the end was near, and remarked to his Swiss doctor that he was prepared to lose the battle ahead.

After receiving news of Mannerheim's death Paasikivi spoke on the radio to the Finnish people: 'One of the greatest men and most illustrious figures in the history of Finland has passed away.' At his funeral in the Lutheran Cathedral in Helsinki on 4 February, K.A. Fagerholm, the speaker of parliament, honoured the memory of 'a great soldier, a great statesman, a great citizen', who now, 'wearied with years and honour, will go to rest in his native soil.' In a special way, said Fagerholm, the Marshal had become the central figure in the history of independent Finland, and no one had impinged on its fateful moments to the same extent. He had done so with the strength of his great personality, and although he had never forced his services on the people, he had always been at their disposal when needed.

The funeral procession through the streets of Helsinki to the war cemetery at Hietaniemi was an unforgettable experience for the great crowds who turned out to show their gratitude and respect. For them Gustaf Mannerheim was and remains a symbol of the republic of Finland and of its freedom.

GLOSSARY OF TOPOGRAPHICAL NAMES
IN FINNISH AND SWEDISH

Finnish	*Swedish*
Hamina	Fredrikshamn
Hanko	Hangö
Helsinki	Helsingfors
Herttoniemi (Helsinki)	Hertonäs (Helsingfors)
Hietaniemi (Helsinki)	Sandudd (Helsingfors)
Ilomantsi	Ilomants
Kaivopuisto (Helsinki)	Brunnsparken (Helsingfors)
Kajaani	Kajana
Kirkniemi	Gerknäs
Koivisto	Björkö
Kultaranta (near Turku)	Gullranda (near Åbo)
Lahti	Lahtis
Lappohja	Lappvik
Lapua	Lappo
Louhisaari	Villnäs
Loviisa	Lovisa
Malmi (Helsinki)	Malm (Helsingfors)
Mikkeli	St Michel
Oulu	Uleåborg
Pietarsaari	Jakobstad
Pori	Björneborg
Porkkala	Porkala
Porvoo	Borgå
Saimaa	Saima
Satakunta	Satakunda
Savo	Savolaks
Sortavala	Sordavala
Suursaari	Hogland
Tamminiemi (Helsinki)	Ekudden (Helsingfors)
Tampere	Tammerfors
Töölö (Helsinki)	Tölö (Helsingfors)
Tornio	Torneå
Turku	Åbo
Uusikaupunki	Nystad
Uusimaa	Nyland
Vaasa	Vasa
Viipuri	Viborg
Vuoksi	Vuoksen

BIBLIOGRAPHY

The biography of Mannerheim in eight volumes by Stig Jägerskiöld, on which this work is based, forms a major source, and each volume contains a bibliography. The volumes are as follows:

IN SWEDISH

Den unge Mannerheim.
Helsingfors, 1964.

Gustaf Mannerheim,
1906–1917.
Helsingfors, 1965.

Gustaf Mannerheim,
1918.
Helsingfors, 1967.

Riksföreståndaren.
Gustaf Mannerheim,
1919.
Helsingfors, 1969.

Mannerheim mellan
världskrigen.
Helsingfors, 1972.

Fältmarskalken.
Gustaf Mannerheim,
1939–1941.
Helsingfors, 1975.

Marskalken av
Finland. Gustaf
Mannerheim, 1941–
1944.
Helsingfors, 1979.

Från krig till fred.
Gustaf Mannerheim,
1944–1951.
Helsingfors, 1981.

IN FINNISH

Nuori Mannerheim.
Helsinki, 1964.

Gustaf Mannerheim,
1906–1917.
Helsinki, 1965.

Mannerheim, 1918.
Helsinki, 1967.

Valtionhoitaja
Mannerheim.
Helsinki, 1969.

Mannerheim rauhan
vuosina, 1920–1939.
Helsinki, 1973.

Talvisodan ylipäällikkö.
Sotamarsalkka Gustaf
Mannerheim, 1939–1941.
Helsinki, 1976,

Suomen Marsalkka. Gustaf
Mannerheim, 1941–1944.
Helsinki, 1981.

Viimeiset vuodet.
Mannerheim, 1944–1951.
Helsinki, 1982.

WORKS IN ENGLISH

Erfurth, Waldemar, *The Last Finnish War.* Washington, D.C., 1979.
Mannerheim, C.G., *The Memoirs of Marshal Mannerheim* (abridged). London, 1953.
——, *Across Asia from West to East in 1906–1908.* Helsinki, 1940. 2 vols.
Nevakivi, Jukka, *The Appeal that was never made: The Allies, Scandinavia and the Finnish Winter War, 1939–1940.* London, 1976.
Rodzianko, Paul, *Mannerheim: An intimate Picture of a great Soldier and Statesman.* London, 1940.
Screen, J.E.O., *Mannerheim: The Years of Preparation.* London, 1970.

WORKS AVAILABLE IN BOTH SWEDISH (1) AND FINNISH (2)

(1)

Donner, Kai, *Fältmarskalken friherre Mannerheim.* Helsingfors, 1934.
Heinrichs, Erik, *Mannerheimgestalten.* Helsingfors, 1957–9. 2 vols.
Mannerheim, G., *Minnen.* Helsingfors, 1951–2. 2 vols.
——, *Brev från sju åartionden.* Sammanställda av Stig. Jägerskiöld. Helsingfors, 1984.
——, *Resa genom Asien. Fältmarskalken C.G. Mannerheims dagböcker förda under hans resa Kaspiska havet – Peking.* Stockholm, 1940. 2 vols.
——, *Marskalken av Finland, friherre Gustaf Mannerheim. Krigaren, statsmannen, människan.* Helsingfors, 1953. (Skrifter utgivna av Finlands adelsför bund, 9)
——, *Marskalken i närbilder.* Sammanställda av Yrjö Kivimies. Helsingfors, 1952.
——, *Med rena vapen. Fältmars kalk Mannerheims dagorder 1918–1942.* Helsingfors, 1942.
Voipio, Anni, *Marskalken av Finland.* Helsingfors, 1943.

(2)

Donner, Kai, *Sotamarsalkka vapaaherra Mannerheim.* Porvoo, 1934.
Heinrichs, Erik, *Mannerheim Suomen kohtaloissa.* Helsinki, 1957–9. 2 vols.
Mannerheim G., *Muistelmat.* Helsinki, 1951–2. 2 vols.
——, *Kirjeitä seitsemän vuosikymmenen ajalta.* Valikoinut Stig Jägerskiöld. Helsinki, 1983.
——, *Matka Aasian halki: päiväkirja matkalta Kaspianmeri – Peking.* Helsinki, 1940–1. 2 vols.
——, *Suomen marsalkka, vapaaherra Gustaf Mannerheim. Sotilas, valtiomies, ihminen.* Helsinki, 1953. (Suomen aatelisliiton julkaisuja, 9)
——, *Suomen marsalkka tuokiokuvina.* Koonut Yrjö Kivimies. Helsinki, 1951.
——, *Puhtain asein. Sotamarsalkka Mannerheimin päiväkäskyjä vv. 1918–1942.* Helsinki, 1942.
Voipio, Anni, *Suomen marsalkka.* Porvoo, 1943.

WORKS AVAILABLE IN FINNISH ONLY

Klinge, Matti, *Mannerheim. Kuvaelämäkerta.* Helsinki, 1968.

Lehmus, Kalle, *Tuntematon Mannerheim. Katkelmia sodan ja politiikan poluilta.* Helsinki, 1967.

Mannerheim, C.G., *Päiväkirja Japanin sodasta 1904–1905 sekä rintamakirjeitä omaisille.* Valikoinut Stig Jägerskiöld. Helsinki, 1982.

Nevakivi, Jukka, *Ystävistä vihollisiksi. Suomi Englannin politiikassa 1940–1941.* Helsinki, 1976.

Selén, Kari, *C.G.E. Mannerheim ja hänen puolustusneuvostonsa 1931–1939.* Helsinki, 1980.

INDEX

Abyssinia, 91

Academic Karelia Society, 185

Agrarian Party, 73, 90, 164, 171, 176, 180, 192

Airo, Maj.-Gen. Aksel: organisation of army, 100; Winter War, 113, 122, 125; Continuation War 147–8, 195; evacuation of German forces, 182–4; arms concealment affair, 191

Åkerman, Gen. Birger, 35, 40

Åland Islands: Swedish claim, 56–7, 59, 71, 73–4; German occupation (1918), 57; defence, 104–5, 112, 130, 132; in Continuation War, 179–80

Albania, 92

Aleksandrov, Adml. A.P., 188

Algeria, 85

Allied Control Commission, 179, 181–96

Aminoff, Lieut.-Gen. Gösta 5

amnesty promulgated, 71, 78

Antell Committee, 23

Arajärvi, J. (Senator), 52

Arapova, Anastasia (wife of Mannerheim), 9–11

arms concealment affair, 190–1

Austria, 33, 35, 37–41, 86, 87, 91

Bailey, Col. Eric, 85, 86

Balfour, Arthur J. (British prime minister), 69, 70

Balkan War (1912), 32

Baltic states, 108, 130–1

Berg, Maj.-Gen. K.E., 82

Bergenheim, Edvard (engineer), 5

Bilderling, Gen. Alexander von (Russian), 5, 15

Blomberg, Gen. W. von (German), 99

Blücher, Wipert von (German envoy), 140, 178

Bobrikov, Nikolai (Russian governor-general of Finland), 11–13, 14, 48

Boheman, Erik (Swedish civil servant), 168

Born, Ernst von (Finnish minister), 176, 179

Born, Victor Magnus von, 12.

Brandestein, Col. von (German), 62

Branting, Hjalmar (Swedish politician), 56, 58, 75

Britain: intervention in Russian civil war, 75–6; policy towards Finland in War of Independence, 68–71; visits by Mannerheim, 69–70, 89, 98–9; arms supplies in Winter War, 100, 118–19; possible intervention in Winter War, 121; release of British volunteers, 146; policy in Continuation War, 146, 156–7, 171, 179, 181–2; member of Allied Control Commission, 181–2

Brusilov, Gen. Aleksei (Russian), 10, 38

Budenny, Marshal S.M. (Soviet), 80

Bulgaria, 41

Bürkner, Commodore L. (German), 142

Buschenhagen, Gen. Erich (German), 137–8, 142, 195

Cadet Corps at Hamina, 3–4, 6

Cajander, Prof. A.K. (Finnish prime minister), 90, 96, 104, 109, 111

Canaris, Adml. W. (German), 164

Castrén, Senator Kaarlo, 73, 77

Castrén, U.J., 180, 183

Cecil, Lord Robert (British statesman), 69

Chamberlain, Neville (British prime minister), 118

Charpentier, Lieut.-Gen. Claes, 48

Chevalier Guards, 7

China, 22–9

Churchill, Winston (British statesman): 75, 89, 118, 121, 126, 146, 156, 171

Civil Guard, 46, 49, 51–3, 71–2, 81–2; dissolved, 185–6

Communist Party, 180, 189–90, 193–4

Conservative Party, 77, 164–5, 180, 189–90

constitution, 76–7, 78

Continuation War: German attack on

203

A NOTE ON THE AUTHOR

Stig Jägerskiöld was born in Sweden in 1911, to a family which had strong connections with Finland. A relative of Mannerheim – through grandparents who were brother and sister – he saw the Marshal often during his childhood and student days, as well as later in life. Jägerskiöld earned his Ph. D. at Uppsala University in 1937 with a study on Swedish diplomacy in the reign of Charles XII (*Sweden and Europe, 1716–1718*), and served from 1937 till 1960 as a docent at Uppsala. He had also studied law and written on legal issues, and from 1960 until his retirement in 1977 was a professor of public law at the universities of Lund and Uppsala. Jägerskiöld now heads the board of the Institute for Research in Swedish Legal History and is a contributor to the Swedish National Biography. *Mannerheim: Marshal of Finland* is his own abridgement of an eight-volume biography which appeared in Swedish and Finnish editions between 1964 and 1981. A sympathetic and admiring portrayal, it brings to English-language readers a survey of Mannerheim's military and political activities during a critical period in modern European history.